Medical-Legal Aspects
of Abused Substances

Old and New—Licit and Illicit

Marcelline Burns, Ph.D.
Thomas E. Page, M.A.

Contributing Authors

Sevil Atasoy, Ph.D.
Tanil M. Baskan, Ph.D.
Martin C. Boorman
Nina J. Emerson
Peter Gerstenzang
Officer Clark John
Sarah Kerrigan, Ph.D.
Officer Chuck Matson
Joel M. Mayer, Ph.D.
Dr. Morris Odell, M.D.
Trinka Porrata
Eric Sills
Philip Swann, Ph.D.

**Lawyers & Judges
Publishing Company, Inc.**
Tucson, Arizona

Lawyers & Judges Publishing Company, Inc.
P.O. Box 30040 • Tucson, AZ 85751-0040
(800) 209-7109 • FAX (800) 330-8795
e-mail: sales@lawyersandjudges.com

Library of Congress Cataloging-in-Publication Data

Medical-legal aspects of abused substances : old and new, licit and illicit
   / [edited by] Marcelline Burns ; contributing authors: Sevil Atasoy ...
   [et al.].
      p. cm.
   Includes bibliographical references and index.
   ISBN-13: 978-1-930056-83-1 (hardcover)
   ISBN-10: 1-930056-83-4 (hardcover)
   1. Drugged driving. 2. Drugs of abuse--Law and legislation.   I.
Burns,
   Marcelline. II. Atasoy, Sevil.
   HE5620.D65M43 2005
   364.1'47--dc22

2005013275

ISBN 1-930056-83-4
ISBN 978-1-930056-83-1
Printed in the United States of America
10 9 8 7 6 5 4 3 2 1

www.lawyersandjudges.com

Contents

Introduction

This book continues a discourse that was begun with *Medical-Legal Aspects of Drugs* (Burns, 2003). As can be noted by the chapter titles, however, the topics extend beyond drugs that have been widely misused and abused over time. The authors discuss newly compounded substances, as well as re-discovered drugs of abuse.

Scientific knowledge about a substance typically lags behind the need-to-know within the criminal justice system and the treatment community. It is only when a particular drug becomes a significant problem and citizens demand attention to the problem that adequate funds become available for research and treatment. Thus, data from rigorous scientific study often do not exist for new or newly popular drugs. Nonetheless, on a daily basis law enforcement, the courts, and many others in the community confront the consequences of drug use—whether old or new, licit or illicit.

Professionals who deal with drug users have written this book. They include police officers, defense attorney, pharmacologist, police physician, prosecutor, psychologist, and toxicologist. Their platforms of expertise are the laboratory, the courtroom, and the streets. Their perspectives are international. They are truly from the front line of the drug problems that are worldwide in scope. They obtained much of the information that they share with the reader from their daily responsibilities. Their limited bibliographies reflect not carelessness but reality; in many cases, there are few if any scientific studies to be cited.

We truly are indebted to the authors for their contributions. We acknowledge their generosity of time and effort, especially since some expressed misgivings about their writing skills and others continued to write during periods of great personal stress. We also thank our assistant, Jené Moio, without whose skills we could not have persevered.

Marcelline Burns
Thomas E. Page

Chapter 1

The Science of Drug Influence

Marcelline Burns

1.1 Introduction

The initial responsibilities for dealing with the consequences of the misuse and abuse of psychoactive substances lie within the criminal justice system. Treatment and rehabilitation facilities, schools, families, and various other social agencies also must cope with the problems created by drugs, but police officers typically are the first responders. They perform the often-difficult task of recognizing the presence of drugs. Analyses of specimens by crime laboratories refute or confirm officers' opinions. The courts then determine appropriate sanctions, and probation departments monitor the offenders.

The science of drugs is incomplete, and the tasks confronting these entities are difficult. Because the accumulation of scientific data progresses from inquiry to inquiry, there always will be some degree of mismatch between the information that the criminal justice system needs and the information that is available from research. It occurs in part because research and the dissemination of findings are labor-intensive and time-consuming activities. It also occurs because research resources, including both funds and personnel, typically are allocated to topics of im-

1

mediate social concerns, which may or may not reflect the most pressing needs of criminal justice professionals.

Information lags behind the development of problems. To illustrate, much of the scientific literature about marijuana's effects came from research conducted during the 1970s. Its relevance now is limited by the fact that the tetrahydrocannabinol (THC) content of marijuana in 2005 is much higher than the THC content of the marijuana that was available more than twenty years ago. Because the issue has not aroused public concern, however, there has been little scientific study of the effects of the higher potency marijuana.

Prudent and timely decisions are often urgently needed when dealing with individuals who may be under the influence of a psychoactive substance. At such times, the decision makers will rely on their real-world experiences, as well as the findings of research. Controlled studies from scientific laboratories provide critically important data, but it would be shortsighted to view such studies as the sole source of valid information. Observational data can serve as reliable indicators, particularly when the observed signs and symptoms are essentially universal. Who would question, for example, that narcotic analgesics constrict pupils? That is an established drug fact, and its occurrence does not require confirmation by scientific study.

Decisions that must be made at roadside, in jails, and in courtrooms will be facilitated by an informed selectivity of information derived solely from experience, as well as by knowledge of both the extent and the limits of research data. To illustrate, consider the question of marijuana effects on pupil size. Arrest documents frequently report that a marijuana suspect exhibited dilated pupils. Those observations must be reconciled with the general failure to observe dilated pupils in controlled laboratory experiments of marijuana.

The resolution of the marijuana-pupil size question will require both field observations and laboratory data. Very high potency marijuana is not available for research, nor can investigators administer high doses over extended time periods. Thus, measurements of pupil size with individuals who have used large amounts or high potency marijuana, possibly for a long time, must be obtained in field studies. Controlled laboratory studies will provide data for known drug amounts with precise measurements insuring that study subjects have not used and are not affected by other drugs. Together, the two kinds of data can determine whether differences between laboratory subjects and arrestees are due to THC level, the environment, the combination of both, or some other as-yet unidentified factor.

1.2 The Study of Drug Effects

Because the media and, on occasion, professional journals report data which ultimately are found to be transitory, contradictory, or non-replicable, an informed consumer must discriminate between good science, pseudo-science, and what truly has no claim to being scientific. Good science is the product of the scientific method. It states a hypothesis, follows established rules to test that hypothesis, and rejects or fails to reject it. Good science (laboratory or field study, significance testing or correlation studies) rigorously and objectively adheres to scientific methods and procedures. Anything less is not scientific study.

At least two kinds of information are essential to fully understand the impact of any drug on human performance: epidemiological data and data from controlled laboratory studies.

1.3 Epidemiological Study

Epidemiology, a term drawn from health sciences, refers to the distribution of a disease within a population. The usage here refers to the distribution of drug use and abuse. Blood specimens are needed to confirm drug presence, but obtaining blood often is not feasible. Until drug measurement is possible with specimens obtained by less invasive sampling, the distribution of drug use in any given population will remain largely unknown. For example, in any given year, how many people drove under the influence of a particular drug? For crash involved and non-crash involved drivers, how many had used a psychoactive drug? Data are not available to answer those questions for many drugs.

Epidemiology provides numbers. How many twelfth-grade students use marijuana? How many heroin addicts are on the road and under-the-influence during morning commutes? What proportion of crash-involved drivers was under the influence of alcohol? These are important numbers, but they reveal nothing about *how* the drug user is impaired. They do not identify the mechanism or severity of impairment or how it differs by driver characteristics.

1.4 Laboratory Experiments

Controlled laboratory experiments provide another kind of essential data. *Some* drugs have been studied with human subjects in laboratory experiments. *Some* drugs have not been studied with human subjects in laboratory experiments but can and may be studied at some time. *Some* drugs have not and will not be studied with human subjects.

Control denotes precision. Subjects with particular attributes are studied (young and old, male and female, rested and sleep-deprived). A measured amount of drug is given at specified times and under specified conditions. Other variables (fatigue, experience with the drug, attitude, motivation) are controlled directly or statistically. Study subjects are free of other drug influence as confirmed by analysis of fluid specimens. With this kind of rigor in a drug vs. placebo experiment, measured performance changes can be attributed to a study drug with a stated level of confidence.

A hypothetical illustrates the relevance of both kinds of data. Drug Z, appears on the street. It is illegal, it is cheap, and it produces a mild high that does not have severe side effects. In roadside surveys, many drivers acknowledge that they sometimes drive after using it. Is it a major problem? Any illicit drug use is a problem, but specifically, is it a roadway safety problem? If laboratory experiments show that Drug Z does not create drowsiness or impair driving skills, it is not. Although the drug is widely used, highway safety countermeasures and law enforcement resources can be directed elsewhere.

Consider a second hypothetical. Drug Y is an expensive, difficult-to-find drug that produces an intense high. Laboratory experiments demonstrate that Drug Y severely impairs driving skills. Survey and crash data reveal that a relatively small number of individuals drive after using it. Does its use create a roadway safety problem that justifies the expenditure of resources? Yes. Even though only a few drivers are affected by it, the extreme impairment creates the potential for a catastrophic crash.

Since *good* science yields valid data, it is reasonable to ask why the findings from one experiment sometimes appear to contradict the findings from another experiment. If the same issue was examined in two experiments and the results differ in ways that matter, those differences must be understood. Begin with a careful reading of the report or journal article. The same hypotheses examined in different laboratories with different measurements by different instruments under different conditions can produce different results. Differences in methods, procedures, instruments, and the sample of subjects may be unintended and unrecognized, neither large nor obvious, and yet they can make significant difference in the results.

Measurement validity, reliability, sensitivity, and relevance are key issues. Measures are valid if they measure what is claimed. To belabor what appears to be obvious but sometimes is not, if a researcher reports results from a laboratory test as evidence that a drug did or did not impair driving, then the test must have measured a driving-related skill. Measures are reliable if they are reproducible, if experiments conducted in different times and places yield results that lead to the same conclusions.

An instrument or a test yields sensitive measures if it can measure small but important changes in performance, and if it measures over a relevant range of doses in alcohol and drug studies. An instrument that measures performance changes at 0.20 percent BAC but not at 0.10 percent BAC is not sufficiently sensitive to alcohol effects to be of value. For studies of medications, instruments must be capable of measuring the effects of therapeutic dose levels.

Relevance is an often-overlooked measurement characteristic. For example, long-term negative health consequences of a hypertension medication are highly relevant to the patient and physician. Medication-induced heart arrhythmias that are undetectable to the patient may be vital information for a physician. Neither drug effect, however, has obvious direct relevance for traffic safety.

A careful reading of the scientific literature reveals a reason for different findings. Investigators have reported that alcohol at 0.10 percent BAC slows reaction time (RT). Other investigators have reported that level of alcohol has no effect on RT. Both findings are correct, but only one is relevant to traffic safety. Studies of simple RT, a test that requires a single type of response to a single type of stimulus, do not find an alcohol-related deficit. The demands of simple RT tasks are insufficient for measurement of the effects of alcohol. Importantly, simple RT is not of critical importance for driving. A first mandate of good science is to ask the right question. Asking whether alcohol impairs simple reaction time may be appropriate for some kinds of experiments, but it is the wrong question for driving studies.

Choice or complex RT tasks involve more than one possible response to multiple stimuli and mirror the complexity of driving demands. If complex responses are slowed, performance of the driving task is degraded. The second finding, that 0.10 percent BAC slows complex RT, is relevant to driving.

1.5 Illicit Drugs

The study of illicit drugs is limited by the nature of the substances. Drugs that may harm or lead to addiction have not been and will not be administered to human subjects. Heroin cannot be studied for any reason within the United States. Codeine can be administered only in therapeutic doses. Limited information is available from the use of LSD several decades ago to ease the fears of terminally ill patients. The early use of Ecstasy as an adjunct to psychotherapy has generated some reports. Information about other Rave and club drugs, e.g., GHB and Ketamine, is limited to users' reports, case studies, and surveys. Two additional data sources are individuals in drug treatment and individuals in custody. In these data, however, the individual's veracity is an issue, as is the lack of verifiable information about dose times and amounts.

Laboratory studies have examined a few illicit drugs, including marijuana, cocaine, and the amphetamines. Marijuana has been studied more extensively than the stimulants, but the body of knowledge is not complete for any of these drugs. Study is limited to drug amounts that can be safely administered to volunteer subjects who report prior use of the drug. In most instances, those amounts are smaller or the drug potency is lower than users ingest during personal use. "First, do no harm," applies in the laboratory as well as in medicine, and investigators have no quarrel with limits on drug doses. Nonetheless, the limits have inevitable and seemingly insurmountable consequences for knowledge of drug effects.

A. Marijuana

Traffic officers regularly encounter drivers who have committed an offense or have crashed, and who are found to have used marijuana. Nonetheless, a decades-long debate continues as to whether marijuana impairs driving. At least three variables can be identified which contribute to differing views: THC content of marijuana, THC dosages, and administration methods.

During the 1970s, the THC content of marijuana used in research was in the range 2-3 percent. Today's marijuana user can obtain much more potent drug. If the effects were known to be linear (doubling the amount doubles the effects), findings from early research could be extrapolated to higher concentrations. There is no evidence, however, of linearity. At this time, it cannot be assumed, for example, that 12 percent THC increases impairment threefold in comparison to 4 percent THC. Critical questions about marijuana effects on driving remain unanswered.

Issues of dose levels and administration procedures are related. Subjects in a laboratory experiment do not socialize and smoke in a party atmosphere over a period of several hours. Instead, they smoke a measured amount in a private room in a short time period following a prescribed and closely monitored method. The controlled smoking procedure standardizes the amount of THC entering subjects' bodies, but it also limits the total maximum dose. With the short smoking period, experienced users are unable to tolerate doses higher than 200-300 mcg/Kg body weight.

Despite the limits imposed on research, there is clear scientific evidence that marijuana impairs driving. Attention, which directly and indirectly affects driving skills, is degraded. Subjects in a driving simulator are less attentive to the task, make more errors, and respond more slowly. Remote observations of eye movements during tests of attention reveal that although marijuana-dosed subjects look at stimuli, they often do not respond to them. It appears that they do not process the visual information.

The following variables affect the results of marijuana studies:

1. The amount of THC that effectively acts on the subject (dose, smoking method).
2. Subject characteristics (age, gender, duration and current level of marijuana use).
3. Time of testing vs. time of dosing.
4. Duration of testing in relation to peak effects, fatigue, or boredom.
5. Apparatus and performance measures (validity, sensitivity, relevance).
6. Data analysis and interpretation.

B. Stimulants

Because stimulants differ one from the other primarily in duration of effects, cocaine and the amphetamines can be considered together. Many of the research problems parallel those for marijuana. Others are unique to stimulants.

An investigator's decision about the amount of cocaine doses involves difficult issues of safety, effectiveness, and relevance. The drug must be obtained from the sole producer of cocaine hydrochloride, but it is unclear how to equate the pure purchased material with illicit cocaine for which quality control is notably lacking.

Amphetamine and methamphetamine are supplied as tablets, and the method for giving them to subjects in the laboratory can match the methods of illicit use. Similarly, powder cocaine can be weighed and packaged for insufflation by subjects. These administration methods are straightforward, but dose amounts are problematic. As much as 126 mg cocaine or 20 mg amphetamine can be given safely to users; however, these amounts, which do not approach private use levels, produce only modest increases in blood pressure and pulse rates. Behavioral changes are subtle and would not be noticed without continual observation. Performance on a variety of laboratory tasks is speeded at these levels, but the speed is associated with an increase in errors and cannot be interpreted as improved performance. These findings provide some direction, but they are not definitive. Individuals in treatment and custody show more dramatic effects, but there are no laboratory data for larger drug amounts.

1.6 Therapeutic Drugs

A large medical literature exists for prescription drugs, but the focus of most of it is the treatment of diseases and disorders. A smaller scientific literature scattered among a variety of journals deals specifically with the effects of medications on behavior and performance, including driving performance.

Two broad statements of fact are relevant to prescription drug research. First, the study of medicinal drugs is beset with complexity. Second, a single study can examine only one or a few of the complex issues. Hence, a questioning and critical mindset is appropriate when reading on this topic. The reader needs to be aware of the study's objective, the source of funding, and the investigator's credentials.

The convergence, or the lack thereof, of data is key to evaluating studies. Are there similar findings from more than one investigator or laboratory? Has an experiment been replicated, especially one that offers breakthrough findings? Do the data converge by drug category? Do the reported findings fit with long established facts about drugs in that specific category? Although new data that do not mesh with what is known about a drug are not necessarily invalid, the differences should raise the bar for additional evidence.

Because the study of medicinal drugs has unique requirements, there has been a moderate amount of study of some drug categories and almost none of others. There are neither enough funds nor enough researchers to examine all new drugs and all those that pre-date current safety concerns. The best hope for traffic safety may be the efforts by pharmaceutical companies to develop non-impairing compounds.

Pharmaceutical companies serve the public by providing medicines. They fund much of the research and thereby set the research agenda. The cost of developing and marketing new drugs, which totals many millions of dollars, includes studies to support new drug applications to the FDA and to support post-marketing label changes. The focus of research is efficacy, and research to determine effects on driving skills is a small part of the total.

The benzodiazepines, as effective anxiolytics, were a major advance in therapeutics, and beginning in the 1980s, they were studied extensively. That research was followed by study of their effectiveness as hypnotics. Extensive study of antidepressants and non-sedating antihistamines followed. An optimal balance is sought between efficacy, adverse effects, safety, and user preference. The benzodiazepines (diazepam, alprazolam, estazolam, midazolam, and their kin) are efficacious. They reduce anxiety, aid sleep, and serve as pre-operative sedatives. They also can be addictive, some more than others, and they can impair; thus, there are adverse effects and safety issues. A non-benzodiazepine, buspirone, is an effective anxiolytic, and is not impairing. It does not produce a subjective high, and it has not captured a large market share, possibly for lack of user preference.

Studies of medications have not been designed to purposefully obtain the kind of information needed for drug recognition. Certainly, the slowed reaction time, drowsiness, and increased errors that can occur with medications, as demonstrated by laboratory research, are relevant to law enforcement. Most research, however, does not provide data about signs and symptoms.

An investigator who undertakes study of medications confronts a number of experiment design issues. Drugs can be expected to differ widely in effects on driving skills, as well as in the signs and symptoms of use. In an oversimplification, stimulants *stimulate* and depressants *depress*, and a given laboratory test may or may not measure both kinds of effects. Tests must be selected to measure the performance deficits that can reasonably be expected for the particular type of drug that is under study. For example, it may not be possible to measure drug-induced drowsiness with tests that are highly demanding and alerting.

When the pharmacokinetics of a drug is not well-understood, the time interval between dosing and testing is a difficult design issue. Testing that occurs either too soon or too late after drug administration will fail to measure the drug's effects at peak blood levels.

The interpretation of drug study findings may not be straightforward. It is possible for a measured performance deficit to be statistically significant but small in magnitude. Statistical significance does not always equate with practical significance. In the individual case, whether the deficit "matters" becomes an issue of interpretation.

The effects of the disease for which a particular medicine will be prescribed complicate the study of that drug. The drug may have adverse and performance-impairing effects, but it may also partially or entirely counteract the consequences of the illness. In that case, its net effects must be weighed. This dilemma can be illustrated with a hypothetical. Assume that a licensed driver experiences unpredictable seizures, a condition of recent origin that is unknown to the licensing authority. Assume that another licensed driver was formerly subject to seizures, but the condition was diagnosed and controlled with a sedative that is known to impair driving skills. Both drivers have an increased probability of crash, but the lack of data to quantify the respective risks makes decisions about their driving privileges very difficult. Similarly, consider whether an untreated, severely depressed individual is a greater or lesser risk on the roadway than a depressed patient whose mood states are controlled with a benzodiazepine.

The study of relative risk from illness versus impairment from a drug requires studies of patients with and without medication. Such data have been obtained for patients with non-life-threatening illnesses and only moderate discomfort (e.g., osteoarthritis, insomnia, allergic rhinitis). Ethical issues, however, preclude study of more devastating conditions. A drug that would relieve a patient's pain or mental distress cannot be withheld solely for the purpose of study.

1.7 Summary and Conclusions

Not all illicit drugs or therapeutic drugs have been studied, and many will not be studied. New drugs and combinations of drugs are subject to abuse. There are neither enough research funds nor research professionals to examine all of them. There are valid, reliable, and relevant data that clearly demonstrate impairment by psychoactive drugs. For the present, criminal justice professionals must rely on the extant scientific literature, together with their observations of and experience with drug-influenced individuals.

Chapter 2

The Role of the Law Enforcement Officer

Thomas E. Page

Synopsis

2.1 Introduction

Many of the day-to-day activities of law enforcement professionals are responses to problems that arise from the use of alcohol and other drugs. Without substance misuse and abuse, the demand for the services of police officers, prosecutors, judges, jailers, correction officers, probation officers, parole officers, and other affiliated professionals would be dramatically lessened. Not only would there be a reduction in crimes directly related to alcohol and drugs, but the incidence of domestic violence, assault, child abuse, robbery, burglary, rape, and aggravated assault would also be reduced. The perpetrators of crimes of all kinds frequently are under the influence of alcohol and drugs. In many instances, the criminal act is a means of obtaining money to purchase more drugs. Note, too, that it is not uncommon for the victims as well as the perpetrators of crime to be under the influence of alcohol and drugs.

The pharmacological actions of a substance may provoke a criminal act. For example, stimulants such as cocaine and methamphetamine activate fight or flight responses via the autonomic nervous system. A user who feels in danger may commit a crime by responding to the perceived threat. Aggressive and violent acts against others often are responses to emotions that arise when drugs have been used. Data from the ADAM (arrestee drug abuse monitoring) surveys of drug use among new arrestees reveal that approximately 70 percent of adult arrestees test positive at the time of booking for illicit substances (National Institute of Justice, 2003).

2.2 Alcohol Versus Drugs

Motor vehicle crashes that involve drivers impaired by alcohol or other drugs are crimes. Note the choice of term, crash vs. accident. The latter term suggests a non-culpable mistake, but driving under the influence (DUI) is rarely a mistake. Rather, the operation of a motor vehicle after consuming alcohol or another impairing substance is almost always an intentional act.

In the United States, approximately 40 percent of traffic fatalities are alcohol-related (U.S. Department of Transportation, 2003). The role of drugs other than alcohol in motor vehicle crashes, however, is less well defined. Data are difficult to obtain, because there are no non-invasive tests for quick and accurate measurement of the presence of drugs in a suspect. Also, the number of potentially impairing drugs is very large, analysis of body fluid specimens is difficult (in part because the amount of drug that must be found often is very small), and data from epidemiological and laboratory studies are not available for many drugs.

Importantly, the relationship between the amount of drug in the person and the extent of impairment is much more complex than it is for alcohol. It appears unlikely that the equivalent of a 0.080 percent BAC limit for driving can be established for most drugs. For such limits, research would have to determine (and legislators accept) that a specific, measured amount of each drug in the blood produces an unacceptably high risk of driving impairment. That large and difficult task may not be possible.

The effort to define the role of drugs in traffic events is further complicated by the pharmacokinetics[1] of drugs. The pharmacokinetics varies and is complex. For example, whereas alcohol is metabolized to water and carbon dioxide, heroin is metabolized to morphine, another psychoactive drug. Also, many of the minor tranquilizers, in particular the benzodiazepines, metabolize intermediately to other benzodiazepines, all of which are impairing substances.

2.3 Trafficking, Manufacturing, and Diversion

Law enforcement, even on the local level, confronts and must respond to drug trafficking, which is related to street sales (on sidewalks and in alleys), as well as to "crack" or dope houses. Manufacturing activities are concentrated in clandestine laboratories, which may be stationary, mobile, or semi-mobile. Drug manufacture involves hazardous chemicals and processes that create a serious risk of explosions and fires. Furthermore, there is a potential for environmental contamination by the chemicals due to improper storage and disposal.

The illegal diversion of legitimate pharmaceutical preparations is another law enforcement issue. Diversion refers to the acquisition and transfer of substances to the illicit drug arena by theft or hijacking or by fraudulent prescriptions. Employees of manufacturing firms, shipping firms, pharmacists, other pharmacy employees, and prescribing physicians have been identified as participants in diversion activities.

2.4 Driving Under the Influence Enforcement

The most common misdemeanor arrest in the United States is for driving under the influence of alcohol (DUI) or other drugs (DUID). DUI and DUID enforcement consumes more physical resources and manpower than enforcement of any other crime. Officers must learn to identify driving behaviors consistent with impairment, to administer and interpret field sobriety tests, to administer breath tests, to collect evidence, and to prepare reports. Officer training is demanding and intensive.

Prior to the 1980s, training and enforcement focused primarily on alcohol-impaired drivers. Even though driving while impaired by other drugs was prohibited, officers received minimal relevant training, and relatively few DUID arrests were made. When the DRE method emerged within the Los Angeles Police Department (LAPD) in the mid-1980s, the focus began to expand. LAPD officers had arrested impaired drivers whose BACs were zero or very low and recognized the need for drug-impairment training and policies.

Alcohol is a central nervous system (CNS) depressant that produces characteristic signs of its presence (bloodshot and watery eyes, slurred speech, unsteady gait). Numerous other drugs also are depressants (e.g., benzodiazepines, barbiturates, GHB, diphenhydramine) and produce signs similar to those of alcohol. Although these drugs mirror many of the effects of alcohol, they do not produce an alcohol odor and cannot be identified with a breath test. Also, unlike alcohol, the relationship of the blood level of other depressants with impairment is either unknown or unpredictable. The difficult task of recognizing impairment, not only by depressants other than alcohol but also by drugs from other categories, was the springboard for development of the DRE methodology.

A certified Drug Recognition Expert (DRE) is trained to recognize the effects of drugs and to identify a drug category in the specific case. The primary focus of the DRE method is impaired driving enforcement, but there are numerous other applications. There are approximately 5,600 DRE officers in thirty-seven U.S. states and Canada, and there are DRE-trained officers in Norway, Sweden, and South Africa. About 10 percent are also DRE instructors. Australia, Germany and the United Kingdom have implemented variations of the program.

The International Association of Chiefs of Police (IACP) oversees DRE training. States and provinces certify DRE-trained officers within their jurisdictions. The National Highway Traffic Safety Administration (NHTSA), of the U.S. Department of Transportation, works closely with the IACP as well as with individual states in administering the DRE program.[2]

A typical DRE investigation begins with a traffic officer's observation of erratic or illegal driving, followed by an enforcement stop. If the officer observes signs of impairment, he directs the driver to step out of the vehicle, and he administers field sobriety tests. Based on all observations (driving, sobriety test performance, the individual's appearance, demeanor, response to instructions), the officer makes a decision to arrest, cite, release, or to summon medical help.[3] If the driver is arrested and transported to a police station, a breath specimen will be obtained for an evidentiary test. If the breath test results are consistent with the observed impairment, and if the BAC exceeds the statutory limit (0.08 percent in most jurisdictions), the driver likely will be processed as a DUI offender.

A DRE officer's assistance in the investigation is requested if the driver's impairment is not consistent with the measured level of alcohol. The DRE officer then assumes responsibility for determining whether impairment is due to drug influence and which category of drug(s) is present. Toxicological analysis of a body fluid specimen for the presence of drugs and metabolites supports this impairment-based approach. Although analysis of a blood or urine specimen can provide scientific proof of consumption of the substance, it does not provide conclusive evidence of impairment. The determination of impairment must be made by the DRE who identifies the signs and symptoms associated with a drug category. Note that a DRE identifies a drug category, not a specific drug within the category.

A clear understanding of the DRE method rests on the definition of impairment. The terms *impairment, intoxication*, and *under the influence*, which are frequently used interchangeably, may be misunderstood. *Impairment* means a loss, abnormality, or decrement of physiological functions, and the term does not apply exclusively to impairment by alcohol or other drugs. Driving impairment may also be due to fatigue, sleep loss, external distractions, and physical or mental illness. *Intoxication* refers to poisoning by a substance, which may be alcohol or another drug, and the term is commonly used to mean obvious impairment. Importantly, note that intoxication is specific to substances; impairment is not. An individual may be too impaired to safely operate a motor vehicle without being intoxicated. An individual who is intoxicated, however, is by definition impaired.[4]

The definition of *under the influence* differs by jurisdiction and occasionally by courts within a jurisdiction. In DUI enforcement, it most often means that a driver's ability to safely operate a vehicle is adversely and appreciably affected by a substance. Officers and attorneys sometimes engage in debate as to whether a driver can be under-the-influence but not impaired. One view is that there is a physiological action on the person by any amount of a substance even though the action may not be observable. That is, although physiologically affected by the substance, the person is not impaired. Although this argument may seem reasonable, by extension it would mean that everyone is *under the influence* at all times due to being continually affected by some substance. A more workable definition, close to the definition of intoxication, restricts the meaning of *under the influence* to detectable *impairment* due to alcohol or other drugs.

A discussion of *under the influence* must also address the situation in which the substance is no longer present in the body, but its use continues to affect the person, as would be the case with a hangover. When alcohol has been metabolized to water and carbon dioxide, it is no longer present as alcohol in the person's body. Nonetheless, the imbiber may experience a number of adverse effects related to the alcohol consumption, including headache, nausea, a decreased ability to concentrate, and dry mouth. Though not *intoxicated*, the individual is *impaired* due to the former rather than the current presence of alcohol. Drugs other than alcohol have similar, acutely impairing hangover effects.

2.5 Non-Driving *Under the Influence* Offenses

Many jurisdictions prohibit the use of controlled substances under health and safety codes. The prohibitions, arising from public health concerns, may specify certain drugs (e.g., phencyclidine, heroin, cocaine, amphetamines). They may be implemented as addiction countermeasures. When these prohibitions are actively enforced, there is a dramatic reduction of other crimes, not just drug-related crimes.

Since arrests under these prohibitive codes generally do not require that the offender use drugs in a public place, they can be made in an individual's residence. Probable cause for the offense, which is known as internal possession, is the display of the signs and symptoms associated with the drug. As with DUID, the arrest requires the support of a positive finding from toxicological analysis of a body fluid specimen.

An individual arrested for DUI or DUID is required to provide a breath or blood test under the implied consent provisions of traffic law. Failure or inability to provide the required specimen may result in both criminal and administrative sanctions. Implied consent provisions do not apply, however, to health and safety code violations. In a non-traffic situation, the individual suspected of using a prohibited substance cannot be compelled to provide a specimen to test for drugs. It can be pointed out that providing a specimen will be advantageous for the arrestee if the specimen is found to be negative for drugs. The suspect can also be informed that failure to provide a specimen may be commented on in court and may be viewed as evidence of consciousness of guilt. The underlying thought, of course, is that an innocent person will freely provide a specimen to obtain a negative test.

Investigations under these prohibitive codes require identification of a specific drug such as cocaine or heroin, but a DUID offense requires only the determination of a drug category. An officer can conclude, for example, that a suspect is under the influence of a stimulant, but cannot identify it as cocaine or methamphetamine. Identification of the specific substance is left to toxicological analysis.

2.6 DRE Drug Categories

The DRE schema posits seven drug categories within which drugs share a pattern of signs and symptoms.[5] A constellation of effects is unique to a single category, and the drugs within that category have similar effects at intoxicating levels. For example, cocaine and methamphetamine both are CNS stimulants that act as sympathomimetics. They dilate pupils, elevate heart rate, and produce hyperactivity and agitation. Because the effects are the same, an officer cannot determine by observations alone which of the two drugs is affecting the person. It may become clear, however, that it is one drug or the other as a result of additional evidence, such as the user's admission, physical evidence (the drug itself), paraphernalia, and drug use trends within the community. Also, cocaine and methamphetamine differ in the duration of the effects. Cocaine is a relatively short-acting drug,[6] and its acute effects typically last only about thirty minutes. Methamphetamine effects persist much longer, typically about four hours, but in some cases as long as twelve hours. Although hangover, carryover, and the crash phase ensure that the user will not revert to a normal state after those periods of time, a dramatic recovery in the short-term would strongly suggest that the stimulant was cocaine. On the other hand, a display of symptoms continuing over several hours is consistent with methamphetamine.

2.7 DRE Procedure

When an arresting officer believes an arrestee may be under the influence of drugs, the officer can request the assistance of a DRE officer. The DRE who responds to that request then is responsible for three determinations:

1. Is the individual's impairment inconsistent with the measured alcohol level?
2. Is the impairment due to a medical condition that may require immediate attention?

3. What category (or categories) of drug is responsible for the impairment?

The signs and symptoms associated with certain medical conditions (e.g., stroke, epilepsy, multiple sclerosis, aphasia, uncontrolled diabetes) can mimic drug effects. DREs must quickly and accurately assess whether the observed impairment may be due to a condition that requires immediate medical attention. Frequently, they do determine that an arrestee, who was appropriately arrested, is not under the influence of drugs and urgently needs medical care. It is only after medical causes of impairment have been ruled out that a DRE proceeds with a drug evaluation. A final opinion then will be delayed until the entire evaluation has been completed, a procedure rooted in standard medical practices for diagnosis of illness or injury.[7]

The twelve steps of the Drug Influence Evaluation (DIE) are:

1. *Measurement of blood alcohol concentration (BAC).* This step usually precedes the involvement of the DRE. If the arresting officer determines that the BAC is consistent with both the type and degree of impairment, a DRE is not called.
2. *Interview of the arresting officer.* The DRE discusses the circumstances of the arrest with the arresting officer. Specifically, the DRE he inquires about the suspect's condition at the time of the arrest, whether the arrestee was involved in a traffic collision, what statements the suspect may have made, whether or not the suspect had drugs in his or her possession, and any other relevant matters. This step is analogous to the interview an emergency room physician conducts when an unconscious individual is brought by ambulance to the hospital.
3. *Preliminary examination.* This is the "fork in the road" that determines whether there is sufficient reason to go forward with an evaluation. It is essential to make an early determination of drug involvement rather than a medical condition. At this point, the DRE makes general observations of the arrestee's condition, inquires about health problems, exam-

ines pupil size and eye tracking, and takes the first of three pulse measures.

If there is evidence of illness or injury, the suspect is referred to medical personnel. If there are no signs of a medical problem or of drug influence, the suspect is returned to the arresting officer for routine processing. Barring these outcomes, the DRE proceeds with the evaluation.

4. *Eye examinations.* The DIE includes examination of three characteristics of eye movement: horizontal gaze nystagmus (HGN), vertical gaze nystagmus (VGN), and eye convergence.

Nystagmus refers to an involuntary but visible jerking of the eyes. HGN is the jerking that occurs as the eyes gaze at a stimulus that is moved side to side in the horizontal plane before the individual's eyes. It reflects the presence of depressants (including alcohol), inhalants, or phencyclidine (PCP). The vertical gaze nystagmus (VGN) examination requires the suspect to visually follow an object that is moved up and down. In sufficient dose, any drug that causes HGN will also cause VGN, but no drug causes VGN without first causing HGN.

For the examination of convergence, the suspect is instructed to look at a stimulus (pen or pencil) that is held about two inches in front of the bridge of his nose.[8] The position forces the suspect's eyes to cross as he focuses on the object. Depressant, inhalants, PCP, and cannabis impair the ability to converge (or cross) the eyes.

5. *Divided attention tests.* Four tests are given in the following order: Romberg Balance, Walk and Turn, One-Leg Stand, Finger-to-Nose.[9] These are divided attention tests that require the individual to balance and coordinate body movements, remember instructions, and perform more than one task at once. Although the suspect would have performed some of the tests at roadside, he is asked to perform them again in the controlled environment of a police station. Frequently, performance during the DIE differs markedly from performance in the field. The differences occur when a drug's effects either

decline or intensify during the time between arrest and evaluation or when a suspect had used multiple drugs with different time courses, resulting in dominant effects changing over elapsed time.

6. *Vital signs examinations*. Measured vital signs include blood pressure, body temperature, and pulse rate (second time). Vital signs are measured precisely and compared with medically accepted normal ranges. Certain drugs elevate specific vital signs, other drugs depress them, and other drugs have no effect on certain signs.[10] If vital signs are dangerously high or low, the arrestee's condition is evaluated by medical personnel.

7. *Darkroom examinations of pupils*. Poets call the eyes the window to the soul, but they are windows to the inner body for a DRE. The pupils enlarge in response to darkness, fear, and excitement and constrict in response to bright light. They also enlarge and constrict in response to certain drugs.[11] The DRE uses a pupillometer to estimate the arrestee's pupil sizes in different light levels, ranging from near total darkness to direct light[12] and also examines nasal and oral cavities for evidence of drug use.

8. *Muscle tone*. Certain drugs cause the skeletal muscles to become rigid, and other drugs, such as alcohol, cause muscle flaccidity. Muscle tone is evaluated throughout the examination by observing the arrestee's movements. During this step, the DRE gently moves the arrestee's arms to determine muscle tone.

9. *Examination of injection sites*. Although a user may inject drugs anywhere on the body, the most common sites are arms, neck, and ankles. Although injection sites, even recent ones, are an indicator of use rather than drug influence, their presence can provide evidence of frequency of use and the type of drug abused. A third pulse is taken at this time.

10. *Statements, interview, interrogation*. In the United States, a suspect must be advised of his or her constitutional rights (Miranda warnings) prior to custodial interrogation. If the warning has not been given, the DRE will do so prior to con-

ducting a structured interrogation, which includes questions about the use of specific drugs. Arrestees often deny illicit drug use and claim to have used a prescription drug.

11. *Opinion.* The DRE records an opinion about drug influence and category. To illustrate, a typical opinion would state, "In my opinion, the arrestee is under the influence of a central nervous system stimulant, and cannot safely operate a vehicle."[13] The informed opinion is guided by objective criteria and is based on the totality of the evidence from the evaluation. DREs are trained that whenever there is any doubt, the opinion should always favor the freedom of the suspect.

12. *Toxicology.* Under implied consent laws, a driver must provide a blood or urine specimen for toxicological analysis. A specimen for drug analysis must be provided even though a breath specimen for alcohol analysis was provided. The laboratory's very important analysis then identifies (or fails to find) a specific substance in the specimen. For example, if a DRE opines that an arrestee was under the influence of a stimulant, the laboratory examines that individual's specimen for amphetamines and cocaine. Toxicological corroboration of drug use is usually necessary for successful prosecution.

2.8 The Art and Science of DRE Reconstruction

In a typical DRE scenario, three components interface: (1) driving behavior; (2) signs and symptoms of alcohol and/or drug influence; (3) toxicological evidence of drug use. Together these three components support a strong prosecution case.

Briefly, the driving behavior component consists of observations of *bad* driving by a police officer. The signs and symptoms component includes the arresting officers' observations, the suspect's performance of roadside tests, and the DIE. The toxicological component is the specimen analysis for psychoactive drugs and/or their metabolites. The DRE's recorded opinion predicts what the toxicologist will find in a specimen, and it is his responsibility to link the signs and symptoms of impairment with the toxicological analysis.

In the best of circumstances, a DRE evaluation is conducted in close proximity to the time of the driving event that gave rise to police involvement. Because of their relatively small number, however, a DRE officer may not be available, or the precipitating event may be a crash of such severity and conditions that prevented or limited field sobriety tests and a DIE. In that case, reconstruction may be the only source of crucial evidence. It requires post-incident collection, analysis, and interpretation of evidence for the purpose of establishing the suspect's state of sobriety at the time of the incident.

2.9 The DRE crime scene

Because a DRE reconstruction often relies on analysis of evidence that was collected by others, it requires exceptional talent and experience. Records of facts, as in police reports, vary widely in quality and completeness. The duration of the signs and symptoms of impairment differ by drug and may persist only minutes or hours. In the best of circumstances, blood or urine and possibly other physical evidence will still be available for analysis. Potential sources of data for reconstruction include:

- reports of driving
- civilian witness observations before, during, and after the incident
- police witness observations
- paramedic/EMT observations
- doctor/nurse observations
- hospital records
- suspect's statements
- direct evidence of drug use (drugs in proximity to the suspect)
- indirect evidence of drug use (paraphernalia)
- collision reconstruction report
- toxicological analysis report

The laboratory report of a specimen analysis is important, because the presence of the drugs or metabolites in the person's body is scientific evidence that the drug was ingested at some time prior to specimen collection. The toxicologist cannot state with certainty when a drug was used, how and how much drug was used, whether the person was legally entitled to use the drug, whether the use was intentional, or how the drug affected the ability to operate a motor vehicle. Importantly, however, presence is proof of use. On the other hand, a negative toxicological finding does not establish non-use with certainty. A negative finding is a function of the specific specimen (urine, blood, or other), and the laboratory's capabilities; i.e., measurement sensitivity and threshold levels. A negative laboratory finding does lessen the likelihood of a convincing reconstruction.

2.10 Direct/Indirect Evidence of Drug Use

A person who is *under the influence* of drugs, by definition, has used drugs that are responsible for impairment. The person's ability to drive safely has deteriorated as a result of drug use, and internal possession of the drug is having a psychoactive effect. Direct and indirect evidence of drug use supports a reconstruction with information about drug type, potency, quantity, and contaminants (cutting agents), ingestion method, and poly-drug use. Direct evidence includes the drug on the suspect's person, in or near the suspect's vehicle, or drug residue on the person or vehicle. Other items, such as drug-related paraphernalia on the person or in or near the vehicle, are indirect evidence of drug use. Paraphernalia includes:

- syringes, matches, soda cans, pipes, lighters, spoons (for *cooking* substances), straws, rolling papers for drug administration
- capsules, pill bottles, paper bindles, balloons, nitrous oxide containers (whippets) for drug storage
- scales, packaging materials, razor blades, pacifiers, glow-sticks
- prescriptions, pharmacy receipts, doctor appointment cards, pill books, drug *recipes*, pill presses
- milk sugar, Novocain, loose tobacco, or other cutting agents

Depending upon the specific items and context, the direct and indirect evidence may support a conclusion that the person was under the influence of a specific category or categories of drugs at the time of the incident. Obviously, the presence of cocaine residue in or around the nose of the suspect is evidence that the individual was using cocaine, a powerful stimulant. Although that evidence requires little interpretation concerning

the type of drug used, it falls short of proving impairment by the drug during the incident in question. It supports that hypothesis, but it doesn't
prove it.

Paraphernalia, which can be similar from drug type to drug type, may
sometimes provide evidence for a specific substance, but both paraphernalia and routes of administration change over time. The changes spring
from trends, idol emulation, and fear of disease, as well as from factors
related to the purity, potency, price, and water solubility of the drug. Most
drugs can be ingested by multiple methods. Heroin can be injected intravenously, intramuscularly and subcutaneously. It can be smoked—*chasing the dragon*—and it can be snorted intranasally. Naïve users who dis-
dain the stigma and infection-potential of injection may initiate use by
snorting or smoking. Since they likely have smoked tobacco, it is a
smaller leap to smoking heroin than to injecting it. Also, with increased
availability of potent, lower cost heroin, snorting has become more attractive. Not only does it carry less risk of disease and stigma, new users believe they can avoid addiction by smoking or snorting. The belief is incor-
rect, because CNS effects do not vary by administration method, and the
addiction potential remains. Cocaine, methamphetamine, and some CNS
depressants are also routinely injected. Hallucinogens (LSD, and others)
and marijuana are not injected. Thus, the presence of injection paraphernalia—a *hype kit*[14]— can narrow an investigation to substances that are
injected. A similar analysis applies to cutting agents, which tend to be substance specific.

Civilian witnesses, who are not part of the law enforcement, public
safety, or medical systems, may be able to provide information about
events that occurred before, during, or after the incident. If the civilian is
related to or has other social, geographic, financial, or economic affilia-
tion with the suspect, he or she may become an alibi witnesses for the suspect. In the most objective circumstance, a witness is disinterested in the
investigation or subsequent criminal/civil actions and wants only to perform the duties of citizenship. On occasion, a civilian witness brings unexpected expertise to the investigation (e.g., medical, engineering, substance abuse, law enforcement, education, behavioral sciences).

Civilian witnesses may have seen the suspect driving erratically or
using drugs *prior to the incident*. He may be able to describe the suspect's
attitude and demeanor as normal, bizarre, or vigilant. The most salient

observations are those that occurred shortly before the incident, but valuable information is not always in close proximity to the event. A witness who is given the opportunity to describe the suspect's behavior and appearance freely may report long-term changes in appearance, friends, hygiene, and behavior that strongly suggest a history of drug use.

During-the-incident refers to the observations of the incident itself. The witness may describe other vehicles, bicyclists, motorcyclists, pedestrians, animals, traffic signals, weather, and distractions. He may have observed erratic driving, evasive actions, and vehicle speed. Such information can be interpreted for purposes of reconstruction in terms of the effects of specific drug categories. CNS stimulants often cause agitated, vigilant behavior. Narcotic analgesics induce sedation and an appearance of drowsiness. Directing the witness to mimic the suspect's behavior and speech may provide surprisingly clear evidence of drug influence.

Witnesses should be encouraged to describe the suspect's actions immediately *after the event*. A serious crash is a traumatic event. Does the witness report that the suspect's behavior was consistent with crash severity? If not, possibly the suspect was reacting to a substance rather than the situation. A competent investigator can obtain key evidence by encouraging a witness to describe details of a suspect's behavior. If unduly vigilant, paranoid or animated behavior is described, that suggests stimulant influence.[15] In direct contrast, if the witness reports that the suspect appeared sedated or was falling asleep in spite of chaotic activities at the crash scene, that suggests a narcotic analgesic such as heroin.

Witnesses sometimes observe the suspect discarding incriminating evidence (alcohol containers, drugs, paraphernalia). There may have been *guilty knowledge* behavior, attempting to switch positions in the vehicle with a passenger. Guilty people do guilt-like things, and directing a witness to recreate the suspect's post-incident movements can yield important evidence.

After-the-incident observations by witnesses can include events that are not in temporal proximity to the precipitating event. Generally, the longer the period of time that has elapsed, the less likely it is that the observations will provide salient information about the state of the suspect's sobriety during the event, but a witness may have heard the suspect admit drug use. The witness may be aware that the suspect attempted to create an alibi after the fact by seeking a drug prescription or by entering a drug treatment facility. The witness may know that the suspect filed a false report of vehicle theft, or repainted, burned or dumped the vehicle. In summary, civilian witnesses can provide compelling evidence, and their observations may lead to a successful DRE reconstruction.

Similar principles apply to obtaining information from police witnesses. They also should be encouraged to explain, expand, and articulate their observations before, during, and after the incident. Police officers differ in training and experience, as well as in their skill in recognizing substance influence. They may not report observations that they consider insignificant but that are, in fact, key information. Officers sometimes report conclusions rather than the facts that were the basis of the conclusions. For example, if an officer opines that a suspect was paranoid, he needs to explain the basis of that opinion.

Officers may administer sobriety tests at the scene of a crash. Due, however, to distractions (sirens, strobe lights, helicopters, people crying hysterically) and unsuitable conditions (wet roads, potholes, sloped surfaces), sobriety testing may not be possible. On occasion, an officer determines that the person is so impaired he would endanger himself or others if required to perform tests at roadside. That decision to forego roadside tests supports a reconstruction conclusion of drug impairment.

Missing evidence is not the focus of skilled reconstruction. Rather, the focus is *all* available evidence. This approach is equally valid for prosecutors when the defense offers alternate explanations for evidence. For example, an elevated pulse is a sign associated with cocaine and other stimulants, and a DRE considers the elevated pulse rate in forming his/her opinion. Defense counsel may challenge the officer's opinion by pointing out alternative causes of an elevated pulse (situational stress such as an encounter with a police officer, excitement, caffeine). The defense may call an expert witness to testify about other causes of an elevated pulse, and the prosecutor must elicit testimony from that expert that stimulant influence is a common cause of pulse rate elevation. Importantly, too, the prosecutor must elicit testimony about the other signs and symptoms of stimulant influence, demonstrating that the DRE's opinion was not based solely on the elevated pulse. The appropriate focus for both the reconstructionist and the prosecutor is observed, documented evidence rather than missing evidence.

Reconstruction occurs most commonly as a result of a serious vehicle crash, often involving grave injuries and fatalities, for which neither sobriety testing nor DRE evaluation were conducted. Lacking these sources of information, EMT (all emergency medical personnel) observations become critical. Who requested an EMT response, what was said, and importantly, how it was said? The investigator will need to listen to an audio recording of the emergency call, especially if it was the suspect who called. The message content as well as the manner of speaking may be inculpatory or exculpatory. Non-responsiveness to questions, repetitive speaking, and cyclic behavior are key indicators of drug influence.

In an effort to preserve life and alleviate trauma, an EMT evaluates the consciousness, responsiveness to pain, awareness of surrounding, and vital signs of crash victims. Pupil size and light reactivity are assessed. A notation of PERL in a report means that the victim's pupils were equal and reactive to light, providing some indication of normal eye function. Readily visible nystagmus is reported, but since the EMT does not perform a rigorous examination, a failure to report nystagmus does not prove that it was not present.

EMTs note whether a victim's pupils were dilated, constricted, or normal. An interpretation of these observations, however, is contingent on the context. Dilated pupils are expected in the dark, and a normal pupil constricts in response to bright lights. The EMT report form may not allow for remarks about light conditions, and an interview of the EMT may be necessary to obtain that information.

EMTs assess and report victims' vital signs. Again, the context must be considered. Since the general pandemonium of a crash scene is expected to elevate vital signs, a low pulse rate may indicate the influence of a drug that depresses the vital signs. Changes in vital signs over time may be significant, and EMT findings can be interpreted in comparison to assessments by police officers and hospital personnel.

EMT reports often, but not always, include comments about the odor of alcohol or other signs and symptoms of drug influence. The reconstructionist must specifically ask the EMT about odor, injection marks, burns on fingers or lips, and drug residue on or about the person.

Nurses, physicians, and other medical personnel have extensive experience assessing trauma victims' physical conditions with and without drug influence. A chronologically ordered interview, beginning with initial observations and continuing through diagnosis and treatment, provides the most comprehensive information. Medical professionals sometimes are reluctant interviewees because of concerns about doctor/patient confidentiality, but the confidentially guarantee generally does not apply to a criminal investigation. Since medical personnel focus on lifesaving activities and may not closely attend to a patient's substance use, the fact that signs of drug influence were not documented does not necessarily mean that the signs were not present. In addition to affecting clinical signs, drugs usually affect behavior, and nursing notes typically document behavior, attitude, and consciousness

A collision reconstructionist recreates the crash environment in an effort to understand the physics and specific causes of the crash. Since DUID drivers are likely to drive in a manner consistent with the drug that has been used, the crash reconstruction often points to specific drugs. A driver under-the-influence of a stimulant, for example, often speeds, makes frequent lane changes, and follows too closely. This driving pattern, which is consistent with stimulation, will be replaced by opposite effects during the ensuing *crash* phase of the stimulant cycle. Ironically, a vehicle crash often accompanies the physiological crash.

Crash reconstruction is a kind of differential diagnosis, similar to "the art or act of identifying a disease from its signs and symptoms."[16] A reconstructionist accumulates measurements and other data, performs needed calculations, and is led to a conclusion by facts. This analytical process yields a final, informed opinion about crash causation.

In summary, a DRE reconstruction may or may not yield a definitive opinion about the influence of alcohol or other drugs. If body fluid specimens were not collected within a relevant time period or witnesses no longer remember the event reliably, the investigation is severely limited. And whatever the limitations and constraints in a particular case, the DRE must adhere to the legal and moral standards that would apply to a full evaluation. Officers who undertake reconstruction are not exempt from the standard of a *reasonable degree of certainty*. Nonetheless, absent a DRE evaluation, a thorough reconstruction is likely to produce the best evidence concerning drug-influence.

Endnote

1. National Institute of Justice. (2003). Drug and alcohol use and related matters among arrestees. Washington, D.C.: National Institute of Justice, Office of Justice Programs, U.S. Department of Justice.

2. National Highway Safety Administration.(2004). Alcohol related fatalities by state, 2003. National Highway Traffic Safety Administration, crash stats report. DOT HS 809 780, August 2004. Washington, D.C.: U.S. Department of Transportation, National Highway Safety Administration.

3. Pharmacokinetics relates to the disposition of the drugs in the body: the absorption, distribution, metabolism, and elimination. In lay terms, pharmacokinetics refers to what the body does to the drug. Pharmacodynamics, on the other hand, refers to the action of the drug on the body.

4. The DRE program is also known by its formal name, the Drug Evaluation and Classification Program (DECP). For the purposes of this chapter, DRE and DECP are synonymous.

5. There are many scenarios that may result in the person being prevented from driving from the scene, although the person may not be under-the-influence of drugs or alcohol. Extreme fatigue is one of those reasons.

6. Traffic enforcement officers occasionally debate the difference between impairment and intoxication in Internet forums. Some officers have maintained that if a person is impaired while driving, then that person can and should be arrested for Driving Under-the-Influence. These officers may believe that if the person is impaired, then that fact alone meets the standard of "probable cause" to affect an arrest. Others, including this author, maintain that there must exist a nexus between impairment and the presence of alcohol and/or drugs; that the officer must have cause to believe that the impairment is due to a substance(s).

7. The seven DRE categories are: CNS Depressants, Inhalants, Phencyclidine (and its analogues), Cannabis, CNS Stimulants, Hallucinogens, and Narcotic Analgesics.

8. The duration of effects of cocaine, as with all drugs, is dependent upon many factors, including the method of administration of the drug. Oral ingestion typically results in longer, but less-acute effects. Smoking, or inhaling the vapors, and injecting the drug produce almost immediate effects of acute intensity.

9. A "history and physical" is the basis for a medical diagnosis.

10. In November of 2004, the Technical Advisory Panel of the IACP revised the procedures for assessing lack of convergence. Prior to this time, the standard procedure was for the pen or pencil to briefly touch the bridge of the nose.

11. Although the Romberg Balance and the Finger-to-Nose tests are not part of the Standardized Field Sobriety Test (SFST) battery, they provide valuable clues of drug impairment.

12. Normal ranges: Pulse rate: 60 to 90 pulsations per minute; Blood Pressure: 120-140 mm Hg systolic, 70-90 mm Hg diastolic; Temperature: 98.6 degrees Fahrenheit +/- 1o.

13. A normal range of 3.0-6.5 mm for pupil size in all light levels was the DRE standard until November of 2004. At that time, the Technical Advisory Panel tentatively approved a curriculum change to: Room light, 2.5-5.0 mm; Direct light, 2.0-4.5 mm; and Near Total Darkness, 5.0-8.5 mm. This change became effective in 2005.

14. The Technical Advisory Panel voted in November of 2001 to eliminate the indirect light portion of the darkroom examination. This is the first significant change in procedures since DRE evidence has been subjected to admissibility hearings under Frye and related standards.

15. The legal definitions of driving under the influence and drugs vary according to jurisdiction. For example, some jurisdictions specify "motor vehicle," but others simply use the word "vehicle."

16. "Hype kit" is law enforcement vernacular for the equipment and paraphernalia used to inject illicit drugs. The typical "hype kit" includes a syringe, matches, tourniquet, cotton balls, and bottle caps or cookers.

17. Sympathomimetics, by definition, mimic the activation of the sympathetic division of the autonomic nervous system. The sympathetic nervous system is commonly called the "fight or flight" system.

18. Merriam Webster's Collegiate Dictionary, 10th Edition.

Chapter 3

Drug Impaired Driving Fundamentals[1]

Sarah Kerrigan

3.1 Introduction

Adjudication of drug-impaired driving cases is inherently complex. Despite the fact that driving under the influence of drugs (DUID) is a widespread problem, these cases may require special consideration and interpretation on a case-by-case basis. This chapter is an overview of this challenging area, focusing on commonly encountered drugs, their effects and how they impair, in addition to issues surrounding scientific testimony and the expert's opinion.

3.2 The Scope of the Problem: *Prevalence of drug-impaired driving?*

Although it is well recognized that drug and alcohol use can be detrimental to safe driving, drug-impaired driving is under-reported and under-recognized. Incidence and prevalence data are relatively sparse. Although it is illegal to drive under the influence of drugs anywhere in the United States, the specific drugs that are prohibited and the statutory language vary widely. Toxicology testing is expensive, resources vary from state to state, and protocols vary between laboratories. Nevertheless, DUID now represents a significant portion of impaired driving casework in laboratories throughout the nation. Studies conducted by the Substance Abuse and Mental Health Services Administration (SAMHSA, 2004, 2003) and the National Highway and Traffic Safety Administration (NHTSA, 2004) indicate the following:

- In 2003, an estimated eleven million persons aged twelve or older reported driving under the influence of an illicit drug during the past year.
- As many as 18 percent of twenty-one-year-olds report drugged driving at least once during the past year.
- Drugs are used by approximately 10-22 percent of drivers involved in accidents, often in combination with alcohol.
- A study of fatally injured drivers from seven states showed that alcohol was present in more than 50 percent of the drivers; other drugs were present in 18 percent of the drivers.
- The incidence of drug-use among drivers arrested for motor vehicle offenses ranges between 15-50 percent.

Although it is well understood that drug use can be detrimental to safe driving, the extent to which drugs impair driving is often difficult to measure, predict or quantify. The degree of impairment depends upon many variables including the dose, drug history and time since drug use. Some drugs have the potential to impair driving performance for extended periods, while others may impair during the "downside," during which time the drug concentration may be decreasing or very low. For this reason, DUID casework is extremely challenging for toxicologists who must take all these factors into consideration.

3.3 Alcohol versus Drug-Related DUI: *Alcohol is a drug, but not all drugs are alcohol*

Driving impairment by a drug other than alcohol is a complex topic. Alcohol is a single substance, and its effects on the body and on driving have been studied extensively. In contrast, there are numerous potentially impairing illicit, prescription, and over-the-counter drugs. Although the scientific literature on the effects of drugs on driving is expanding, many drugs have not been fully investigated. Furthermore, drugs are often used in combination with alcohol or other drugs, requiring a case-by-case evaluation of the potential for interaction and possible impairment. Whereas most people are familiar with the effects of alcohol to some degree, the same is not true for many drugs. In the courtroom, jurors require sufficient information to enable them to understand the effects that drugs can have on driving skills.

Per se limits establish the legal limit of ethanol for driving as 0.08 g/ 100 mL blood. Above that concentration, a driver is deemed to be impaired. There are no widely accepted standards for other drugs. Statutory approaches to drugs and driving are generally approached in one of three ways:

- statutes that require the drug to render a driver *incapable* of driving safely;
- statutes that require the drug to impair a driver's ability to operate a vehicle safely or require a driver to be *under the influence, impaired* or *affected* by an intoxicating drug; or
- *per se* laws that make it a criminal offense to have a specified drug or drug by-product (metabolite) in the body while operating a vehicle. Some states' per se drug laws incorporate a *zero tolerance* standard in which any detectable level of a specified drug or metabolite constitutes a violation while a few states list actual drug concentrations at which a violation occurs.

The first two approaches, which are the most prevalent, require evidence that a driver was affected by a drug at the time of the offense. Because this is technically complicated, some states have adopted per se or zero-tolerance drug laws. States with zero-tolerance statutes make the presence of any specified drug or metabolite in blood or urine obtained from a person who was operating a motor vehicle a crime in and of itself; i.e., distinct from a charge of drug-impaired driving. These laws facilitate the identification, prosecution and treatment of drivers who use drugs, and they typically are used in conjunction with incapacity or under the influence statutes. Zero-tolerance drug laws do not supplant drugged driving laws that require demonstration that the driver was affected by the drug.

3.4 Prevalence of Drugs in DUI: *Which drugs are most frequently encountered?*

Marijuana, stimulants, depressants and opiates are the most frequently encountered drugs in impaired drivers. Prevalence of specific drugs varies, however, by geographical location; for example, there is more methamphetamine use on the West coast, and more oxycodone use on the East coast. Table 3.1 lists licit and illicit drugs by drug class. Many abused substances also have legitimate uses, and in those zero-tolerance states where a valid prescription constitutes a legitimate defense, prosecution must proceed under an incapacity or an under the influence statute with evidence that the person was affected to some degree. The necessary degree to which a driver must be impaired is usually defined by statute or case law.

In 2003, marijuana was the most commonly used illicit drug in the United States (14.6 million users) followed by the non-medical use of prescription drugs (6.3 million) (SAMHSA, 2004). Of those persons who abused prescription drugs, an estimated 4.7 million abused pain relievers, 1.8 million abused tranquilizers, 1.2 million abused stimulants and 0.3 million abused sedative medications. In the same year, estimates for cocaine and hallucinogens were 2.3 million and one million.

Measures of drug prevalence are also a function of drug testing methodology and specimen type (blood, urine, saliva, other). A drug's detection time (the time that the drug or its metabolite is present in a given bio-

Drug Class	Uses	Examples
Depressants	**Anticonvulsants** **Antidepressants** **Antihistamines** **Anxiolytics** **Hypnotics** **Muscle relaxants** **Anticataplectic** **Sedatives**	**Alprazolam, Amitriptyline, Caramazepine, Carisoprodol, Diazepam, Diphenhydramine, Gamma-Hydroxybutyrate** *(Goop, Grievous Bodily Harm, Good Hormones at Bedtime, Max, Soap)* **Meprobamate, Phenobarbital, Temazepam, Trazodone, Zolpidem**
Stimulants	**Anorectics** **Attention Deficit** **Disorder** **Narcoleptics** **Local anesthetic**	**Amphetamine, Cocaine** *(Blow, Horn, Nose Candy, Jelly Beans (crack), Rooster (crack), Tornado (crack), Moonrock (crack and heroin), Wicky Stick (crack, PCP, and marijuana), Snowball (cocaine and heroin))* **Methamphetamine** *(Bikers coffee, Chalk, Chicken Feed, Crank, Crystal Meth, Glass, Go Fast, Ice, Meth, Poor Man's Cocaine, Shabu, Speed, Stove Top, Trash, Yellow Bam),* **MDMA*** *(Disco Biscuit, Hug Drug, Go, XTC)*
Opioids	**Analgesics** **Antitussives** (cough suppressaants)	**Codeine, Fentanyl, Heroin*** (Smack, Hell Dust, Big H, Thunder, Nose drops, (liquefied heroin), Crop (low-quality heroin), Dragon Rock (heroin and crack), A-Bomb (marijuana and heroin)) **Hydrocodone, Methadone, Morphine, Oxycodone, Propoxyphene**
Hallucinogens	**Anethetic adjunct** **Appetite stimulant** **Antiemetic**	**Ketamine** (Cat Valium, K, Jet, Super Acid), **Lysergic Acid Diethylamide* (LSD)** Acid, Acid Cube, Backbreaker, Battery Acid, Doses, Dots, Elvis, Loony Tunes, Superman, Window Pane, Zen), **MDMA*** *(Disco Biscuit, Hug Drug, Go, XTC)*, **Mescaline*, PCP*, Peyote*, Tetrahydrocannabinol (THC)** (Bud, Dope, Ganja, Herb, Hydro, Indo, Mary Jane, Shake)

* Indicates no currently approved medicinal use in the United States.

Table 3.1 *Licit and illicit drugs by drug class*

logical specimen) varies with dose, route of administration and elimination rate.

3.5 Common Drug Effects: *Pharmacology Basics*

Drugs that affect the central nervous system (CNS) produce characteristic effects by class, such as depressants, stimulants, opioids (narcotic analgesics) or hallucinogens (Table 3.2). Although drugs within a class produce predictable effects, such as the ataxia, slow movements and slurred speech associated with depressant drugs, other effects are more complicated.

Some substances have characteristics of more than a single drug class. For example, tetrahydrocannabinol (THC), the principal active component of marijuana, has both hallucinogenic and depressant effects; Methylenedioxymethamphetamine (MDMA, Ecstasy) acts as both a stimulant and a psychedelic; Phencyclidine (PCP) and ketamine have both depressant and psychedelic effects. Although observable signs of drug use are determined, to a large extent, by the pharmacology of the drug, a user's behavior will also be affected by the amount of drug ingested, the environment or setting of use, and the concomitant use of other substances. The individual's history of drug use, mood, and expectation of drug effects are also important variables.

Drug	Effects
Depressants	Ataxia, disorientation, decreased inhibitions, fumbling, ptosis (droopy eyelids), sluggishness, slowed reflexes, sedation, slurred speech
Hallucinogens	Body tremors, dazed appearance, diaphoresis (perspiration), disorientation, dysarthria (difficulty in articulating words), memory loss, muscle rigidity, nausea, paranoia, poor coordination, poor time and distance perception, synesthesia (blending of the senses), visual/auditory disturbances
Marijuana	Ataxia, body tremors, disorientation, eyelid tremors, increased appetite, poor time and distance perception, paranoia, reddened conjunctiva, reduced inhibitions, transient muscle rigidity
Opioids	Ataxia, constipation, dry mouth, dysphoria, euphoria, facial itching, low, raspy voice, ptosis (droopy eyelids), mental clouding, muscle flaccidity, nausea, nodding off, sedation, slow reflexes, vomiting
PCP	Agitation, ataxia, blank stare, confusion, cyclic behavior, diaphoresis, dissociative anethesia, dysarthria, hallucinations, "moon walking," muscle rigidity
Stimulants	Anxiety, body tremors, bruxism (teeth grinding), dry mouth, excitation, eyelid tremors, euphoria, hyperreflexia (overactivity of physiological reflexes), hypervigilance, insomnia, irritability, jaw tightness, muscle rigidity, reduced appetite, rhinorrhea (runny nose), reddening of nasal mucosa, talkativeness

Table 3.2 *Effects by drug class.*

Drugs with a high potential for abuse may also produce characteristic withdrawal effects (Table 3.3). These are sometimes the exact opposite of the desired or expected effect of the drug. For example, during withdrawal or the "crash" phase following binge use of methamphetamine, a potent stimulant, the user experiences profound lethargy, exhaustion and hypersomnolence.

Knowledge of characteristic appearance, behavior and other observable effects is extremely important to the toxicologist who provides expert testimony. The presence of a drug or drugs in a biological specimen provides valuable insight, but most toxicologists also consider other factors.

Drug	Withdrawal Symptoms
Stimulants	Muscular aches, abdominal pain, tremors, anxiety, hypersomnolence (extreme fatigue), lack of energy, depression, suicidal thoughts, exhaustion
Opioids	Dilated pupils, rapid pulse, piloerection (erection/bristling of hairs), abdominal cramps, muscle spasms, vomiting, diarrhea, tremulousness, yawning, anxiety
Depressants	Tremulousness, insomnia, sweating, fever, anxiety, cardiovascular collapse, agitation, delirium, hallucinations, disorientation, convulsions, shock
Marijuana	Anorexia, nausea, insomnia, restlessness, irritability, anxiety, depression

Table 3.3 Withdrawal symptoms by drug class.

A. Pharmacology

The pharmacology of a drug encompasses two disciplines: pharmacokinetics and pharmacodynamics. Pharmacokinetics comes from the Greek words *pharmacon* meaning drug and *kinesis* meaning movement, and together the terms refer to how the drug moves about the body. Pharmacokinetics addresses questions such as "When was the drug used?" and "How much was taken?" Pharmacodynamics refers to the way in which the drug interacts with receptors in the brain. It answers the questions, "What are the effects?", "What type of impairment is expected?"

B. Pharmacokinetics

Pharmacokinetics involves the processes of absorption, distribution, metabolism and elimination, which determine the efficacy of the drug, its concentration at the active site, and the intensity and duration of its effects. The pharmacokinetic properties of drugs enable scientists and clinicians to develop new therapeutics, understand the factors that govern abuse, and determine how drugs can be detected over time, as well as to predict and describe their effects on human performance.

C. Route of administration

The onset of action, the duration of effects, and the intensity and quality of the experience depend upon the route of administration (Table 3.4). Intravenous drug administration provides maximum drug delivery and rapid onset of effects. Injection of a drug bypasses the body's natural safeguards, however, and can lead to complications such as infection, virus transmission, emboli, blood vessel occlusion, thrombosis and irritation. In part due to these risks, inhalation and smoking are popular alternatives. A smoked drug is rapidly absorbed in the lungs and transported to the brain via the arterial blood supply. Smoking is a preferred route of crack cocaine administration due to rapid onset and the intensity of the experienced euphoria. Efficient delivery and speed increase a drug's reinforcing effects and thereby its potential for abuse.

Route	Drugs
Oral	Cannabinoids, opiates, LSD, mescaline, peyote, GHB, benzodiazepines
Inhalation	Solvents, gases, low boiling point alkaloids
Intravenous	Opiates, cocaine, methamphetamine, PCP
Smoking	Marijuana, PCP, crack cocaine, methamphetamine (ice)
Intranasal	Cocaine, heroin, methamphetamine
Dermal	Fentanyl, nicotine

Table 3.4 Routes of administration

D. Absorption

To exert a pharmacologic effect, a drug must gain entry to the body by absorption, a process largely determined by the drug's physical and chemical properties. For example, a drug's tendency to be acidic, basic or neutral influences its absorption, as does its preference for water (water-soluble) or fat (fat-soluble).

E. Distribution

Once a drug has been absorbed, the distribution phase begins. Depending on the properties of the drug, it undergoes diffusion, filtration or transportation that distributes it to surrounding tissues and organs. Lipid (fat) soluble drugs are distributed readily into the tissues. THC is a fat-soluble drug and is distributed and stored in tissues and fat depots within the body. This accounts for its gradual release and long half-life.

The extent to which a drug is distributed in the body is related to its volume of distribution (Vd). Essentially, the volume of distribution is a proportional constant between the dose and the total plasma drug concentration. Highly water-soluble (hydrophilic) drugs, like ethanol (Vd 0.5 L/kg), are distributed predominantly in body water and have low volumes of distribution. Conversely, drugs with large volumes of distribution, such as heroin (Vd 25 L/kg), are extensively distributed throughout the body and into the tissues (Table 3.5).

F. Metabolism

Relatively small amounts of most drugs are excreted from the body unchanged, the remainder of the drug undergoes metabolism. The process speeds elimination and prevents accumulation of the drug in the body. Many variables affect drug metabolism, including age, sex, genetic polymorphisms, health, disease, and nutrition.

Metabolism increases the water solubility of the drug thereby facilitating its elimination via urine. It also affects pharmacological activity. For example, cocaine is metabolized to benzoylecgonine and THC to 11-nor-9-carboxy-delta-9-THC (carboxy-THC), both of which are pharmacologically inactive. The metabolites of some drugs are pharmacologically active and contribute to the overall effects. Examples of drugs with pharmacologically active metabolites include diazepam, which is metabolized to nordiazepam, carisoprodol, which is metabolized to meprobamate, and codeine, which is metabolized to morphine.

G. Elimination

Ethanol clearance is described as "zero order," which means that it is eliminated at a fixed rate with the average rate being 0.015 g/100mL/hour. Most other drugs are eliminated by "first order" kinetics, which means that clearance is non-linear. Figure 3.1 depicts zero and first order kinetics. Because the elimination rate for most drugs is non-linear, it is described by its half-life ($T_{1/2}$), which is the time taken to eliminate half of the drug (Table 3.5).

H. Pharmacodynamics

The effect of a drug depends on its action at a receptor site. An increase in drug concentration modulates the receptor response and enhances the pharmacologic effect. This relationship underlies dose response with the effect becoming more pronounced as the dose increases. Although the duration of effect can be estimated, it varies with dose and residual effects may persist in time beyond the drug's acute effects (Table 3.5). The link between drug amount and drug effect over time is the basis for establish-

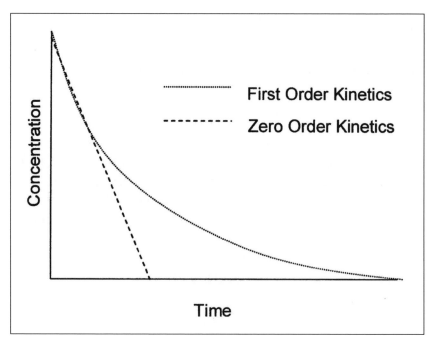

Figure 3.1 *Zero and first order kinetics*

Drug	Clinical Dose	Half-Life	V_d (L/kg)	Duration of Effect[#]	Excreted unchanged in urine	Principal Metabolite(s)
Alprazolam	0.25-2 mg	6-27 h	0.9-1.3	4-8 h	20%	Alpha-hydroxyalprazolam[+]
Carisoprodol	200-350 mg	0.9 - 2.4 h	-	4-6 h	<1%	Meprobamate[+]
Cocaine	40-100 mg	0.5-1 h	1.6-2.7	1-2 h	<10%	Benzoylecgonine, Ecgonine methyl ester
Diazepam	4-40 mg	21-37 h	0.7-2.6	4-8 h	<1%	Nordiazepam,[+] temazepam,[+] oxazepam[+]
GHB	2-4 g	0.3-1 h	0.4	3-6 h	-	-
MDMA	-	8 h	5-8	1-4 h	65%	Methylenedioxyamphetamine (MDA)[+]
Methadone	20-200 mg	15-55 h	5	12-24 h	5-50%	2-ethylidene-1, 5-dimethyl-3, 3-diphenylpyrrolidine (EDDP)
Methamphetamine	2.5-15 mg	6-15 h	3-7	2-4 h	10-20%	Amphetamine[+]
Morphine	5-30 mg	4-6 h	2-5	4-6 h	<10%	Conjugated morphine
Oxycodone	2.5-10 mg	4-6 h	1.8-3.7	4-5 h	15%	Oxymorphone,[+] conjugated oxycodone
THC	2.5-10 mg	20-57 h	4-14	3-6 h	<1%	11-nor-9-carboxy-delta-9-THC (Carboxy-THC)

Sources: Baselt, R.C. (2001). *Drug effects on human performance and behavior*, Baselt, R.C. (2004). *Disposition of toxic drugs and chemicals in man* (7th ed.), and Wilson, J. (1994). *Abused drugs*.

Residual effects may last for extended periods   + Pharmacologically active metabolite

Table 3.5 *Drug distribution in the body.*

ing therapeutic and toxic drug concentrations. These ranges are widely published for clinical purposes, but there are no therapeutic concentrations for many illicit drugs. Furthermore, habitual drug users may develop tolerance to a drug's toxic effects, allowing them to withstand concentrations of drug that would be highly toxic or fatal in a naïve subject.

The pharmacologic effect is a function of time elapsed since ingestion as well as the blood-drug concentration. For this reason, a given concentration can produce widely varying effects with time, a phenomenon referred to as hysteresis. To illustrate, during the absorption phase after ethanol consumption, a person usually feels more excited and euphoric than during the elimination phase. CNS stimulants like methamphetamine follow a similar cycle. At a given concentration during the absorption phase (when the drug concentration is *increasing*) methamphetamine may produce euphoria, exhilaration, restlessness and stimulation. Several hours later during the elimination phase (when the drug concentration is *decreasing*), the same drug concentration may be associated with confusion, depression, anxiety and exhaustion. THC exhibits a counterclockwise hysteresis, indicating a slight delay between the effects and blood concentration.

Because the presence of a drug or metabolite in urine only indicates exposure at some previous time or times over a period of hours, days or even weeks, blood is the matrix of choice for the purpose of determining impairment. Nonetheless, with the exception of ethanol, there is no direct correlation between the concentration of a drug in the blood and the level of impairment.

Tolerance affects the pharmacodynamic response to a drug. A cocaine blood concentration sufficient to produce mild effects in a chronic user could be acutely cardiotoxic in a naïve user, resulting in coma and death. The pharmacologic effects being experienced by a drug user may be apparent from vital signs, involuntary reflexes, and behavior. These signs, symptoms and behaviors, as observed by clinicians and law enforcement personnel, are highly relevant to toxicological interpretations of drug concentrations in blood.

3.6 How Do Drugs Affect Driving? *Relating drug effects to driving impairment.*

Drugs may impair driving, because they have the potential to impair basic skills that are essential to safe motor vehicle operation (Figure 3.2). Driving is a time-shared task with a high demand for information processing and division of attention. Any drug that affects cognition could potentially impair attention, concentration, risk avoidance, and emergency decisions. CNS depressants can slow information processing, impair decision-making, and attention, and interfere with tracking (steering) or the maintenance of the vehicle's position in the lane. Agitation, preoccupation, or distractibility which may result from the use of potent stimulant drugs and can interfere with essential driving skills. Judgment, a key component of safe driving, is affected by mood-altering drugs.

Vehicle control depends on coordination and psychomotor responses. Thus, drugs that affect nerves and muscles and impair braking, steering, and acceleration are inconsistent with safe driving. Characteristic impaired-driving errors, e.g. striking a fixed object or rear-ending another vehicle, often are the result of slowed response time.

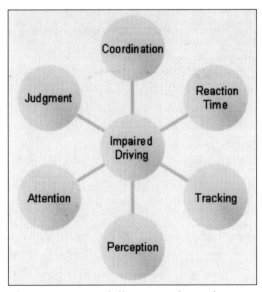

Figure 3.2 Basic skills essential to safe motor vehicle operations.

Perception is an important component of driving skill, and misperceptions or perception deficits underlie many crashes. Hallucinogens can distort visual perception, and marijuana can interfere with the perception of time and distance Cocaine can produce visual disturbances in the form of snow lights or flashes of light in peripheral vision, and many depressant drugs and therapeutics can blur vision.

Progressive symptoms and the impairment associated with some commonly encountered drugs are summarized in Table 3.6. Responses vary, however, due to both inter and intra-individual differences. For this and other reasons, the scientific evaluation of driving performance is technically and logistically complex, and it is extremely unlikely that an individual under the influence of a drug can correctly assess his or her own fitness to drive.

3.7 Measuring Impairment: *The scientific literature*

The scientific study of drug effects on driving skills is ongoing and likely will remain so due to the number of drugs that are potentially impairing and the ethical and safety issues that limit controlled study. For the foreseeable future, toxicologists must rely on a combination of sources, including those that have data only for a limited number of drugs. Collectively, information from a variety of sources enables a toxicologist to determine, in many cases, whether a drug's effects are consistent with safe driving.

- empirical considerations (drug pharmacology, uses and effects)
- epidemiological studies
- case reports
- laboratory studies
- simulator studies
- actual driving studies

Different sources of data have differing merits and limits (Table 3.7). Also, the data from studies of drugs in combination may be misleading or misinterpreted. For example, laboratory studies report that a single, low dose of stimulant (methamphetamine) can offset sedation caused by a depressant (alcohol). This finding does not equate to a reversal of effects or

Drug	Progressive Symptoms	Impairment
Alprazolam*	Drowsiness, confusion, lightheadedness, weakness, lack of coordination, blurred vision, fatigue, irritability	Subjective sedation, impaired vision, reaction time, memory, tracking, vigilance, cognitive function, psychomotor function
Carisoprodol*/Meprobamate*	Drowsiness, dizziness, ataxia, slurred speech, tremor, irritability, syncope, weakness	Attention, reaction time, subjective sedation, psychomotor function
Cocaine	Restlessness, euphoria, dizziness, mydriasis, hyper-activity, irritability, dyskinesia, anxiety, tremor, dysphoria, insomnia, psychosis, fatigue, lethargy	Subjective confusion, perception, hallucinations, judgment
Diazepam*	Drowsiness, lethargy, ataxia, dizziness, confusion	Vigilance, reaction time, memory, subjective sedation, attention, perception, anticipation of hazards, speed control, tracking, psychomotor function
GHB*	Drowsiness, lethargy, euphoria, confusion, disorientation, slurred speech, ataxia, nausea, vomiting, mydriasis, reduced inhibitions, dizziness, unconsciousness	Cognitive function, psychomotor function, loss of peripheral vision, visual disturbances
MDMA	Sensory disturbances, nausea, dizziness, ataxia, diaphoresis, muscular rigidity, restlessness, tremor	Subjective excitability, perception, cognitive function, attention, memory, psychomotor function
Methadone*	Drowsiness, dizziness, weakness, disorientation, miosis, lightheadedness, visual disturbances	Vision, reaction time, subjective sedation

*Warning from manufacturer

Table 3.6 [2-5] *Progressive symptoms and impairment associated with commonly encountered drugs.*

Drug	Progressive Symptoms	Impairment
Methamphetamine*	Restlessness, euphoria, dizziness, mydriasis, dyskinesia, tremor, dysphoria, insomnia, irritability, nervousness, rapid speech, confusion, agitation, hyperactivity, psychosis, fatigue, somnolence, anxiety, delusions	Perception, judgment, attention, psychomotor function
Morphine*	Drowsiness, dizziness, lethargy, ataxia, miosis, visual disturbances, weakness, confusion	Subjective sedation, reaction time, psychomotor function, cognitive function
Oxycodone*	Drowsiness, dizziness, lethargy, miosis, weakness, confusion	Psychomotor function, subjective sedation, reaction time
THC*	Ataxia, confusion, dizziness, somnolence, euphoria, relaxation, hallucinations, speech difficulty, weakness, malaise, visual disturbances, paranoia	Perception, subjective sedation, reaction time, memory, vigilance, attention, emergency decision making, psychomotor function, cognitive function

*Warning from manufacturer

Table 3.6 (cont.) Progressive symptoms and impairment associated with commonly encountered drugs.

a zero net effect. Alleviation of sedation may not be accompanied, for example, by a reversal of effects on judgment, attention, and psychomotor skills.

Psychoactive drugs affect driving by enhancing or impairing human performance. The same drug may either enhance or impair performance, depending, in part, on the dose and pattern of drug use. For example, in the laboratory a single, low doses of amphetamine (5-15 mg) and methamphetamine (10-30 mg) improved alertness and psychomotor performance in healthy, sleep-deprived individuals. Real-world doses of methamphetamine, however, often far exceed those that can be administered to

Approach	Advantages	Disadvantages
Empirical	Readily supportable; Extensively published; can draw inferences for similar drugs	Does not anticipate an atypical response; does not account for poly-drug use or drug interactions; Not driving: individual, environment or situation specific
Epidemiological studies	Can measure population differences; can identify trends	Largely descriptive and non-specific; require large numbers; difficult and expensive; may be time/location sensitive
Case reports	Real-world doses; Reports of actual effects in relevant populations; First hand accounts;	Anecdotal; Lack of control data;
Laboratory studies	Identifies, measures specific skills under controlled conditions	Real-world drug doses may not be administered. Does amounts limited by safety and ethical issues; simulated driving lacks some characteristics of real driving
Simulator studies	Safe, controlled environment; Aaproximate, the driving task	Real-world drug doses may not be administered. No risk of harm to driver; dynamics of simulator differ from dynamics of real vehicles
Actual driving	Realistic driving situation; potential for real consequences	Real-world drug doses may not be administered. Liability and ethical constraints; conditions and demands of task not reproducible across subjects and sessions

Table 3.7 *Advantages and disadvantages of different data sources.*

human subjects for purposes of study. Epidemiological studies, as well as empirical knowledge of methamphetamine effects at elevated doses indicate that it impairs the skills necessary for safe driving.

3.8 Case Interpretation: *Is this driver impaired by drugs?*

Toxicological interpretation in a specific case often is difficult, because drug effects vary as a function of dose, individual metabolism, frequency of drug use, and the presence of other drugs. Information about one or more of these factors frequently is not available. It may be possible to estimate drug ingestion time using pharmacokinetic principles such as drug half-life. If a drug is eliminated by first order kinetics, 99 percent of will be eliminated in seven half-lives, and less than 1 percent will remain in the body. Given ten half-lives, 99.9 percent will have been eliminated. Detection times in body fluids can be estimated, but these vary by drug, dose, metabolism, as well as age, sex and health of the user.

Since drug detection times in blood are typically shorter than in urine, a blood specimen that contains a drug is better evidence of recent use than a urine specimen. Because the dose of drug is usually unknown, it is generally not possible to determine exactly when the drug was administered, but a "window of drug use" may be estimated. For example, THC blood concentrations increase rapidly during smoking but decline rapidly upon cessation of smoking. As a result, elevated THC blood concentrations indicate recent drug use.

Quantification of drug blood concentrations sometime is sufficient for pharmacological interpretation based upon known effects and reference data. There is, however, a limited detection window of time for blood specimens.

The therapeutic, toxic and lethal blood concentrations of licit and illicit drugs must be interpreted with caution due to inter-individual differences. Therapeutic and toxic ranges overlap for some drugs, and human performance may be impaired at therapeutic concentrations. Hypnotics and sedatives, for example, can impair driving at therapeutic concentrations due to CNS depression. Though drug blood concentrations are typically low during the "crash" phase of chronic stimulant use, the user will experience extreme fatigue and exhaustion. For these reasons, toxicological interpretation relies not only on the results of specimen analyses but must also consider other case information and the observations of law enforcement personnel or clinicians who had timely contact with the individual.

Urine is easily collected and can readily be screened for drugs. Although for most drugs detection times are longer in urine than in blood, they are affected by fluid intake, diuresis, and the effect of urinary pH on drug elimination. Urine drug concentrations have limited quantitative meaning, and collection conditions may allow adulteration. Urine drug results may be useful, however, for determinations of approximate times of exposure. For example, the detection time of 6-acetylmorphine in urine is approximately two to eight hours.

Multiple drug use complicates interpretation, because drug combinations interact in different ways:

- *additive* effects occur when a combination of drugs produce a total effect that is equal to the sum of the individual effects,
- *synergistic* effects occur when a combination of drugs produce a total effect that is greater than the sum of the individual effects, and

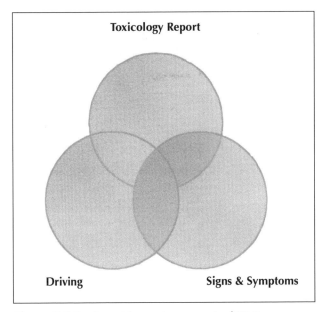

Figure 3.3 *Basic evidence in support of DUI allegation*

- *antagonistic* effects occur when the effect of one drug is lessened due to the presence of another drug.

The interpretation of toxicological analyses is complicated by the number of drugs found in a specimen, the user's health status and history of drug use, as well as by metabolism, duration of drug effects, and withdrawal. The same drug at the same dose will produce similar effects in two individuals, but severity varies and idiosyncratic responses may occur. The presence of a drug in a person's blood or urine may or may not be sufficient evidence to support an allegation of impairment. Ideally, these findings should be augmented with other information such as driving pattern, appearance, behavior, performance on standardized field sobriety tests, and a drug recognition expert (DRE) evaluation.

3.9 Testing Methodology: *The forensic toxicology laboratory*

Most forensic toxicology laboratories that routinely analyze specimens for DUI cases use a two-tiered approach. Initially, specimens are screened for common drugs or drug classes with an antibody-based test. Specimens that screen positive with this test are then confirmed with a more rigorous technique. Since it would not be feasible to initially use a confirmatory test for all drugs that a specimen possibly might contain, this two-tiered approach is time and cost effective.

A. Screening tests

An *immunoassay* test, which uses an anti-drug antibody, is the most common screening test. If a drug is present the antibody can bind to it. The degree to which binding occurs is measured, and this is the basis for the screening test. Common immunoassays for drugs of abuse include enzyme linked immunosorbent assays (ELISA), enzyme mediated immuno technique (EMIT), fluorescence polarization immunoassay (FPIA), cloned enzyme-donor immunoassay (CEDIA) and radioimmunoassay (RIA).

Immunoassay test results are considered presumptive, because the antibodies may cross-react with analogs or substances that are structurally similar to the drug to produce a false positive. For example, over-the-counter cold medicines that contain pseudoephedrine may cause a false positive for some methamphetamine immunoassays. Levels above established cut-off values or threshold concentrations are considered positive. Although cut-off concentrations are mandated for workplace testing by SAMHSA, they do not apply to forensic testing in DUI casework. The workplace levels are set high enough to avoid false positives due to inadvertent drug exposure (e.g. poppy seed ingestion). Most toxicology laboratories must use lower cut-off concentrations for criminal cases. Also, because of shorter detection times and lower concentrations in blood, the cut-off concentrations for blood specimens are typically lower in blood compared to urine.

B. Confirmatory tests

A confirmatory test is more specific and sensitive than an immunoassay test. The most frequently used technique is gas chromatography-mass spectrometry (GC-MS), but high performance liquid chromatography (HPLC), liquid-chromatography-mass spectrometry (LC-MS) and others are also used.

The specificity of confirmatory techniques allows unequivocal determination of the drug that is present. GC-MS can distinguish between structurally related drugs such as pseudoephedrine and methamphetamine. Quantitative analysis can determine blood drug concentration. A screening test requires little or no specimen preparation, but confirmatory tests require that the drug first be isolated from the biological sample, typically by using liquid-liquid extraction or solid phase extraction.

The gas chromatograph separates individual components of a specimen based on chemical and physical characteristics. The specimen then enters the mass spectrometer, where fragmentation of the drug molecule produces a characteristic mass spectrum. This molecular fingerprint of the drug, together with the characteristic retention time from the gas chromatograph identifies the drug.

3.10 Conclusions

The impact of drugs on traffic safety is undisputed. Certain drugs are capable of producing effects that are clearly inconsistent with safe driving. Yet, the mere presence of a drug or drug metabolite in a blood or urine sample does not, by itself, constitute impairment. The effect of a drug or combination of drugs on an individual driver is often difficult to predict, measure or quantify. Interpretation requires careful evaluation on a case-by-case basis. A toxicologist will consider multiple factors, including the driving pattern, observed behavior and signs or symptoms, together with the toxicology results. Using this approach, the basis of the opinion can be determined conservatively and in a scientifically justified manner.

3.11 Acknowledgements

My sincere thanks to past and present colleagues, toxicologists from other states, and the Society of Forensic Toxicologists for providing insight, training and collective experience in this challenging field.

Endnotes

1. Abbreviated from *Drug Toxicology for Prosecutors, American Prosecutors Research Institute*, National Traffic Law Center, August 2004. Reproduced with permission.

2. Baselt, R.C. *Drug Effects on Human Performance and Behavior*. Foster City, CA: Biomedical Publications, 2001.

3. Baselt, R.C. *Disposition of Toxic Drugs and Chemicals in Man* (7th ed.). Foster City, CA: Biomedical Publications, 2004.

4. *Forensic Science Review* (2002); Vol. 14 (1&2).

5. *Forensic Science Review* (2003); Vol. 15 (1).

References

Baselt, R.C. *Drug Impaired Driving*. National Highway Traffic Safety Administration, US Dept. of Transportation, http://www.nhtsa.gov. Retrieved 2004.

Substance Abuse and Mental Health Services Administration (SAMHSA) (2004). *2003 National survey on drug use and health: National findings.* Washington, D.C.: Department of Health and Human Services, Substance Abuse and Mental Health Services Administration, Office of Applied Studies. Retrieved 2004 at http://www.DrugAbuseStatistics.samhsa.gov.

Substance Abuse and Mental Health Services Administration (SAMHSA) (2003). *The NSDUH report: Drugged driving, 2002 update.* Washington, D.C.: Department of Health and Human Services, Substance Abuse and

Mental Health Services Administration. Retrieved 2004 at http://www.samhsa.gov.

Wilson, J. (1994). *Abused drugs*. Washington, D.C.: AACC Press.

Chapter 4

The Legal and Prosecution Perspective of Drug Impairment

Nina J. Emerson

4.1 Introduction

The use and abuse of mind-altering substances is not new. Since the beginning of time, people have imbibed, ingested, and smoked whatever would make them high. In fact, drug use is as old as recorded history. For example, alcohol in the form of mead was popular in the Paleolithic age (8000 B.C.), the use of opium was recorded on Sumerian tablets (4000 B.C.), and marijuana was known in China in 2737 B.C.[1] Today, in the United States, there are approximately 50 million nicotine addicts, 15 million alcoholics; 3 million marijuana addicts, about 2.5 million cocaine addicts and 1 million heroin addicts.[2] Both addiction and intoxication appear to encourage careless and combative behavior, which often results in illegal activities. Thus, most crimes are committed by people who are under the influence of alcohol, illegal drugs, or a combination of the two.[3] One of those crimes involves driving or operating a motor vehicle. In any given year, millions of Americans operate their motor vehicles while impaired by alcohol or drugs or both.[4]

This chapter will provide the reader with a general background on drugs, both legal and illicit. It is not intended to be exhaustive but rather to act as a springboard for the reader to explore the more complex issues related to drug impairment from a prosecutorial perspective. In this respect, the chapter will address the problem of drug impairment, how it intersects with the driving task, and how it is dealt with in the criminal justice system. Further, this chapter will look at how prosecutors can successfully handle cases involving drug impairment, which may not always result in prosecution. In addition, it will address alternative ways for the judiciary to deal with drug-impaired defendants. Finally, the chapter will look at how the overarching problem of drug impairment can be addressed so that it does not have to enter the criminal justice system.

4.2 Drugs In General

In comparison to what is known about alcohol impairment, much less is known about drug impairment. More is known about the relationship between alcohol consumption and driving than about any other drug.[5] This is because alcohol is a legal, socially acceptable drug and perhaps the world's oldest known drug.[6] As such, researchers have been able to dose willing subjects to varying levels of intoxication to evaluate how they perform on a wide variety of tasks.[7] Perhaps the most notable of these research studies involved the development of a standardized field sobriety test battery to be used by police officers in making drunk driving arrest decisions.[8]

In another notable study, commonly referred to as The Grand Rapids Study,[9] researchers went to crash sites, interviewed the responsible drivers and obtained breath specimens to determine the relative probability of being in an alcohol-involved crash.[10] From this and numerous other studies, it is safe to say that all people with a 0.08 percent blood alcohol concentration (BAC) are impaired to some degree. Hence, the federal government mandated that all states institute 0.08 percent as the proscribed legal level for driving and/or operating a motor vehicle. To date, all states (including Puerto Rico and Guam) have passed 0.08 percent laws, some more begrudgingly than others.[11] That being said, it does not change the fact that we know more about alcohol consumption, impairment and its affects on driving. For some people, the knowledge may come from personal experience. For others, the knowledge may come from dealing with intoxicated individuals in an arrest and prosecution setting.

4.3 Legal and Illegal Drugs

One definition of "drug" says quite simply, "a substance which has a physiological effect when ingested or otherwise introduced into the body..."[12] A definition of "drug" used by law enforcement states, "any substance, when ingested into the human body, that can impair the ability of the person to operate a vehicle safely."[13] If we were to stick with either of the definitions above, we would not get bogged down with the legal distinctions of whether a drug is "legal" or "illicit." But when working within the criminal justice system, we must work with how drugs are categorized. For example, statutes categorize drugs by schedule depending upon whether they have any legitimate medical application and abuse potential. The federal statute that sets out the authority and standards for classifying controlled substances is the Comprehensive Drug Abuse Prevention and Control Act of 1970 as amended and in effect on April 1, 1985.[14] The Attorney General makes the findings and places substances on the Schedules, per its authority under 21 USCS § 811. The standards for which substances should appear on each schedule are as follows:

- Schedule I

a. The drug or other substance has a high potential for abuse.
b. The drug or other substance has no currently accepted medical use in treatment in the United States.
c. There is a lack of accepted safety for use of the drug or other substance under medical supervision.

- Schedule II

a. The drug or other substance has a high potential for abuse.
b. The drug or other substance has a currently accepted medical use in treatment in the United States or a currently accepted medical use with severe restrictions.

   c.   Abuse of the drug or other substances may lead to severe psychological or physical dependence.

•   Schedule III

   a.   The drug or other substance has a potential for abuse less than the drugs or other substances in Schedules I and II.
   b.   The drug or other substance has a currently accepted medical use in treatment in the United States.
   c.   Abuse of the drug or other substance may lead to moderate or low physical dependence or high psychological dependence.

•   Schedule IV

   a.   The drug or other substance has a low potential for abuse relative to the drugs or other substances in Schedule III.
   b.   The drug or other substance has a currently accepted medical use in treatment in the United States.
   c.   Abuse of the drug or other substance may lead to limited physical dependence or psychological dependence relative to the drugs or other substances in Schedule III.

•   Schedule V

   a.   The drug or other substance has a low potential for abuse relative to the drugs or other substances in Schedule IV.
   b.   The drug or other substance has a currently accepted medical use in treatment in the United States.
   c.   Abuse of the drug or other substance may lead to limited physical dependence or psychological dependence relative to the drugs or other substances in Schedule IV.

Although federal law does not require them to do so, most states classify drugs in the same manner as the federal system. At least forty-two states have adopted or incorporated the Comprehensive Drug Abuse Prevention and Control Act of 1970.

A more casual definition refers to "recreational drugs" as "drugs taken on an occasional basis for enjoyment, especially when socializing."[15] The term "recreational drugs," which encompasses a wide range of narcotic and hallucinogenic drugs, was originally used literally to distinguish the form of use from that of medical necessity. In the 1980s, however, it came increasingly to reflect the view that it was possible to have intermittent and pleasurable recourse to substances of this kind without the user becoming addicted or being seen as part of the 'drug scene.' "Recreational drug users (RDUs) are not those who followed the 1960s injunction to 'tune in, turn on, and drop out', but are those who regard the preferred drug as something which could enhance without damaging the chosen lifestyle."[16] The term "designer drug" refers to "a synthetic analogue of an illegal drug, especially one devised to circumvent drug laws; a fashionable artificial drug."[17]

Another definition of drug states, "A substance used in the diagnosis, treatment, or prevention of a disease or as a component of a medication."[18] Here, the word "medicine" is defined as "a compound or preparation used for the treatment or prevention of disease, especially a drug or drugs taken by mouth." Recorded from Middle English, the word comes via Old French from Latin *medicina*, from *medicus* 'physician'.[19]

Today, entire industries are built around pharmaceutical drugs. There are underground markets, managed care markets, and federally subsidized markets. The American dream may well include better living through chemicals—legal pharmaceuticals, that is. Physicians write approximately 200,000 prescriptions for Viagra every week. In addition, about one of every fourteen people takes antidepressants.[20] Perhaps this should come as no surprise, given the expensive marketing efforts of pharmaceutical companies that now appeal directly to the consumer in both print and on television to "Ask your doctor about..."

Prescription drugs play a vital role in the lives of millions and millions of people. For example, a time-released morphine medication allows migraine suffers to lead normal lives. Although prescription drugs provide medical relief to patients, the drugs also are abused by users with and without valid prescriptions. The focus here is whether the person was impaired to a degree that he or she was less able to safely operate a motor vehicle.[21]

4.4 Drug Impairment

One defense attorney noted that in his over twenty-eight years of handling DUI cases, the number of clients taking medication prior to drinking and driving has increased by 250 to 300 percent. The combined consumption of alcohol with prescription drugs can cause an unexpected and increased impairment beyond the expected impact of either drug alone, be it alcohol or prescription drug.[22] In terms of illicit drugs, the 2003 National Survey on Drug Use and Health (NSDUH) indicated that an estimated 19.5 million Americans had used an illicit drug during the previous month. Further, an estimated eleven million people in the same survey reported driving under the influence of an illicit drug during the past year.[23] In the 1996 National Household Survey on Drug Abuse, nine million drivers self-reported driving within two hours of drug use. The most commonly reported drugs used were cocaine and marijuana.[24]

Given the increased incidence of drugged driving, there is a growing body of literature dedicated to the topic of drugs and drug impairment. Drug risk factors, however, are still not known with acceptable precision. Currently available data do not allow one to predict with confidence whether a driver who tests positive for a drug, even at a measurable concentration, was actually impaired by that drug at the time of a crash. This is in stark contrast to what is known about alcohol concentrations and corresponding levels of impairment.[25] Similarly, there is relatively little information available concerning the true incidence and prevalence of illicit drug use in impaired driving. Most of the research data concern the prevalence of illicit drugs in fatally injured drivers.[26]

Understanding drug impairment does not require a complete understanding of the psychopharmacology of drugs. Rather, it is possible to look at the resulting signs and symptoms to assess whether a person is impaired. For example, most people can describe how a drunken person acts and looks. The telltale signs include bloodshot eyes, slurred speech, an odor of intoxicants, disheveled appearance, unsteady balance, swaying, wobbling, and a general lack of coordination. But would most people be able to describe how a person looks or acts when under the influence of cocaine or heroin? The difference is that although the effects of alcohol are within the ken of most people, the same cannot be said for most drugs. A notable exception may be marijuana, the use of which has been comically portrayed by characters Cheech and Chong in *Up in Smoke*[27] and

Still Smokin'.[28] Numerous other films have included marijuana use[29] so that even if a person has not smoked marijuana, he or she would probably be able to identify signs and symptoms of its use such as bloodshot eyes, thick tongue, slow responses, increased appetite, and distinct odor. The pharmacology of marijuana and its effects on driving have been studied more extensively than any other illicit drug.[30]

One way to better understand non-alcohol drugs is to become familiar with the seven drug categories established by a nationally recognized drug enforcement program. Specifically, the Drug Evaluation and Classification (DEC) Program is an advanced program that trains law enforcement officers to detect and arrest drug impaired drivers. The program is based on a systematic method for examination of impaired individuals to identify drugs within specific categories. The method does not identify a specific drug, but it narrows the focus of testing to one or more of the seven drug categories. When officers complete the training and certification, they are known as Drug Recognition Experts or DREs.[31]

The seven drug categories are: 1) central nervous system (CNS) depressants, 2) CNS stimulants, 3) inhalants, 4) narcotic analgesics, 5) cannabis, 6) hallucinogens, and 7) phencyclidine (PCP). The drugs are grouped according to the shared patterns of symptoms and signs, and the categories are associated with identifiable symptoms and observable signs in users. Therefore, drugs in one category will be unique and distinct from the drugs in the other six groups. For example, CNS depressants slow the operations of a person's brain and central nervous system. They depress heart rate, blood pressure, and other processes controlled by the brain.[32] Alcohol is the most commonly used CNS depressant, but the category includes anti-anxiety tranquilizers, antidepressants, anti-psychotic tranquilizers and various derivatives of barbituric acid.[33]

Drugs impair the ability to operate a motor vehicle, because they affect the skills necessary to the driving task. Specifically, coordination, judgment, decision-making, perception, tracking, reaction time, and divided attention/multitasking are impaired. In fact, many prescription medicines contain advisory information that a drug "may impair the mental and/or physical abilities required for the performance of potentially hazardous tasks such as driving a car or operating machinery; patients should be cautioned accordingly."[34] The information may also caution users against combining the medication with alcohol. For example, medical information for Vicodin states, "Alcohol and other CNS depressants may produce an additive CNS depression, when taken with this combination product, and should be avoided."[35] Additional caution should be taken when combined with different medications as well. "Patients receiving other narcotic analgesics, antihistamines, anti-psychotics, anti-anxiety agents, or other CNS depressants (including alcohol) concomitantly with Vicodin tablets may exhibit an additive CNS depression. When combined therapy is contemplated, the dose of one or both agents should be reduced."[36]

The DEC program provides a detailed summary (DRE Matrix) of the effects associated with each drug category. The matrix provides the general indicators, duration of effects, usual methods of administration, and overdose signs for each of the seven drug categories. This information can be obtained from the National Traffic Law Center of the American Prosecutors Research Institute or the International Association of Chiefs of Police (IACP).

4.5 Drug *Per Se* Laws

One response to the lack of knowledge about the relationship between drug quantification and drug impairment is to make it illegal for a person to have any amount of an illicit drug in his or her system at the time of driving or operating a motor vehicle. This is often considered an absolute sobriety requirement for drugs. To date, ten states have drug *per se* laws; Arizona, Georgia, Illinois, Indiana, Iowa, Minnesota, Pennsylvania, Rhode Island, Utah and Wisconsin. Nevada law prohibits a person from driving or being in actual physical control of a vehicle on a highway or on premises to which the public has access with a specific amount of a prohibited substance in his or her blood or urine. For example, the law prohibits a person from having 100 nanograms of amphetamine per milliliter of blood or 500 nanograms of amphetamine per milliliter of urine.[37]

In contrast, Georgia's per se law prohibits a person from having "any amount of marijuana or a controlled substance," as defined in Code Section 16-13-21, present in the person's blood or urine, or both, including the metabolites and derivatives of each or both without regard to whether or not any alcohol is present in the person's breath or blood.[38] Wisconsin's per se law prohibits a person from driving or operating a motor vehicle with a "detectable amount of a restricted controlled substance" in his or her blood.[39] Unlike other per se statutes, the Wisconsin statute does not include marijuana metabolites but is limited to delta-9-tetrahydrocannabinol, which is the principal active ingredient in marijuana. On the other hand, cocaine or any of its metabolites are prohibited as restricted controlled substances.

For the remaining states, a person who is driving or operating under the influence of a controlled substance or illicit drug would likely be charged with a violation of the "under the influence" statute or some derivation of that language. In fact, all states, with the exception of Texas and New York, use the phrase "under the influence" in their driving prohibitions.[40]

A number of states have further defined the standard within the statute to require that the person who is under the influence is rendered incapable of safely driving. Thus, proof of unsafe driving must be linked to the drug ingested. This places a greater burden on the prosecutor to prove a causal connection between the drug consumption and the capacity of the person to drive.[41] It was this issue that prompted the Wisconsin legislature to pass a law that prohibits driving or operating a motor vehicle with a detectable amount of a restricted controlled substance in his or her blood regardless of whether one's ability to operate safely has been impaired.

4.6 Possible Solutions

People understand that immunizations save lives and money. If addiction were treated like immunizations, taxes would be lower and society would be better. But drug use and abuse is treated as a legal and moral problem, which is subject to punitive public policy within the criminal justice system. A person formally enters the criminal justice system at the time a case is charged out by the prosecuting attorney. Once individuals get into the legal system, it is very difficult to get them into treatment. Prosecutors are often judged by their conviction rates. Yet, if offenders received the treatment they need, many of them wouldn't need to be in jail.[42] Further, findings from a number of studies in New York State indicate that individuals with alcohol addiction problems are less likely to be deterred from drinking and driving regardless of the sanctions they have experienced in the past. These findings also suggest that drunk drivers, especially the multiple offenders, need to be screened for substance abuse problems, and, if necessary, provided with treatment.

The typical response to drug-related criminal activity is to deal with the crime and hope the drug problem goes away while the person is in prison. Whether due to inadequate availability or poor quality of substance-abuse treatment services, incarceration amounts to a missed opportunity to control crime. Consider the fact that criminal activity of addict-offenders seems to rise and fall in step with their drug consumption. If drug consumption is reduced, be it unassisted or through formalized treatment that is either coerced or voluntary, then criminal activity will drop as well. Thus, a treatment-induced reduction in demand is an unequivocal winner from a crime control perspective.[43] Findings from a comprehensive study of treatment effectiveness; namely, Treatment Outcome Prospective Study (TOPS) indicate that most of the treatment related reduction in criminal activity occurs during treatment.[44] While these findings may not comport with a conventional definition of success (complete abstinence one year later), the treatment approach is a viable alternative to incarceration.

Although the New York State studies focused on the drinking-driving offender, it is reasonable to consider the application for both alcohol and other drug-related crimes. Here again, punishment by itself may not effectively reduce recidivism of alcohol and drug-related crimes by offenders who are dependent on a substance. Offenders who commit alcohol and drug-related offenses should be screened for substance abuse and dependence problems so that sanctions and rehabilitative/treatment efforts can be effectively integrated to produce the optimal results in decreasing recidivism.[45]

One solution has been successfully implemented in Brooklyn, New York. The Drug Treatment Alternative to Prison (DTAP) program, which originated in 1990, is much like a drug court in that it places offenders in a fifteen to twenty-four month intensive residential substance abuse treatment program in place of incarceration. The DTAP program is different than a drug court, because prosecutors run it. It requires less judicial interaction with participants and fewer judicial resources.

The target population for the DTAP program is repeat felony offenders who, if convicted, face mandatory imprisonment. To be eligible for the program, offenders must be drug addicted and in need of substance abuse treatment, and the addiction must have been a significant contributing factor to the crime. The prosecutor offers a plea agreement in which the defendant pleads guilty to the felony charge and agrees to a term of incarceration to be served if he or she does not complete the DTAP program. If an offender fails the program, the agreed upon prison sentence of the plea agreement takes effect. If an offender successfully completes the program, the guilty plea is withdrawn, and the felony charges are dismissed. The participant then continues with the program's employment assistance services that include job training and work experience. When ready to re-enter the community, program graduates are assisted with finding housing and employment.[46]

One of the keys to the success of this program as opposed to drug courts is that it is more flexible. Participants who break the rules at the treatment center are not automatically eliminated from the program. For example, if a participant leaves the facility without permission but later decides to return without being forced to do so, that person can be given another chance in the program. The DTAP program officials and the treatment facility staff recognize that recovery is a process in which setbacks can occur, and that a setback does not necessarily mean the participant will not ultimately succeed in treatment.

Like drug courts, but unlike incarceration, the DTAP program affords participants the skills and ability to remain sober and to become productive members of society. They are much less likely to re-offend than their incarcerated counterparts, and this results in a substantial cost savings. An independent report in 2003 determined that the average cost of DTAP participation is $32,975, whereas the average cost to incarcerate the same offenders would be $64,338. In addition to the monetary savings, society benefits in increased public safety and greater productivity when drug offenders are treated and then helped with their transition into the community.

Another less intensive approach involves mandatory desistance from the use of drugs for people on probation, parole, or pretrial release. When coupled with frequent drug tests that have predictable and fairly immediate sanctions for each missed test or incident of detected drug use, this approach can reduce drug use for non-addicted offenders who use drugs based on availability.[47] This "testing-and-sanctions" approach may be sufficient for offenders whose drug use is subject to their own volitional control. In contrast, those who are unable to control their drug use, even under threat, will be quickly identified in a way that is likely to break through the denial that often goes hand-in-hand with addiction. Identifying people with substance abuse issues will allow treatment resources to be directed to those most in need of them. Further, an effective testing-and-sanctions program would impact the volume illicit drug trade by reducing the number of illicit drug users.[48]

4.7 Educate Thyself

Lack of knowledge about drug impairment cannot be attributed to a lack of information. There is a growing body of literature about the effects of drugs and their impact on driving skills. This information is accessible through the Internet. A simple Google search using the word "drugs" pulled up 62,400,000 results. This chapter is offered as a springboard for the reader to explore the literature and the more complex issues related to drug impairment.

A police ride along, especially with an officer who is a trained Drug Recognition Expert, is instructive for prosecutors. Even if there is no encounter with someone under the influence of drugs, the officer will be able to share a great deal of information based upon his experience in dealing with people under the influence. It is also worthwhile to attend the portion of a DRE class during which the officers conduct their evaluations. The session will provide ample opportunity to see people under the influence of many of the categorized drugs. Also, consider attending the DWI Detection and Standardized Field Sobriety Testing[49] class for officers. Although this curriculum is designed for detection of alcohol-impaired drivers, the SFST battery is an integral part of the DRE 12-step protocol.[50]

Finally, watch movies that depict drug use. There are many movies that illustrate a broad spectrum of drug use. See the list at the end of this chapter. Read widely about drugs and proposed countermeasures. Keep an open mind when working with offenders who have identifiable substance abuse needs. Don't assume that their problems will be addressed in prison.

4.8 Conclusion

Alcohol continues to be America's drug of choice, but more and more people are driving after having ingested an illicit drug. Less is known about drugs than about alcohol, although studies are ongoing. A specific level of an illicit drug may not establish that the driver was actually impaired at the time of driving.

In theory, it should be enough that the person had ingested an illicit substance and was operating under the influence of that substance, but the reality is that it is not that easy. Hence, some states have passed per se laws that prohibit people from driving with any amount of a controlled substance or illegal drug. Once a person enters the criminal justice system for a drug-related crime, consideration should be given to whether the person has substance abuse issues that need to be addressed. When drug use is reduced, criminal activity also decreases. Demand reduction as a result of treatment is a winner from the crime control perspective. In lieu of treatment, a testing-and-sanctions program also can reduce the frequency of drug use and thereby reduce drug-related criminal activity. Prosecutors who are educated about these complex issues will be better equipped to deal with crimes involving drug impairment.

Suggested Movies

Reefer Madness, U.S. 1936, Kino International Corp., 1999.

The Cocaine Fiends, distributed by Sinister Camera home video, 1937.

The Man with the Golden Arm, Carlyle Productions, Inc., 1955. Assigned Otto Preminger Films, Ltd.

Valley of the Dolls, Twentieth Century Fox Film Corp. and Red Line Productions, Inc., 1967. Renewed 1995 Twentieth Century Fox Film Corp. and Red Line Productions.

Up in Smoke, Paramount Pictures, 1978.

Dazed & Confused, MCA Home Video, Inc., 1994.

Hurly Burly, New Line Productions, Inc., 1998. New Line Home Video, Inc., 1999.

Annie Hall, United Artists Corporation, 1977.

New Jack City, Warner Brothers Pictures.

Scarface, Universal Home Video, Inc., 1998.

Pulp Fiction, Buena Vista Pictures Distribution.

Fear and Loathing in Las Vegas, Universal Home Video, Inc., 1998.

Drugstore Cowboy, Avenue Pictures, 1989.

Traffic, USA Films, 2000.

Trainspotting, Buena Vista Pictures Distribution, 1996.

Requiem for a Dream, Requiem For A Dream, LLC, 2000.

Blow, New Line Productions, Inc., 2001. New Line Home Entertainment, Inc., 2001.

28 Days, Columbia Pictures Industries, Inc., 2000. Layout and Design Columbia TriStar Home Video, 2000.

Go, Columbia Pictures Industries, Inc., 1999. Layout and Design Columbia TriStar Home Video, 2000.

Clean and Sober, 1988 Warner Brothers, Inc., 1988.

Homegrown, TriStar Pictures, Inc., 1998. Layout and Design Columbia TriStar Home Video, 1998.

Gridlock'd, PolyGram Film Productions B.V., 1996.

Permanent Midnight, Artisan Pictures, Inc., 1998.

Rush, MGM-PathÈ Communications, Co., 1991.

Still Smokin', Cheech and Chong's Comedy Film Festival Number One, Inc.

Jesus' Son, Universal Studios, 2000.

Lady Sings the Blues, Paramount Pictures (1972). Paramount Pictures Corp., 1979.

Weed, Vanguard Films, 1998.

Sid and Nancy, Zenith Productions. Ltd., 1986.

Endnotes

1. J. Brick and C. Erickson, *Drugs, the Brain, and Behavior,* at 3 (1998).

2. Michael Jonathan Grinfeld, "Decriminalizing Addiction," *Psychiatric Times,* Vol. XVIII, No. 3, March 2001, quoting Herbert D. Kleber, M.D., professor of psychiatry, Columbia University College of Physicians and Surgeons.

3. When state and federal prisoners were asked about the circumstances of the offenses that landed them in prison, 24 percent said they wee under the influence of illicit drugs (but not alcohol) at the time, 30 percent cited intoxication with alcohol alone, and 17 percent named drugs and alcohol together. D. Boyum and M. Kleiman, "Breaking the drug-crime link," *The Public Interest,* Summer 2003, at 21.

4. S. Kerrigan, American Prosecutors Research Institute, *Drug Toxicology for Prosecutors,* October 2004, at 3.

5. A. Cavaiola and Wuth, *Assessment and Treatment of the DWI Offender,* 2002.

6. Alcohol has historically been known as a food, a nutrient, a palliative, and today as a drug. Brick and Erickson, *supra* note 1, at 55.

7. *See* S. Mongrain and L. Standing, "Impairment of Cognition, Risk-Taking, and Self-Perception by Alcohol," *Perceptual and Motor Skills,* 1989, 69, 199-210; D. Heacock and R. Wikle, "The Effect of Alcohol and Placebo on Reaction Time and Distance Judgment" *The Journal of General Psychology,* 1974, 91, 265-268; H. Moskowitz, et al., "Skills Performance at Low Blood Alcohol Levels," *Journal of Studies on Alcohol,* Vol. 46, No. 5, 1985, 482-495; M. Nicholson, et al., "Variability in Behavioral Impairment Involved in the Rising and Falling BAC Curve," *Journal of Studies on Alcohol,* Vol. 53, No. 4 , 1992, 349- 356; D. Damkot, "Alcohol, Task Demands, and Personality Affect Driving: Beware the Interactions," *Alcohol, Drugs and Traffic Safety,* 923-937 (L. Goldberg, ed., Vol. III 1981); and E. Geller, et al., "Knowing When to Say When: A Simple Assessment of Alcohol Impairment," *Journal of Applied Behavior Analysis,* No. 1, 1991, 24, 65-72.

8. M. Burns and H. Moskowitz, U.S.-DOT, NHTSA, *Psychophysical Tests for DWI Arrest,* June 1977. See also V. Tharp, M. Burns and H. Moskowitz, U.S.-DOT, NHTSA, *Development and Field Test of Psychophysical Tests for DWI Arrest,* March 1981.

9. R. Borkenstein, et al., Department of Police Administration, Indiana University, *The Role of the Drinking Driver in Traffic Accidents* (A. Dale, ed. 1964).

10. The curve from this study, which has been displayed and referred to countless times, is the single most significant demonstration of alcohol's affect on driving related skills. At a 0.08% BAC, the probability of being involved in a crash was 8 times that of an alcohol-free driver. R. Forney, "Toxicology and Pharmacology of Alcohol," University of Wisconsin Law School, Resource Center on Impaired Driving, *8th Annual Traffic and Impaired Driving Law Program,* 2002.

11. Legislators in several states, for example, Wisconsin, considered the federal government's mandate a form of blackmail in that it tied the receipt of federal highway dollars to the passage of the 0.08% BAC law.

12. The word is recorded from Middle English, and comes from Old French *drogue,* and perhaps ultimately from Middle Dutch *droge vat,* literally 'dry vats', referring to the contents (i.e., dry goods). *The Oxford Dictionary of Phrase and Fable,* Elizabeth Knowles, ed. (2000) at 313, Oxford University Press Inc., New York.

13. U.S. DOT, NHTSA, *Drugs That Impair Driving,* Student Manual, HS 178B R2/00 at 1-2.

14. 21 USCS Sec. 812.

15. *The Oxford Dictionary, supra* note 12, at 905.

16. *Id.*

17. *Id.,* at 286.

18. *The American Heritage College Dictionary,* 3rd ed., Houghton Mifflin Company, Boston, New York (2000).

19. *Id.,* at 270.

20. Schlosser, E., *Reefer Madness, Sex, Drugs, and Cheap Labor in the American Market,* First Mariner Books Edition, 2004.

21. Wis. JI-Criminal 2600, 2004.

22. William C. Head, "'Combination' DUI Cases: Alcohol and Other Drugs— The Explosion of New Polydrug Arrests," *DWI Journal: Law & Science,*

Vol. 19, No. 5, May 2004.

23. S. Kerrigan, *supra* note 4, at 3.

24. *Id.*

25. R. Jones, et al., Mid-America Research Institute, *State of Knowledge of Drug-Impaired Driving,* September 2003 at ix.

26. *Id. See also* J. de Gier, "Prevalence of Illegal Drugs in Drivers," *Developing Global Strategies for Identifying, Prosecuting and Treating Drug-Impaired Drivers,* Symposium Final Report 2004 (available on line at http://www.walshgroup.org).

27. Paramount Pictures 1978.

28. Cheech and Chong's Comedy Film Festival Number One, Inc.

29. "Dazed and Confused," MCA Home Video, Inc., 1994, "Fast Times at Ridgemont High," Universal Studios, 1999, "The Big Chill," Columbia Pictures Industries, Inc., 1998.

30. *For example, see* H. Robbe and J. O'Hanlon, U.S.-DOT, NHTSA, *Marijuana, Alcohol and Actual Driving Performance,* July 1999; H. Robbe and J. O'Hanlon, U.S.-DOT, NHTSA, *Marijuana and Actual Driving Performance,* November 1993; H. Moskowitz, "Marihuana and Driving," *Accid. Anal. & Prev.,* Vol. 17, No. 4, 323-345, 1985; H. Moskowitz, S. Hulbert and W. McGlothin, "Marihuana: Effects on Simulated Driving Performance," *Accid. Anal. & Prev.,* Vol. 8, 45-50, 1976; S. Peeke, R. Jones, and G. Stone, "Effects of Practice on Marijuana Induced Changes in Reaction Time," *Psychopharmacology,* Vol. 48, 159-63, 1976; A. Smiley, "Marijuana: on Road and Driving Simulator Studies," *Alcohol, Drugs, and Driving,* Vol. 2, No. 3-4, 121-134, 1986.

31. N. Sines and P. Schroth, Resource Center on Impaired Driving, University of Wisconsin Law School, *Compendium on Drug Impaired Driving,* October 1996.

32. U.S. DOT, NHTSA, *Drugs That Impair Driving,* Student Manual, HS 178B R2/00. *See also* American Prosecutors Research Institute, *The Drug Evaluation and Evaluation (DEC) Program,* October 2004.

33. American Prosecutors Research Institute, *The Drug Evaluation and Evaluation (DEC) Program,* October 2004, at 6.

34. Physicians' Desk Reference, 57 ed., 2003, at p.510.

35. Id.

36. Id.

37. Sec. 484.379 Nev. Rev. Stat. Ann.

38. Sec. 40-6-391, Code of Georgia Ann.

39. Sec. 346.53(1)(am), Wis. Stats. 2003-04.

40. The Walsh Group, *Driving Under the Influence of Drugs (DUID) Legislation in the United States,* Nov. 2002, at 2.

41. Id.

42. Esty Dinur, "Battling addiction: When drug and alcohol users bottom out, help is at hand," *Isthmus,* May 28, 2004.

43. D. Boyum & M. Kleiman, "Breaking the Drug-Crime Link, *The Public Interest,* No. 152, Summer 2003, at 34-35.

44. Id., at 35.

45. John Yu, "Addiction and Sanctions: Deterring Drinking Drivers," *Impaired Driving Update,* Vol. VII, No. 4, Fall 2003.

46. Approximately 52.6 percent of program participants graduated, of those put in the program before November 2000. Of those studied in 2000, DTAP participants, whether they graduated from the program or not, were 67 percent less likely to return to prison two years after leaving the program than were members of the comparison group of non-DTAP defendants that were studied. *Id.*

47. "Substance abuse" as a legal matter means use of a prohibited drug, or use of prescription medication for non-medical reasons; "substance abuse" as a medical matter is defined by criteria such as escalation of dosage and frequency, narrowing of the behavioral repertoire, loss of control over use, and continued use despite adverse consequences. In contrast, the most common pattern of substance abuse is a single active period followed by "spontaneous" or non-treatment initiated remission. D. Boyum & M. Kleiman, *supra* note 43, at 34.

48. One estimate is that a national testing-and-sanctions program could reasonably be expected to shrink total hard-drug volumes by 40 percent. *Id.*, at 35.

49. U.S. DOT, NHTSA, *DWI Detection and Standardized Field Sobriety Testing,* Student Manual, HS 178 R1/02.

50. Specifically, 1) Breath Alcohol Test, 2) Interview of the Arresting Officer, 3) Preliminary Examination and First Pulse, 4) Eye Examination (includes the horizontal gaze nystagmus test), 5) Divided Attention Psychophysical Tests (includes the Walk and Turn and One Leg Stand), 6) Vital Signs and Second Pulse, 7) Dark Room Examinations, 8) Examination for muscle Tone, 9) Check for Injection Sites and Third Pulse, 10) Subject's Statements and Other Observations, 11) Analysis and Opinions of the Evaluator, and 12) Toxicological Examination. *The DEC Program,* supra note 33, at 3-5.

Chapter 5

A True Double Standard: A Defense Perspective on the Inherent Unfairness in the Administration of the Impaired Driver Laws

Peter Gerstenzang and Eric H. Sills

Synopsis
5.1 Introduction
5.2 The Initial Stop
5.3 Roadside Detention/Interrogation
5.4 Post-Arrest Detention/Interrogation
5.5 Chemical Tests
5.6 Chemical Test Refusals
5.7 Miscellaneous Issues
5.8 Conclusion
Endnotes

5.1 Introduction

Due to the intense pressure placed upon legislators, prosecutors and judges to wage war on impaired drivers—by interest groups such as Mothers Against Drunk Driving—it is rare that a year goes by without an increase in the penalties imposed for driving under the influence of alcohol (DUI) or drugs (DUID). This pressure, combined with the lack of any organized lobbying on behalf of the drinking or drug-using driver, has led to a true double standard in which the criminal justice system has created two classes of criminals: (1) impaired drivers, and (2) all other criminals.

The inherent unfairness in the administration of the DUI laws pervades virtually every aspect of a DUI case, from the initial stop of the defendant's vehicle, through the administration of the chemical test. In addition, the courts routinely find that the use of so-called "civil penalties" to exact extra punishment on DUI offenders (e.g., driver's license suspensions pending prosecution, chemical test refusal revocations, vehicle seizures or forfeitures, and so on), do not violate either the double jeopardy clause or the due process clause.

In this regard, this article will demonstrate that the Constitution has been interpreted to provide less protection where the defendant is accused of DUI than it does where the defendant is accused of virtually any other crime, regardless of how serious or despicable. Notably, the inherent bias against DUI defendants is evidenced not only by the actual holdings and reasoning of the cases cited below but also by the comments in many of the decisions lamenting the "carnage caused by drunk drivers," the "increasing slaughter on our highways," the "national tragedy" of drunken driving, and so on.

5.2 The Initial Stop

Although the Supreme Court has "never approved a checkpoint program whose primary purpose was to detect evidence of ordinary criminal wrongdoing," *City of Indianapolis v. Edmond*, 531 U.S. 32, 41,121 S.Ct. 447, 454 (2000), it has nonetheless approved of the use of sobriety (i.e., DUI) checkpoints. See *Michigan Department of State Police v. Sitz*, 496 U.S. 444, 110 S.Ct. 2481 (1990). See also *Illinois v. Lidster*, 540 U.S.419, 124 S.Ct. 885 (2004) (Fourth Amendment not violated where motorist was stopped at "information-seeking" checkpoint yet arrested for DUI).

In addition, as if it wasn't easy enough for the police to lawfully stop a motor vehicle, the Supreme Court has expressly authorized the use of "pretext stops" by the police, see *Whren v. United States*, 517 U.S. 806, 116 S.Ct. 1769 (1996)—despite the fact that the term "pretext stop" had previously been synonymous with the term "illegal stop." Thus, pursuant to *Whren*, a police officer can lawfully stop a motor vehicle[1] whenever the officer has probable cause to believe that a traffic infraction (or equipment violation) has occurred—no matter how minor the infraction (and regardless of whether the officer is assigned to a traffic enforcement detail)—even if the officer's true purpose in stopping the vehicle is to "fish" for drunk drivers.

In *Welsh v. Wisconsin*, 466 U.S. 740, 104 S.Ct. 2091 (1984), the Supreme Court issued a rare ruling upholding the rights of a drunk driver. However, as will be demonstrated below, *Welsh* has turned out to be a Pyrrhic victory.

In *Welsh*, the defendant, who was driving erratically, ultimately drove his car off the road and into an open field. A civilian witness, who observed the defendant's driving, used his truck to block the defendant from driving back onto the road and asked a passerby to call the police. Before the police arrived, however, the defendant fled the scene on foot, walked home, went upstairs to his bedroom, stripped naked and went to sleep. The police located the defendant's home (by checking the registration of the abandoned car), and proceeded thereto, arriving at approximately 9:00 P.M. Without obtaining a warrant, the police entered the home, went upstairs, woke the defendant and arrested him for DUI.

In holding that the warrantless nighttime entry into the defendant's home violated the Fourth Amendment, the *Welsh* Court found that, "*in the circumstances presented by this case*, there were no exigent circumstances sufficient to justify a warrantless home entry." *Id.* at 749 n.11, 104 S.Ct. at 2097 n.11 (emphasis added). The "circumstance" of the case that the *Welsh* Court found to be critical to its ruling was the fact that "[t]he State of Wisconsin has chosen to classify the first offense for driving while intoxicated as a noncriminal, civil forfeiture offense for which no imprisonment is possible." *Id.* at 754, 104 S.Ct. at 2100. In this regard, the Court held that "an important factor to be considered when determining whether any exigency exists is the gravity of the underlying offense for which the arrest is being made." *Id.* at 753, 104 S.Ct. at 2099. The Court further noted that there was no "hot pursuit" of the defendant. *Id.* at 753, 104 S.Ct. at 2099.

Not surprisingly, various state courts have eviscerated *Welsh*, distinguishing it "on three main grounds:(1) the officer was in hot pursuit; (2) there was a need to preserve evidence of the defendant's blood alcohol level; and (3) the ordinance or statute under which the defendant was arrested provided for criminal penalties and not merely noncriminal civil forfeitures." *State v. Paul*, 548 N.W.2d 260, 266 (Minn. 1996). See also *City of Middletown v. Flinchum*, 95 Ohio St. 3d 43, 45, 765 N.E.2d 330, 332 (Ohio 2002); *Matter of Stark v. New York State Department of Motor*

Vehicles, 104 A.D.2d 194, 196-97, 483 N.Y.S.2d 824, 826 (N.Y. App. Div. 1984), *aff'd*, 65 N.Y.2d 720, 492 N.Y.S.2d 8 (N.Y. 1985).

5.3 Roadside Detention/Interrogation

Once the vehicle stop has been made and a DUI investigation has commenced, the issue arises as to when a DUI suspect is "in custody" for purposes of *Miranda v. Arizona*, 384 U.S. 436, 86 S.Ct. 1602 (1966). In this regard, the *Miranda* Court repeatedly made clear that "[b]y custodial interrogation, we mean questioning initiated by law enforcement officers after a person has been taken into custody *or otherwise deprived of his freedom of action in any significant way*." *Id.* at 444, 86 S.Ct. at 1612 (emphasis added). See also *Id.* at 445, 86 S.Ct. at 1612 (same); *Id.* at 467, 86 S.Ct. at 1624 (same); *Id.* at 477, 86 S.Ct. at 1629 (same); *Id.* at 478, 86 S.Ct. at 1630 (same). See generally *Id.* at 461, 86 S.Ct. at 1620 ("In this Court, the privilege has consistently been accorded a liberal construction").

It would seem clear that when the police (a) pull a motorist over, (b) seize the motorist's driver's license and registration, (c) preliminarily interrogate the motorist, (d) order the motorist to exit the vehicle, and (e) demand that the motorist remain outside the vehicle and perform field sobriety tests, the motorist has been deprived of his or her freedom of action in a significant way, and thus that the motorist is "in custody" for purposes of *Miranda*. Nonetheless, the Supreme Court has held that, in the absence of extraordinary circumstances, such a detention does *not* constitute custodial interrogation, and thus is not protected by the Fifth Amendment. *See, e.g., Pennsylvania v. Bruder*, 488 U.S. 9, 109 S.Ct. 205 (1988); *Berkemer v. McCarty*, 468 U.S. 420, 104 S.Ct. 3138 (1984).

5.4 Post-Arrest Detention/Interrogation

Even where a DUI defendant is in custody, virtually none of the evidence typically gathered by the police in connection with a DUI case (e.g., odors, observations of the defendant's speech, physical condition and motor coordination, results of field sobriety tests, results of breath, blood or urine tests, test refusals, routine booking questions, etc.) is Constitutionally protected. At the outset, the Fifth Amendment only protects the defendant from disclosing "testimonial or communicative" evidence (as opposed to "real or physical" evidence), *see, e.g., Pennsylvania v. Muniz,*

496 U.S. 582, 589, 110 S.Ct. 2638, 2643 (1990); *South Dakota v. Neville*, 459 U.S. 553, 559, 103 S.Ct. 916, 920 (1983); *Schmerber v. California*, 384 U.S. 757, 764, 86 S.Ct. 1826, 1832 (1966) — and almost every significant piece of evidence in a DUI case has been found to either (a) constitute "real or physical" evidence, (b) arise from custodial questioning that does not constitute "interrogation," and/or (c) fall within an exception to *Miranda*.

The primary case in this regard is *Pennsylvania v. Muniz*. The *Muniz* Court held that "any slurring of speech and other evidence of lack of muscular coordination revealed by Muniz's responses to Officer Hosterman's direct questions constitute nontestimonial components of those responses." 496 U.S. at 592, 110 S.Ct. at 2645. In addition, the Court noted that many state courts have found and Muniz did not dispute that "standard sobriety tests measuring reflexes, dexterity, and balance do not require the performance of testimonial acts." *Id.* at 603 n.16, 110 S.Ct. at 2651 n.16. *See also People v. Berg*, 92 N.Y.2d 701, 703, 705, 685 N.Y.S.2d 906, 907, 908(09 (N.Y. 1999); *People v. Jacquin*, 71 N.Y.2d 825, 826, 527 N.Y.S.2d 728, 729 (N.Y. 1988); *People v. Hager*, 69 N.Y.2d 141, 142, 512 N.Y.S.2d 794, 795 (N.Y. 1987).

The *Muniz* Court also found that, "with two narrow exceptions not relevant here," "Officer Hosterman's dialogue with Muniz concerning the physical sobriety tests consisted primarily of carefully scripted instructions as to how the tests were to be performed. These instructions were not likely to be perceived as calling for any verbal response and therefore were not 'words or actions' constituting custodial interrogation." 496 U.S. at 603, 110 S.Ct. at 2651. "The two exceptions consist of Officer Hosterman's requests that Muniz count aloud from 1 to 9 while performing the 'walk and turn' test and that he count aloud from 1 to 30 while balancing during the 'one leg stand' test. Muniz's counting at the officer's request qualifies as a response to custodial interrogation."[2] *Muniz*, 496 U.S. at 603 n.17, 110 S.Ct. at 2651 n.17.

The *Muniz* Court did not decide, "whether Muniz's counting (or not counting) itself was 'testimonial' within the meaning of the privilege." *Id.* at 603 n.17, 110 S.Ct. at 2651 n.17. Similarly, the *Bruder* Court declined to "reach the issue whether recitation of the alphabet in response to custodial questioning is testimonial and hence inadmissible under *Miranda v. Arizona*." 488 U.S. at 11 n.3, 109 S.Ct. at 207 n.3. In this regard, however, most state courts that have addressed the issue have found that counting and reciting the alphabet are not "testimonial or communicative" in nature, and thus do *not* fall within the ambit of *Miranda. See, e.g., People v. Berg*, 92 N.Y.2d 701, 705, 685 N.Y.S.2d 906, 909 (N.Y. 1999) ("Reciting the alphabet and counting are not testimonial or communicative because these acts do not require a person to reveal knowledge of facts relating to the offense or to share thoughts and beliefs with the government. Instead, these tests attempt to determine whether alcohol has impaired the reflexive process by which the alphabet and numbers are recalled from memory and spoken").[3] *State v. Devlin*, 294 Mont. 215, 221, 980 P.2d 1037, 1040 (Mont. 1999) ("We . . . hold that neither counting aloud nor reciting a portion of the alphabet is testimonial in nature and that therefore Fifth Amendment protections do not attach when a driver suspected of DUI is asked to recite either or both as part of field sobriety tests"); *Vanhouton v. Commonwealth*, 424 Mass. 327, 335 36, 676 N.E.2d 160, 166 (Mass. 1997); *State v. Maze*, 16 Kan. App. 2d 527, 533, 825 P.2d 1169, 1173 (Kan. Ct. App. 1992).

Furthermore, the *Muniz* Court found the limited questioning of a DUI defendant either (a) during the instructional phase of field sobriety tests (e.g., inquiries as to whether the defendant understood the officer's instructions), and/or (b) in conjunction with the defendant's breath test (e.g., inquiries as to whether the defendant understood the nature of the test and the implied consent law, and whether the defendant would submit to the test), to be "attendant to" the legitimate police procedure, and thus not protected by *Miranda*. 496 U.S. at 603-05, 110 S.Ct. at 2651-52. Thus, according to the Court, any incriminating utterances by the defendant during such instructions (or in response to such questioning) are "'voluntary' in the sense that they [are] not elicited in response to custodial interrogation." *Id.* at 604, 110 S.Ct. at 2651. *See also People v. Jacquin*, 71 N.Y.2d 825, 826, 527 N.Y.S.2d 728, 729 (N.Y. 1988) ("Performance tests need not be preceded by *Miranda* warnings and, generally an audio/visual tape of such tests, *including any colloquy between the test-giver and the defendant not constituting custodial interrogation*, is admissible") (emphasis added).

Moreover, although the *Muniz* Court found that "Officer Hosterman's first seven questions regarding Muniz's name, address, height, weight, eye color, date of birth, and current age qualify as custodial interrogation," 496 U.S. at 601, 110 S.Ct. at 2650, the Court created a brand new exception to the *Miranda* requirement (i.e., the so-called "routine booking question" or "pedigree" exception) which permits such custodial interrogation without the reading of *Miranda* warnings. *Id.* at 601, 110 S.Ct. at 2650.

Thus, while the *Muniz* Court made clear that "'[t]he vast majority of verbal statements . . . will be testimonial' because '[t]here are very few instances in which a verbal statement, either oral or written, will not convey information or assert facts,'" (*Id.* at 597, 110 S.Ct. at 2648 (quoting *Doe v. United States*, 487 U.S. 201, 213, 108 S.Ct. 2341, 2349 (1988)), out of all of the questions asked of Muniz, and out of all of the "incriminating utterances" made by Muniz during the entire course of his DUI stop, arrest and detention, the only utterance that the Court found to be protected by the Fifth Amendment was Muniz's response to the following question: "Do you know what the date was of your sixth birthday?" 496 U.S. at 586, 598-600, 110 S.Ct. at 2642, 2649.[4] This lack of Fifth Amendment protection is particularly disturbing considering that the police questioning of a DUI suspect occurs at a time when the suspect is purportedly intoxicated, and is thus less likely to be able to adequately protect whatever rights he or she does have.

5.5 Chemical Tests

The lack of Constitutional protections afforded to DUI defendants extends to the issue of chemical testing. At the outset, although the procuring of a breath or blood sample from a DUI suspect constitutes a "search and seizure" within the meaning of the Fourth Amendment, see *Skinner v. Railway Labor Executives' Association*, 489 U.S. 602, 616-17, 109 S.Ct. 1402, 1413 (1989); *Schmerber v. California*, 384 U.S. 757, 767, 86 S. Ct. 1826, 1834 (1966), the Supreme Court has nonetheless held that "a person suspected of drunk driving has no constitutional right to refuse to take a blood-alcohol test." *South Dakota v. Neville*, 459 U.S. 553, 560 n.10, 103 S.Ct. 916, 921 n.10 (1983). In this regard, the taking of a DUI suspect's blood for chemical testing has withstood due process as well as Fourth, Fifth and Sixth Amendment challenges. See, e.g., *Schmerber, supra*; *Breithaupt v. Abram*, 352 U.S. 432, 77 S.Ct. 408 (1957). In addition, a DUI suspect's blood can be withdrawn for alcohol and/or drug testing regardless of whether the suspect is conscious or unconscious, and regardless of whether the suspect consents or refuses to submit to such test (i.e., a DUI defendant can be forcibly compelled to submit to a blood test). *See, e.g., Pennsylvania v. Muniz*, 496 U.S. 582, 593, 604 n.19, 110 S.Ct. 2638, 2646, 2652 n.19 (1990); *Neville*, 459 U.S. at 554, 559, 103 S.Ct. at 917, 920; *Schmerber, supra.*

Furthermore, so-called "implied consent" laws literally force motorists to implicitly consent to chemical testing in order to drive (and punish those who withdraw such implied consent with driver's license suspension/revocation and use of the refusal by the prosecution at trial). As such, the normal rules pertaining to "consent searches," *see, e.g., Florida v. Royer*, 460 U.S. 491, 497, 103 S.Ct. 1319, 1324 (1983) ("where the validity of a search rests on consent, the State has the burden of proving that the necessary consent was obtained and that it was freely and voluntarily given, a burden that is not satisfied by showing a mere submission to a claim of lawful authority"); *Schneckloth v. Bustamonte*, 412 U.S. 218, 222, 248-49, 93 S.Ct. 2041, 2045, 2059 (1973) (same); *Bumper v. North Carolina*, 391 U.S. 543, 548-49, 88 S.Ct. 1788, 1792 (1968) (same), appear not to apply in DUI cases.

Moreover, the Constitution has been found not to require the state to preserve a sample of the defendant's breath for independent testing by the defense, *see California v. Trombetta*, 467 U.S. 479, 104 S.Ct. 2528 (1984) —despite the fact that such preservation has been technologically feasible at least since the early 1980s. Id. at 482 and n.3, 104 S.Ct. at 2530 and n.3. In this regard, the *Trombetta* Court asserted that "[i]n all but a tiny fraction of cases, preserved breath samples would simply confirm the Intoxilyzer's determination that the defendant had a high level of blood-alcohol concentration at the time of the test." *Id.* at 489, 104 S.Ct. at 2534. Notably, the Court was only made aware of three ways in which erroneous test results could occur—"faulty calibration, extraneous interference with machine measurements, and operator error," *Id.* at 490, 104 S.Ct. at 2534—yet it is well known that there are at least several more significant potential causes of inaccurate breath test readings (e.g., mouth alcohol contamination of the defendant's breath sample, elevated temperature of the defendant's breath sample, and/or variations between the blood/breath ratio presumed by the machine and the defendant's actual blood/breath ratio).

5.6 Chemical Test Refusals

Similarly, a DUI defendant's *refusal* to submit to a chemical test, which is clearly "testimonial or communicative" in nature,[5] and which is obtained after the defendant has been arrested for DUI, is not protected by the 5th Amendment. See, e.g., *Pennsylvania v. Muniz*, 496 U.S. 582, 604 n.19, 110 S.Ct. 2638, 2652 n.19 (1990); *Welsh v. Wisconsin*, 466 U.S. 740, 744, 104 S.Ct. 2091, 2094 (1984); *South Dakota v. Neville*, 459 U.S. 553, 564, 103 S.Ct. 916, 923 (1983); *People v. Thomas*, 46 N.Y.2d 100, 103, 412 N.Y.S.2d 845, 846 (N.Y. 1978). In this regard, the *Neville* Court reasoned that "[i]n the context of an arrest for driving while intoxicated, a police inquiry of whether the suspect will take a blood-alcohol test is not an interrogation within the meaning of Miranda." 459 U.S. at 564 n.15, 103 S.Ct. at 923 n.15. See also *Muniz*, 496 U.S. at 604, 110 S.Ct. at 2651-52. *Neville* further held that the use of a DUI defendant's refusal to submit to a chemical test against him or her at trial does not violate Due Process, 459 U.S. at 566, 103 S.Ct. at 924, and *Muniz* further held that *Neville* applies to breath test refusals as well as to blood test refusals. 496 U.S. at 604 n.19, 110 S.Ct. at 2652 n.19.

Thus, although the *Miranda* Court held that "it is impermissible to penalize an individual for exercising his Fifth Amendment privilege when he is under police custodial interrogation, the prosecution may not, therefore, use at trial the fact that he stood mute or claimed his privilege in the face of accusation," 384 U.S. at 468 n.37, 86 S.Ct. at 1624 n.37; see also *Schmerber v. California*, 384 U.S. 757, 760-61, 86 S.Ct. 1826, 1830 (1966) (same) — if a DUI suspect stands mute in the face of a request that he or she submit to a chemical test, such silence *can* be used against the suspect at trial.

Simply stated, where the police ask an in-custody DUI defendant to take a chemical test, the defendant's response is "testimonial"—but the request is not an "interrogation." On the other hand, where an in-custody DUI defendant is asked to count (or to recite the alphabet) during field sobriety testing, the request is an "interrogation"—but the defendant's response is not "testimonial". In other words, the courts seem to almost always find a way to deny Constitutional protections to DUI defendants.

Turning to the issue of civil sanctions for chemical test refusals, in *Mackey v. Montrym*, 443 U.S. 1, 99 S.Ct. 2612 (1979), the Supreme Court held that, upon a driver's alleged refusal to submit to a chemical test, his or her driver's license can be suspended *prior to the holding of a hearing* without violating the driver's due process rights. In this regard, the *Mackey* Court summarily declared, without any basis, both (a) that "[t]he officer whose report of refusal triggers a driver's suspension is a trained observer and investigator," id. at 14, 99 S.Ct. at 2619, and (b) that "as this case illustrates, there will rarely be any genuine dispute as to the historical facts providing cause for a suspension." *Id.* at 14, 99 S.Ct. at 2619.

In *Illinois v. Batchelder*, 463 U.S. 1112, 103 S.Ct. 3513 (1983), the Supreme Court issued a *per curiam* decision even more unfavorable to drivers accused of refusing to submit to a chemical test. In *Batchelder*, the Illinois chemical test refusal statute required the arresting officer to complete and file a sworn statement (commonly known as a Report of Refusal) which was required to include, *inter alia*, "a statement that the arresting officer had reasonable cause to believe the person was driving the motor vehicle within this State while under the influence of intoxicating liquor." 463 U.S. at 1113, 103 S.Ct. at 3514 (quotation omitted).

The arresting officer's sworn statement in *Batchelder* technically complied with this requirement, as it summarily and conclusorily parroted the statutory language. In this regard, the pre-printed portion of the arresting officer's Report of Refusal stated that, "I hereby certify that I have placed the above named person under arrest, and that I had at the time of arrest reasonable grounds to believe that said person was driving a motor vehicle in this State while under the influence of intoxicating liquor." *Id.* at 1114-15, 103 S.Ct. at 3514-15 (quotation omitted). However, the narrative portion of the officer's report failed to state a single fact pertinent to the issue of *Batchelder's* alleged intoxication.

Nonetheless, despite the fact that the Illinois courts ruled that the arresting officer's Report was legally insufficient, the Supreme Court held that:

> [W]e conclude that the Constitution does not require arresting officers in Illinois, in enforcing that state's implied consent statute, to recite in an affidavit the specific and concrete evidentiary matters constituting "the underlying circumstances which provided him with a reasonable belief that the arrested person was driving under the influence of intoxicating liquor." The driver's right to a hearing before he may be deprived of his license for failing to submit to a breath-analysis test accords him all, and

probably more, of the process that the Federal Constitution assures. *Id.* at 1119, 103 S.Ct. at 3517 (quotation omitted).

5.7 Miscellaneous Issues

The Supreme Court has upheld the use of a prior *uncounseled* misdemeanor DUI conviction to increase the level of a subsequent DUI charge (from a misdemeanor to a felony), see *Iowa v. Tovar*, 541 U.S. 77, 124 S.Ct. 1379 (2004), as well as to increase the sentence that the defendant can receive for a subsequent criminal conviction. See *Nichols v. United States*, 511 U.S. 738, 114 S.Ct. 1921 (1994) (overruling *Baldasar v. Illinois*, 446 U.S. 222, 100 S.Ct. 1585 (1980)). Notably, despite the fact that a DUI charge can be one of the more complex crimes to prosecute, and despite the fact that many potential defenses are available to competent defense counsel, the *Tovar* Court indicated that it is unclear what assistance defense "counsel could have provided, given the simplicity of the charge." 541U.S. at 79, 124 S.Ct. at 1390.

Furthermore, the Supreme Court has twice found that DUI is not a "serious" offense for purposes of the Sixth Amendment right to a jury trial. See *United States v. Nachtigal*, 507 U.S. 1, 113 S.Ct. 1072 (1993); *Blanton v. City of North Las Vegas*, 489 U.S. 538, 109 S.Ct. 1289 (1989).

Finally, most States have enacted so-called "suspension pending prosecution" laws, pursuant to which DUI defendants' drivers' licenses are suspended while the underlying DUI charges are pending. In this regard, unlike defendants charged with most other crimes, DUI defendants are not afforded the presumption of innocence, which has always been a basic tenet of the American criminal justice system. Rather, DUI defendants are presumed guilty upon the mere accusation of driving under the influence. Nonetheless, such laws have been found to pass Constitutional muster. *See, e.g., Pringle v. Wolfe*, 88 N.Y.2d 426, 646 N.Y.S.2d 82 (N.Y. 1996); *State v. Hochhausler*, 76 Ohio St. 3d 455, 668 N.E.2d 457 (Ohio 1996); *Commonwealth v. Crowell*, 403 Mass. 381, 529 N.E.2d 1339 (Mass. 1988).

5.8 Conclusion

As this article demonstrates, the Constitution has been interpreted to provide less protection where the defendant is accused of DUI than it does where the defendant is accused of virtually any other crime, regardless of how serious or despicable. In this regard, it is not much of an exaggeration to say that the police have virtual *carte blanche* to stop, question, field sobriety test, arrest and chemical test a DUI suspect without even implicating the suspect's Fourth, Fifth, Sixth and/or Fourteenth Amendment rights. Simply stated, although the police, the prosecution and the public routinely claim that "the system" favors the defense bar and/or the drinking driver, the reality is quite the opposite.

Endnotes

1. It is well settled that the stopping of a motor vehicle by the police constitutes a "seizure" within the meaning of the 4th Amendment. See, e.g., *Lidster*, 540 U.S. at 425-26, 124 S.Ct. at 890; *Edmond*, 531 U.S. at 40, 121 S.Ct. at 453; *Whren*, 517 U.S. at 809-10, 116 S.Ct. at 1772; *Sitz*, 496 U.S. at 450, 110 S.Ct. at 2485; *Berkemer v. McCarty*, 468 U.S. 420, 436-37, 104 S.Ct. 3138, 3148 (1984), *Deluware v. Prouse*, 440 U.S. 648, 653, 99 S.Ct. 1391, 1396 (1979).

2. This is because the tests at issue were performed at the police station after Muniz had been placed in custody. Requests that a DUI suspect count during field sobriety testing (or recite the alphabet) at the roadside prior to arrest do not fall within this rule. See *Bruder*, *supra*; *Berkemer*, *supra*.

3. The authors were defense counsel in *Berg*.

4. Even so, Muniz's incriminating response to that question would have been admissible if the question had been asked either (a) at the roadside prior to his arrest, see *Bruder*, *supra*; *Berkemer*, *supra*, or (b) if he had been read his *Miranda* warnings before the question was asked.

5. See, e.g., *People v. Thomas*, 46 N.Y.2d 100, 106, 412 N.Y.S.2d 845, 849 (N.Y. 1978) ("the evidence of the defendant's refusal to take the test [can] be classified as communicative or testimonial"); *id.* at 106, 412 N.Y.S.2d at 848 (chemical test refusal "evidence may be characterized as 'communicative or testimonial' rather than 'real or physical' evidence").

Chapter 6

Examining MDMA: 3,4-methylenedioxymethamphetamine (Ecstasy)

Charles Matson

6.1 Introduction

The term "ecstasy," which originates from the Greek word *Exstas Sirxs*, means *the flight of the soul from the body*. This meaning closely mirrors the drug experiences of MDMA users. It also provides insight into the belief of some individuals and groups that this Schedule 1 drug is not only harmless but that it is beneficial. Ecstasy is a synthetically prepared psychoactive substance 3,4-methylenedioxymethamphetamine, or MDMA. Despite the positive opinions of users and the ongoing studies of its psychotherapeutic use, the drug presents significant potential danger.

MDMA is often described as a mixture of mescaline and amphetamine. From a chemical structure perspective, as well as that of its behavioral effects, the description is fairly accurate. Although MDMA is not the actual equivalent of a mixture of the two drugs, the reference reflects the sensations that users may experience under its influence. They expect and often experience psychedelic and stimulant effects.

One unusual feature of MDMA is that users, addicts, scientists and drug officials typically refer to it by its street name, Ecstasy. In contrast, official statements about other drugs, LSD or "acid" for example, aren't commonly referred to with street nomenclature.

6.2 History and Background

MDMA is not a new drug. Merck Pharmaceuticals patented the formula for the chemicals in 1914 (Greer and Tolbert, 1998). Although several sources allege that Merck was looking for an appetite suppressant when MDMA was produced, the company was actually attempting to synthesize the vasoconstrictive styptic medicine, Hydrastinin. MDMA was an unintentional outcome and was never marketed by Merck. During the 1950s MDMA attracted attention as a potential psychological warfare tool. U.S. Army intelligence investigated it and several other substances with possible *brain washing* functions.

Although MDMA was known to be a precursor in the manufacture of other therapeutically effective drugs, it was not tested on human subjects. Instead, the drug's longer lasting and more hallucinogenic analogue, 3,4-methylenedioxyamphetamine (MDA), was part of the MK-ULTRA program carried out in the 1950s and 1960s. The program was a governmental research effort that studied drugs, as well as hypnosis, as tools to aid in interrogation and mind programming of adversaries. The U.S. Army studies, which were declassified in 1969, identified MDMA as the most toxic substance investigated (Cohen, 1998).

MDMA remained obscure until the 1970s when it emerged as a treatment for depression and related mental conditions (Greer and Tolbert, 1998; Holland, 2001). Although there were no controlled studies, it was investigated informally when psychiatrists gave it to clients in psychotherapy sessions and reported such benefits as lowered inhibitions and increased bonding between couples. Additionally, they reported that it assisted in the re-establishment of memories and in the treatment of traumatic disorders. At the time, the drug was not illegal, and the anecdotal reports about its beneficial uses were not subjected to scientific scrutiny. Note that one very important topic received little, if any, consideration at the time, namely patients' experiences after they left the clinical setting.

What were the downside experiences, if any, and did the drug have long lasting effects, either positive or negative?

An increase in the recreational use of MDMA became evident in the U.S. in the early 1980s. It is possible that the reports of Ecstasy increasing users' warm feelings toward others contributed to its emergence as a drug of abuse. It was legal, and it was sold openly. Its reputation grew, as did its use.

The Drug Enforcement Administration (DEA) initiated action to classify MDMA as emergency Schedule 1 in 1984. Despite significant resistance, especially by some psychotherapists, MDMA was formally classified as a Schedule 1 drug in March of 1988.

MDMA use escalated within the Rave community. Raves are dance parties, usually held in remote locations and sometimes attended by thousands of young people. Some attendees are as young as 12 years old, and the oldest are very young adults. In unsupervised settings of loud electronic music and continuous dancing, there is minimal capability for responding to medical emergencies. Nonetheless, the attendees ingest a variety of drugs (www.streetdrugs.org; www.emedicinehealth.com/articles/28418-1.asp).

"Ecstasy makes you want to hug and to be hugged."

Most users experience warm feelings. It is understandable that they then enthusiastically tell friends that a state of joy and happiness can be achieved just by taking a tablet of MDMA.

To begin to comprehend the dynamics of Raves, consider that the environment has many celebratory characteristics. The young attendees typically know only a few of the hundreds or thousands of other young people present at the event. They take and encourage others to take MDMA in anticipation of unbridled ecstasy. Positive emotions, peer pressure, lowered inhibitions, and the influence of music, sleeplessness, and fatigue all contribute to drug use. Exactly how many Rave attendees take the drug is unknown and will vary as a function of circumstances, but it can be reasonably assumed that many participants are drawn to the events because of the availability and accepted use of MDMA.

The growth of Raves seems to have slowed and possibly has reversed in many parts of the U.S. (MDMA (Ecstasy) Report, 2004). Although the reasons for the slowdown are debatable and not fully understood, it appears that new laws have had an impact. Legislation at both state and federal levels has curtailed the sale of the drug. The federal Illicit Drug Anti-Proliferations Act, which was enacted in April of 2003, has effectively reduced the number of Raves by providing for criminal and civil prosecution of the planners, facilitators and promoters of events who knowingly allow drug activity by those in attendance.

The popularity of MDMA grew rapidly between 1998 and 2001. In January of 2002 the Partnership for a Drug-Free America and the White House Office on National Drug Control Policy unveiled a series of print and TV advertisements designed to expose MDMA as dangerous and potentially lethal. The president of the non-profit Partnership for a Drug-Free America, Stephen Pasierb, stated "We've got 2.8 million kids who have used Ecstasy and millions more who think they might want to try it. If we wait another five years to talk about this, the monster could be out of the box." (Leinwand, 2002). In September 2002 Congressional testimony, DEA representatives identified MDMA as the number one drug problem facing America's urban youth (Hanson, G. R., 2002).

The trend in MDMA use now may have been reversed. As early as 2001, the yearly Monitoring the Future (MTF) survey of secondary students across the country revealed that a higher proportion of students viewed MDMA as a dangerous drug. In 2002, use began to decline, and it plunged in 2003 (Johnston, et al., 2003, 2004). As reported at a White House news conference, 2003 data showed that the proportion of American tenth and twelfth grade students who had used MDMA in the prior twelve months dropped by more than half compared to 2001.

6.3 Development and Delivery

Synthesizing MDMA involves setups and equipment akin to those needed for making d-methamphetamine, but the comparison falls short in important ways. Compared to d-methamphetamine, the chemical skill level required for making MDMA is greater, it is more difficult to obtain the necessary precursor chemicals, and it involves the acquisition and management of hazardous chemicals. The primary precursors for MDMA syntheses are safrole, issafrole and pipernol, which are volatile, unstable and explosive.

European labs, many in the Netherlands and Belgium, provide most of the MDMA for the world market. It is manufactured, smuggled, distributed, and sold primarily through criminal networks. Illegal delivery relies on traditional smuggling methods including transport by mail, concealment in luggage, and individuals transporting it on or within their bodies.

The criminal enterprise is a lucrative pyramid of activities, and the illicit drug market has been inundated with MDMA tablets since the early 1990s. DEA documents place the average cost per tablet in the Netherlands and Belgium area at $.50 to $2.00. In the U.S., wholesale prices jump to $8.00 to $10.00 per tablet. Retail prices reflect several factors including location, supply and purity. Good quality tablets cost $15.00 to $20.00 in coastal cities and $30.00 to $50.00 in rural areas. Anywhere within the manufacture-to-sales system, the tablets can be crushed into powder, mixed with similar-looking substances and reformulated into tablets or capsules. The *fillers* may or may not be psychoactive, but they increase bulk with less expensive material and produce a more profitable product.

6.4 Appearance and Routes of Administration

MDMA is a crystallized powder, similar in appearance to d-methamphetamine. As with methamphetamine, the chemical ingredients, processes of manufacture, and diluents determine its color. Individuals or groups of suppliers anywhere along the pyramided selling system compact the powder into a pill form or insert in into empty digestible gelatin capsules, and the drug is most frequently taken orally as a tablet or capsule. For quick absorption, the tablet sometimes is crushed and wrapped in a piece of tissue, a practice called *parachuting*. For even faster absorption, the drug is taken as a suppository either as a whole tablet, crushed and wrapped in tissue, or mixed in with a liquid enema. Less frequently, the drug is insufflated, a practice referred to as railing. It also is injected or mixed with other material and smoked.

Typical MDMA tablets are about the size of an aspirin, and most are imprinted with lettering or logos. Shapes and colors vary. Imprints may be cartoon characters, designer labels, drug symbols, angels, shapes, or many others (see Table 6.1).

Although there are no reliable observable indicators of the chemical composition of an MDMA tablet, users believe the symbols and shapes indicate its worth. They report their experiences with specific pills via Internet bulletin boards with the result that others believe that tablets with certain characteristics have greater strength or purity. The drug manufacturers also monitor the Internet sites, learn what is believed about markings, and produce tablets with the sought-after appearance.

Numerouse nicknames based on the tablet imprint	
E	Beans
Vitamin E	Rolls
X	Tickets
XTC	Love drug

Table 6.1 Common street names for MDMA

6.5 Counterfeits

Hollywood used the sale of over-the-counter capsules as Ecstasy in the story line of the 1999 dark comedy, *GO*. Criminal manufacturing and dispersal networks do not insure drug quality, and quality control for MDMA rests entirely in the hands of criminals. Not surprisingly, Ecstasy tablets containing other substances are routinely sold to unsuspecting buyers. A 300 mg tablet represented to be Ecstasy on average contains 69 to 120 mg MDMA (Hanson, 2002).

The supplement Remifemin® is an extreme example that demonstrates that almost anything can be sold as Ecstasy. Remifemin® is an aid for the treatment of menopausal symptoms. Because it carries a butterfly logo, which is recognized as a symbol of Ecstasy, naive individuals purchase Remifemin® and are confident that they have acquired Ecstasy. Kits are available for the purpose of testing for MDMA in a tablet. Also, there are Internet sites to which tablets can be submitted anonymously. The tablets will be tested and the results posted on the site. The only certain method for determining the content of an illegal tablet, however, is a competent chemical testing facility.

6.6 Analogs

A drug analog is chemically similar to the original substance, produces comparable behavioral effects and is referred to as a chemical first-cousin (see Table 6.2). Synthetically produced analogs, sometimes referred to as

MDA	3,4-methylenedioxyamphetamine
MDE	3,4 methylenedioxy-n-ethylamphetamine
MMDA	3-metoxy-4,5-methlenedosyamphetamine
DOM	2,5-dimethoxy-4-methylampetamine
PMA	para-methoxyamphetamine
TMA	3,4,5-trimethoxyphenethylamine
2C-B	4-bromo-2,3 dimethoxyphenethylamine

Table 6.2 Common MDMA analogs

designer drugs, are produced for the purpose of circumventing criminal laws. This approach relies on slight alterations of the structure of an illegal chemical to avoid prohibitions. In 1986, however, the Controlled Substances Analog Act was enacted to deal with this ploy. It bans the manufacture and sale of all designer drugs. The amphetamine-based drugs, which appear in the following table, have hallucinogenic properties and are examples of MDMA analogs.

6.7 Effects

MDMA increases the action of a least three neurotransmitters: serotonin, dopamine and norepinephrine. Some of the amplified activity mimics the activity of abused stimulants. Investigators, who have studied stimulants, including the amphetamines and cocaine, have concluded that even moderate use alters the brain's production of neurotransmitters. Such changes in dopamine and serotonin interfere with the regulation of mood states and the formation of memories and possibly will lead to long-term depression (Ali et al., 1993).

MDMA affects the sensory system. With increased sensitivity to stimuli, color appears vibrant and bright, sound seems clearer, odor is more intense, and touch is more sensitive. Effects on emotions are even greater. With a major release of serotonin, sensitivity is enhanced and empathy and introspection increase. Although many medical texts classify MDMA as a hallucinogen, it only rarely produces a hallucination.

The route of ingestion and strength of the substance have an effect on the time course and duration of effects. With the most common route of administration, swallowing, the greatest effects are experienced within thirty to sixty minutes. Drug purity, on the other hand, determines the duration of effects, which averages three to six hours (Beck and Rosenbaum, 1994; Hanson, 2002). Significant variations in intensity and duration of effects can and do occur with dosage, route of administration and tolerance levels.

The context of use, that is, the user's mood state and the social surroundings, contributes to the ultimate effect of all drugs, especially those with emotional properties. For this reason, MDMA-using groups advise, "You get out of it what you put into it," and users arrange mental and environmental conditions to be consistent with the experience they seek. Careful control of environment and mind set can protect against negative effects to some extent. Nonetheless, the potential remains for this methamphetamine-based drug to produce the negative effects associated with methamphetamine alone. Pupils dilate, body temperature, pulse and blood pressure increase. Muscles become rigid and sweating becomes profuse. Spasm-like movements of the fifth cranial nerves cause bruxism. Users can become hyperactive and experience long bouts of energy and sleeplessness.

Several sources list nystagmus as a side effect of MDMA, but the observed twitching of the eyeballs is not horizontal gaze nystagmus. Rather, with this drug, the eyes are sometimes observed rolling upward toward the forehead. The movement, at times referred to as jittery eyes, may be the origin of the slang term for Ecstasy, "rolling,"

Common reported psychological effects	
Empathy	Improved communications
Euphoria	Relaxation
Decreave of inhibitions	Improved self esteem
Increased confidence	Increased understanding
Common reported physiological effects	
Elevated body temperature	Increased pulse
Dilated pupils	Increased blood pressure
Slow reaction to light	Bruxism
Visual distortions	Decreased libido

Table 6.3 Common psychobiological effects

As the body metabolizes MDMA, its effects diminish and the phase known as a drug's downside follows. The user experiences emotions and energy levels in direct opposition to those experienced while under the influence of the drug. The major depletion of serotonin can result in deep depression. Mental despair typically follows within two days following the last MDMA intake, giving rise to the phrases "terrible Tuesdays" and "suicidal Tuesdays." The Tuesday reference reflects the fact that drug use often occurs during weekend partying. Depression lasts two to three days, but it may persist longer following prolonged use. If MDMA is ingested during these periods of despondency when there is a depleted level of serotonin, it will produce stimulation without the desirable emotional effects. Within the MDMA sub-culture, the phrase "less is more" acknowledges that the drug's use must be minimized to consistently achieve pleasure from it.

In an effort to avoid the downside of the drug, users take vitamins, minerals and nutrients, which they believe will augment serotonin levels. This pre-loading may include serotonin precursors such as 5-hydroxytryptophan (5HTP), sometimes referred to as the brain's tryptophan. The substance is found in foods (e.g., turkey, Ovaltine) and vitamins. Kits with powders, herbs and vitamins that contain 5HTP are touted as a means to modulate the emotional descent from MDMA. Users may also self-medicate with antidepressants, alcohol, marijuana, and other drugs. These additional psychoactive drugs introduce the possibility of drug interactions with serious consequences.

Self-proclaimed experts offer advice via the Internet for optimal breaks from MDMA with non-use advocated for periods of three days to three months. If these suggested longer intervals were followed, MDMA use would create little, if any, chemical dependency. Whenever users are confronted with drug-using opportunities and they recall the pleasures associated with use, the advocated period of abstinence likely will not be heeded. Limited use of any psychoactive substance is likely to be less damaging then heavy and frequent use. Nonetheless, any ingestion of MDMA carries the potential for physical and psychological damage. A single use can result in overdose death, inappropriate behavior, increased sexual proclivity, driving under-the-influence, and other dangerous activities.

6.8 Toxicity

Opinions vary widely about the potential for physical and mental damage from MDMA use. Myths and mistakes abound. The view that the so-called love drug is the world's most dangerous chemical of abuse occupies one extreme of opinion. The view that there is little or no risk is at the other extreme of opinion. Science-based evidence supports neither extreme but raises concerns about recreational use of the drug and suggests a need for additional research about utilization in therapeutic settings.

A drug's capacity to cause harm and its addiction potential impose limits on its administration to human subjects for the purpose of study. Thus, controlled study of MDMA with human subjects is sparse, but animal studies partially fill the void. The data accumulated over fifteen years of investigations demonstrate that MDMA damages specific neurons in the brains of animals. Some researchers working with animals have reported evidence of axon regeneration, whereas other investigations have found no rejuvenation. It appears that MDMA-related damage may be species-specific and may vary as a function of the method and amount of ingestion.

There is near-universal agreement among scientists that MDMA diminishes serotonin levels in human brains. When it crosses the blood brain barrier, it floods the area with serotonin, a neurotransmitter that the brain normally releases and stores in small amounts. Unusually large release results in depletion, and the larger the release of serotonin, the longer time needed to replace it.

A study led by Dr. George Ricaurte of Johns Hopkins University School of Medicine has been controversial. Dr. Ricaurte was the lead author of a September 26, 2002 report in *Science* titled "Severe Dopaminergic Neurotoxicity in Primates After a Common Recreational Dose Regimen of MDMA (Ecstasy)" (Ricaurte et al., 2002). The report stated that nonhuman primates given three sequential doses of MDMA experienced a 60-80 percent loss of dopaminergic nerve endings. The investigators concluded that permanent brain damage could result from one large dose. In September of 2003, however, the research team retracted their report (Ricaurte et al., 2003). Due to a labeling error, the primates had been dosed with methamphetamine instead of MDMA.

MDMA use was at an all-time high when the initial report was released. For drug enforcement officials, the news seemed to be proof that

MDMA is a risky drug. Prior to the retraction, however, proponents of MDMA legalization had already noted that scientists had not been able to replicate the study. The retraction then served to bolster theories of political motives and unwarranted attempts to prevent use of a beneficial medicine.

6.9 Driving

The Drug and Human Performance Fact Sheet for MDMA (Cooper and Logan, 2004) summarizes the potential effects of the drug on driving skills as follows:

> Low to moderate single doses of MDMA can cause acute changes in cognitive performance and impair information processing, which in turn would impair driving ability. Basic vehicle control is only moderately affected; however, subjects may accept higher levels of risk.

> Risk taking behavior and impulsivity are frequently observed in those who are under-the-influence of MDMA in non-driving situations. It can be logically assumed that those behind the wheel of an automobile will also take greater chances. Not to be lost in the possible hazards of operating a motor vehicle after ingestion of the drug is the heightened effects on the sensory systems of the body, particularly that of vision.

> Determining the instances and percentages of motor vehicle crashes involving the drug is difficult, because many investigating law enforcement personnel lack the specialized training for detecting drug influence and thus may not require a chemical test for the substance.

6.10 Summary

Many MDMA users consider the drug to be harmless. It is an empathogen; that is, it induces feelings of empathy. Users experience increased understanding of others, as well as gaining some insight about themselves. The drug state has been described as being akin to a religious experience. The chemicals activate the brain's pleasure centers and increase energy. Is it any wonder the drug is known as Ecstasy?

Still, troubling questions remain. MDMA users are young. Most of the drivers and passengers in fatal motor vehicle crashes, for whom MDMA is found in blood specimens, are adolescents and young adults.

Little is known about the drug's effects on developing brains. Essentially nothing is known about long-term effects when use begins as early as age twelve. Animal studies suggest brain changes with potentially serious consequences, and scattered anecdotal evidence from teenage users paints a picture of severe and irreversible damage.

There are no final answers about the consequences of MDMA use. It is, however, a cautionary tale.

The FDA approved the use of MDMA in research with patients suffering form Post-Traumatic Stress Disorder in 2001, and in March of 2004 the DEA issued its first Schedule 1 possession license for research purposes. Studies of the possible therapeutic benefits of the drug are ongoing, but the results of those studies will be largely irrelevant to issues about its use by young people solely for pleasure-producing effects. The brain of an adolescent or young adult clearly is not an appropriate place for experimentation with a powerful drug.

References

Ali, S. F., Newpart, G. D., Scallet, A. C., Binienda, Z., Ferguson, S. A., and Bailey, J. R. (1993). Oral administration of MDMA produces selective 5-HT depletion in non-human primate. *Neurotoxical. Teratol.* 15, 2, Mar-Apr, 91-96.

Bankson, M.G., Cunningham, K.A. (2001). 3,4-Methylenedioxymethamphetamine (MDMA) as a unique model of serotonin receptor function and serotonin-dopamine interactions. *J Pharmacol Exp Ther*, 297, 3, June, 846-852.

Beck, J., and Rosenbaum, M. (1994) *Pursuit of ecstasy: The MDMA experience.* Albany, NY: State University of New York Press.

Burns, M. (2003). *Medical-legal aspects of drugs.* Tuscon, AZ: Lawyers & Judges Publishing Co., Inc.

Cohen, R.S. (1998). *The love drug: Marching to the beat of ecstasy.* Haworth Medical Press, Binghamton, NY.

Concar, D. (June 21, 1997) "After the rave, the ecstasy hangover." *New Scientist Plant Science.* (http://www.bassdove.demon.co.uk/rave.htm).

Drug Identification Bible (2004/2005 Edition). Grand Junction, CO: Amera-Chem, Inc., (http://www.drugbible.com).

Goldstein, A. (2001). Addiction from biology to drug policy. New York: Oxford University Press.

Greer, G., and Tolbert, R. (1998). A method of conducting therapeutic sessions with MDMA. *Journal of Psychoactive Drugs*, 30, 4, 371-379.

Holland, J. (2001). *Ecstasy: The complete guide*. Inner Traditions International, Limited.

Grob, C. S. (2000). Deconstructing ecstasy: The politics of MDMA research. *Addiction Research*, 8, 6, 549-588.

Hanson, G.R. (2002). Testimony before the subcommittee on Criminal Justice, Drug Policy and Human Resources, Committee on Government Reform, United States House of Representatives, Research on MDMA. Acting Director National Institure on Drug Abuse and National Institute of Health Department of Health and Human Services September 19, 2002.

Harris, D., Baggott, M., Jones, R.T., and Mendelson, J.E. (2000). MDMA pharmacokinetics and Physiological and Subjective Effects in Humans, In L.S. Harris (Ed.), *Problems of Drug Dependence 1999. Proceedings of the 61st Annual Scientific Meeting, the College on the Problems of Drug Dependence. NIDA Research Monograph Series 180*:131.

Jerome, L. (2004). MDMA investigator's brochure update #2. A review of research in humans and non-human animals. Multidisciplinary Association for Psychedelic Studies. (http://www.maps.org/mdma/protocol/litupdate2.pdf).

Johnston, L.D., O'Malley, P.M., Bachman, J.G., and Schulenberg, J.E. (2004). *Monitoring the future national survey results on drug use, 1975-2003. Volume I: Secondary school students*, p. 545 (NIH Publication No. 04-5507). Bethesda, MD: National Institute on Drug Abuse.

Johnston, L.D., O'Malley, P.M., Bachman, J.G., and Schulenberg, J.E. (2004). Monitoring the future national results on adolescent drug use: *Overview of key findings, 2003*, p. 59 (NIH Publication No. 04-5506). Bethesda, MD: National Institute on Drug Abuse.

Johnston, L.D., O'Malley, P.M., and Bachman, J.G. (2003). *Monitoring the Future national survey results on adolescent drug use: Overview of key findings, 2002*, p. 56 (NIH Publication No. 03-5374). Bethesda, MD: National Institute on Drug Abuse.

Kuhn, C., Swartzwelder, S., and Wilson, W. (1998) *Buzzed: The straight facts about the most used and abused drugs from alcohol to ecstasy.* New York: W. W. Norton.

Leinwand, D. (2002). More teens try ecstacy. *USA Today*, February 11, 2002. Retrieved 2004 at http://www.usatoday.com/news/nation/2002/02/11/ecstasy.htm

MDMA/Ecstasy Research: Advances, Challenges, Future Directions, A Scientific Conference. (http://www.drugabuse.gov/Meetings/MDMA/MDMAExSummary. html).

Nelson, K. T. (1999). MDMA and memory impairment: Proven or not? *Multidisciplinary Association for Psychedelic Studies*, 9, 3, 6-8.

National Institute of Drug Abuse. MDMA (Ecstasy) Report (2004). (http://www.drugabuse.gov/ResearchReports/MDMA/default.html).

National Institute of Drug Abuse. NIDA Info Facts (February 2004) MDMA (Ecstasy) (www.drugabuse.gov).

NIDA Research Report MDMA (Ecstasy) Abuse. (http://www.drugabuse.gov/ResearchReports/MDMA).

Ricaurte, G.A., Yuan, J., and McCann, U.D. (2000). (+/-) 3, 4-methylenedioxymethamphetamine ("Ecstasy") - induced serotonin neurotoxicity: Studies in animals. *Neuropsychobiology*, 1, 5-10.

Ricaurte, G.A., Yuan, J., Hatzidimitriou G., Cord B.J., and McCann U.D. (2003). Severe dopaminergic neurotoxicity in primates after a common recreational dose regimen of MDMA ("ecstasy"). *Science*, September 26, 2002, paper retracted September 2003.

Ricaurte, G.A., Yuan, J., Hatzidimitriou, G., Cord, B.J., McCann, U.D. (2003). "Retraction," Letter to Science Magazine, Sept. 12, 2003, Vol. 31, p. 1479.

Saunders, N., and Doblin, R. (1996). *Ecstasy dance trance and transformation.* Oakland, CA.: Quick American Archives.

Saunders, N. (1995). *Ecstasy and the dance culture.* London: Saunders: published by author. .

Shulgin, A.T., and Nichols, D.E. (1978). Characterization of three new psychotomimetics, In R.C. Stillman, and R.E. Willette (Eds.). *The pharmacology of hallucinogens.* New York: Pergamon.

Tranceer, M., & Schuster, C. R. (1997). Serotonin and dopaimine system interactions in the reinforcining porpoerites of psychostimulants: A research strategy. *Multidisciplinary Association for Psychedelic Studies*, 7, 3, 5-11.

Vollenweider, F.X., Gamma, A. Liechti, M., and Huber, T. (1999). Is a single dose of MDMA harmless? *Neuropsychopharmacol*, 21, 598-600.

Chapter 7

Examining Methamphetamine

Charles Matson

7.1 Introduction

Methamphetamine, a Schedule II drug, is one of the amphetamines, a group that also includes dextroamphetamine and assorted salts. Methamphetamine is a very potent stimulant that is relatively easy to obtain or manufacture. It appears to undermine an individual's self control more quickly than most other psychoactive drugs.

Use of methamphetamine, or meth as it is commonly called, has increased rapidly in recent years. The decades-long predictions of law enforcement officers, treatment providers, government officials and others are becoming reality. Millions of drug tests during 2003 showed a 68 percent increase for amphetamine use compared to 2002. Methamphetamine accounted for most of the increase (Jones, 2004). If there is any question that the drug's use is greater than ever, consider that drug-related emergency room visits involving amphetamine/methamphetamine increased 54 percent between 1995 and 2002 (DAWN, 2002). As use of this drug moves from the West Coast to the eastern United States, it is possible that addiction to methamphetamine may become the worst drug epidemic in our country's history. Prevention, treatment, and enforcement officials, who must try to find answers to meth-related problems within their individual agencies, face a challenge.

7.2 Forms

Although some amphetamine-based medications are prescribed for legitimate medical purposes, (e.g., Desoxyn®, Dexedrine®, Adderall®, Benzedrine®, DextroStat®, Biphetamine®, and Gradumet®), all CNS stimulants have a potential for abuse and addiction. As with other chemicals that cross the blood-brain barrier, methamphetamine's potency largely determines the effects that a user experiences. The chemical strength of three types can be characterized as follows:

- L-Methamphetamine *(L=Levo)* is the least potent form of the drug, with a short duration of effects. Over-the-counter (OTC) cold medicines such as Vicks Inhalers® contain l-methamphetamine. The inhaler is used as a treatment for nasal congestion and is rarely abused. Excessive use can create stomach pain and body tremors, and there are few, if any, pleasurable effects.

- D/L-Methamphetamine *(D/L=Dextro-Levo)* sometimes is the unplanned result of production methods, and it does not produce effects that are as desirable as those of d-methamphetamine. Users report that they experience body tremors and stomach cramps. It cannot be smoked.

- Methamphetamine *(D=Dextro)* the most potent substance is the form most often used by abusers and addicts. Even small amounts stimulate the brain and produce changes in emotions and basic drives. Meth generates intense feelings of euphoria, confidence, and superiority. Users also report an elevation in sensory acuity, increased energy and a decrease in appetite. It increases heart rate, blood pressure and respiration. Its use will almost always result in addiction, destruction of the mind and body, and a shorter life span.

7.3 History

The organic substance ephedra, which is derived from the stems of a small shrub, has been used medically for centuries. Ephedrine, which is synthesized from the organic material, has bronchial dilator properties. Amphetamine, the parent of methamphetamine, was first synthesized from ephedrine in 1887 by German chemist L. Edeleano, and was known as phenylisopropylamine (Anglin et al., 2000). Japanese chemists produced methamphetamine, which has more acute effects than amphetamine, in 1919. It is water soluble, and can be injected and smoked.

During the 1920s, amphetamines were investigated as treatments for maladies that included alcoholism, epilepsy, migraines, opiate addiction and schizophrenia. In 1932 the pharmaceutical company, Smith, Kline and French, marketed Benzedrine, known on the street as bennies, as an OTC inhaler. The stimulant constricts inflamed nasal passageways and dilates the lung's bronchial tubes, enabling asthma patients and those with other respiratory disorders to breath more freely. Other pharmaceutical companies produced similar products.

Users discovered that the drug made them feel good. As a result, the abuse of amphetamines began. During the era of alcohol prohibition in the United States, individuals removed the soaked strips of paper from inhalers and put them into coffee to achieve a "buzz." The brew may have been quite potent since some of the inhalers contained the equivalent of as many as fifty-six amphetamine tablets. In the United States the intravenous injection of the contents of inhalers was first reported in the late 1950s.

Although Smith, Kline, and French withdrew Benzedrine from the market in 1949, other companies continued to sell similar OTC inhalers.

With the advent of the amphetamines, the popularity of cocaine had declined, and it remained relatively low as long as non-prescription amphetamines were available. Sales of the inhalers ended with the enactment of the Controlled Substances Act of 1970.

American, British, German and Japanese troops used amphetamines during World War II to increase stamina and alertness and to reduce the need for sleep. During the forty-four days between German troops first crossing the French border and their march through Paris, the French were astonished by the Germans' aggressive, relentless attack. It is believed that access to stimulants was the reason they seemed to never need rest. In that case, the blitzkrieg could have been called the *speedkrieg*. In 1941, however, Nazi officials banned the use of methamphetamine, most likely due to incidents of psychosis and deaths from exhaustion. It has been reported that the Nazis added meth to Schokokloa, a chocolate bar, which is available even today albeit with caffeine instead of methamphetamine. The chocolates were available in containers outside Adolph Hitler's office, and it is probable that he was addicted to the drug toward the end of his life. A method of clandestine manufacture in the U.S. currently is known as the Nazi method.

Methamphetamine was also available to Japanese combatants. The reported injections by Kamikaze pilots with meth prior to their suicide missions is striking evidence that it encourages aggressive behaviors and increases confidence. As a drug that promotes alertness and self-confidence, it would have been an ideal choice for the pilots.

Methamphetamine use reached epidemic proportions in Japan after the end of WWII. During that postwar period, the nation needed to increase production of goods if they were to recover from the economically disastrous war. Apparently, workers were allowed, if not encouraged, to tap the leftover stores of stimulants. As use skyrocketed, however, authorities changed the free-access policy and created programs to discourage use.

It was generally believed during the late 1950s and early 1960s that there were few, if any, negative consequences of amphetamine use. Methedrine and Dexedrene/Dexdrine, amphetamine-based drugs, were legal and easily obtainable in the U.S. They were prescribed for weight loss and depression and were used by truck drivers who needed to stay awake during long hours of driving, as well as by college students who needed to study long hours to prepare for an exam.

Beginning in the 1960s and continuing through the 1980s, outlaw motorcycle gangs were the principal distributors of illicit methamphetamine. According to street lore, the slang term for methamphetamine, "crank," came about because the gangs transported the drug in their motorcycle crankcases.

Currently many citizens believe that local clandestine labs are responsible for the methamphetamine problem. The evening TV news and the local paper may report that the police shut down a dangerous drug lab. There are images of residents being removed from homes, children being taken from parents, and cops walking around in strange looking protective gear. These items are newsworthy, but in reality these small labs produce only 10 to 15 percent of the illicit meth that is consumed in the United States. Most comes from super labs that are controlled by highly organized, sophisticated criminal cartels and are driven by large profits.

Mexican national crime organizations with a history of cocaine and marijuana smuggling were attracted to methamphetamine commerce. Unlike cocaine, they could make the drug themselves, and they could introduce it to potential users by including it with shipments of cocaine. Since they had well-established smuggling routes, the addition of another drug added no costs to their operations.

The motorcycle gangs and the Mexican cartels made methamphetamine with a method known as the Phenyl-2-Propanone (P2P) method until the 1980s. At that time, tighter restrictions on chemicals prompted a switch to the ephedrine reduction method. In those early days, the labs usually remained in one location and took major precautions with site security, often relying on aggressive guard dogs and booby traps to protect their profitable operations. When Congress passed the Comprehensive Methamphetamine Control Act in 1996 placing tight restrictions on ephedrine, the labs switched to pseudoephedrine as the precursor chemical. The updated technique is faster, produces a drug of much higher purity, and yields greater profits.

The number of methamphetamine labs in the U.S. began to increase dramatically in the early 1990s, a trend that continues today. The Drug Enforcement Administration (DEA) reports that the number of labs in the U.S. in 1995 was 327. In 2001 there were 12,715 labs and in 2003 there were 14,908. A third of all labs were in California in 1995, but that percentage has been reduced to less than 15 percent.

In 1999, more than 95 percent of the total of 228 super labs were in California, mainly in the Central Valley or Southern California area. These labs can produce ten pounds or more of methamphetamine per twenty-four hour period and supply approximately 80 percent of the drug that reaches the street throughout the U.S. Mexican cartels use sophisticated purchasing and smuggling operations to obtain the equivalent of 800-1,000 tablets of ephedrine/pseudoephedrine that are required to produce an ounce of methamphetamine.

There also are small independent operations that are referred to variously as mom and pop, coffeepot, bathtub, kitchen, mobile and Beavis and Butthead labs. Most are users/dealers who make the drug for personal use and sell enough to obtain money to buy more ingredients for more drugs. Most are mobile and can quickly transport their equipment and chemicals from one location to another. Although they produce a relatively small amount of drug, the quality typically is higher (90 percent purity) than that seized from super labs.

Methamphetamine that can be smoked first appeared in Japan and Korea in the late 1980s and later appeared in Hawaii and the western U.S. This form, which is known as "ice," is attractive to users, because smoking the drug produces exhilarating effects but avoids the hazards associated with needle use. Ice is to methamphetamine as crack is to cocaine. Impurities have been removed, and rapid absorption produced powerful effects.

7.4 Appearance

Illicit methamphetamine is produced in a number of different shapes and colors with the final appearance limited only by the imagination of the manufacturer. All non-liquid forms are crystals, although the very small particles may appear to be powder. Much of the product is white, but the color is dependent on the precursor chemicals, as well as adulterants that are introduced during production. "Ice" resembles small glass fragments or rock candy. It is clear or semi-clear, or it may have a translucent yellow tint.

Methamphetamine is also available as "Yaba," a multicolored methamphetamine tablet to which caffeine and sometimes flavorings (chocolate, vanilla, grape, orange) have been added. Although presently Yaba is smuggled into the United States predominantly for sale and use in the Asian community, it is certainly possible that this form will become popular in the future. Use of the tablets, which are also called Hitler's drug, Nazi speed, "Myanmar" and "crazy medicine," has reached epidemic proportions in Southeast Asia, most notably in Thailand.

Meth	Poor man's cocaine	Speed	Ice
Crystal	Crystal meth	Yaba	Crank
Glass	Tina	Go fast	Bikers coffee
Amp	Chalk	Zip	

Table 7.1 Common street names for methamphetamine.

7.5 Methods of Administration

Methamphetamine enables the user to experience euphoria, heightened energy, and increased confidence. When it enters the blood system and circulates throughout the body reaching the limbic area of the brain, it triggers an eruption of neuro-chemical actions. It produces highly reinforcing feelings of pleasure, energy and self-confidence.

A stronger addiction produces a greater desire for methods of ingestion that are rapid and efficient. Oral ingestion, snorting, injecting, and smoking differ in the onset time and the intensity of effects.

A. Oral: Because of their bitter taste, tablets usually are swallowed without chewing. Tablets or crystals are dissolved in fluid for drinking. Meth does not have local anesthetic effects as cocaine does, and is not ingested by rubbing on the gums. *Onset:* fifteen to thirty minutes. *Intensity:* CNS stimulation without the euphoria associated with injecting or smoking.

B. Snorting: The ground crystals are insufflated using a straw. This method may produce an extreme burning sensation. *Onset:* three to five minutes. *Intensity:* more CNS stimulation than with oral ingestion but no extreme euphoria.

C. Injection: The drug is mixed with water and injected into a vein.

    Onset: a rush occurs within thirty seconds. Because spikes in dopamine can occur as the user anticipates the effects of injecting the drug, preparing for injection may become psychologically addictive.

    Intensity: extreme euphoria.

D. Smoking: Ice is commonly smoked with a glass pipe. The drug is heated to its melting/vaporizing point of 347° Fahrenheit. When heat is removed from the pipe, the ice re-coagulates. It can be vaporized again allowing a user to obtain ten to twenty-five hits from one gram of drug. Other forms can be smoked by placing the meth on a piece of folded aluminum foil, heating it and inhaling through a straw, a method known as "foiling" or "chasing the dragon."

    Onset: immediate.

    Intensity: intense euphoria.

Meth also is mixed with water and squirted into the nostril with a nasal spray bottle or dropped into the fluid of the eye. Users with severe formication (the belief that bugs are crawling under the skin) obtain relief by rubbing it onto open lesions for absorption into the bloodstream.

7.6 Legislative Control of Methamphetamine

Drug laws are expected to continue to focus on a few key areas. Legislation can limit the amount of over-the-counter cold medications that can be purchased by individuals and groups. Laws also may increase the mandatory minimum sentences for possession and distribution of methamphetamine. It is possible that laws will make it illegal to communicate information about the manufacture of illegal drugs, thereby eliminating the recipes that proliferate via the Internet. The latter possibility is a complicated free speech issue.

7.7 Patterns of Use and Abuse
A. Low-intensity abuse

Low-intensity abuse sometimes stems from the desire to lose weight or a need to be awake and alert over prolonged periods. The users administer the drug orally or by insufflation (snorting). Because the powdered drug is abrasive, the latter method often results in irritation of the nasal membranes. This level of use generally produces no overt signs that can be recognized by the untrained observer. Although the individual's vital signs will be elevated, outward appearance and behavior may not appear unusual. As tolerance to the drug's effects develops, the user may use larger amounts. If he or she progresses to smoking or injecting, the risk of binging increases.

B. High-intensity abuse

A high-intensity abuser is fixated on recapturing the orgasmic feeling experienced with the first injection or smoking of meth. This behavior often brands the addict as a speed freak. As tolerance for the drug increases and more meth is needed to obtain inferior highs, the user eventually uses the drug not to feel good but just to feel something.

A high-intensity abuser may appear nearly normal to an untutored observer. Signs commonly associated with intoxication (bloodshot eyes, slurred speech, poor balance, an unstable gait) may not exist. The constriction of blood vessels within the eyeballs makes the sclera and conjunctiva appear clear and bright. In addition, droopy eyelids do not occur, because the stimulant action causes a retraction of the eyelids. Speech typically is slightly to moderately rapid, the voice may tremble slightly, and thought may be disorganized. The misleading physical appearance may result in a hazardous failure to recognize emotional instability and paranoia. Driven by continuous craving, the user can be unpredictable, even dangerous. Seemingly minor behavioral and physical clues, however, can assist a trained observer's assessment of possible methamphetamine use. Rapid eye movements and an inability to focus attention are clues.

C. Binge and crash

When methamphetamine is first smoked or injected, the user experiences a tremendous rush that some individuals describe as being similar to multiple orgasms. The orgasmic rush is due to the activation of the adrenal gland and the resulting discharge of the hormone epinephrine. Dopamine floods the pleasure center of the brain. Within seconds, the effects on the autonomic nervous system cause vital signs to soar. Pupils dilate, the jaw tightens, the teeth grind, and hair on the back of the neck stands up. Unlike the rush associated with crack cocaine, which lasts for approximately two to five minutes, the methamphetamine rush can continue for up to thirty minutes.

The user will continue to experience a high that will last four to twelve hours depending upon his or her tolerance and the potency of the drug itself. They will frequently become assertive and self-confident. As the high dissipates they may consume more of the chemical or binge to delay the inevitable crash. The binging can last for several days or even weeks.

The terms tweaking, tweaker, and tweaked refer to the descending stage of a stimulant binge. It is a downward spiral of emotional and physical collapse accompanied by physical pain and unstable thinking. Efforts to stop the crash with additional ingestion of meth are futile due to the depletion of dopamine in the brain. Although more and more drug may be ingested, the crash inevitably occurs. The tweaker then often seeks relief from the dysphoria of a crash by taking depressants or narcotics.

A crash is characterized by exceedingly long periods of sleep, during which it may not be possible to awaken the individual. The addict eventually returns to a physiological and psychological state somewhat below his or her homeostatic level—a state which may last as long as fourteen days.

D. Withdrawal

The transition into withdrawal is gradual, frequently occurring thirty to ninety days after the last drug use. The first symptom is a decreased ability to experience pleasure. The addict feels lethargic and lacks motivation thereby creating problems in his or her personal life. Finding and maintaining employment becomes difficult. Personal and family relationships are disturbed. No aspect of the addict's life is immune during this difficult period. The great challenge of addiction, of course, is the memory of previous drug experiences and the knowledge that the discomfort of withdrawal can be escaped by using methamphetamine again.

E. Methamphetamine psychosis

Methamphetamine abuse can cause hallucinations, delusions, and paranoia. The delusions may be of control, grandeur, or persecution. Hallucinations may be auditory, gustatory, olfactory, tactile, or visual. This loss of contact with reality is, by definition, a psychotic state. It is clinically similar to paranoid schizophrenia and may persist after cessation of drug use.

7.8 Identifying a Methamphetamine Addict

Many methamphetamine addicts appear thin and even anorexic. The appearance is due at least in part to the suppression of appetite by the drug and to CNS stimulation. Also, food intake is reduced, because the meth user does not experience pleasure from eating. Drug seeking is a higher priority than finding food.

Also, methamphetamine users sometimes appear feeble and anemic, a condition known as central pallor; i.e., a deficiency of facial color. It occurs because the stimulant action on the CNS diverts blood away from the surface of the skin.

Extreme elevation of body temperature causes the user to feel warm to the touch. Excessive levels of perspiration often are observable on the skin surface, particularly on the upper lip and forehead. The user's body odor may be offensive. Although there are various explanations for the odor, most are conjecture and none have been systematically examined. The cause of odor may be as simple as the failure of addicts to bathe and launder regularly.

Methamphetamine addicts often have severe dental decay due to:

- lack of dental hygiene—their first priority is obtaining and using the drug, not brushing and flossing;
- poor nutrition—they fail to eat a balanced diet, instead consuming sugary foods and empty calories that contribute to tooth decay;
- bruxism—stimulants trigger spasm actions in the Trochlear (fifth) cranial nerve and cause grinding of the teeth, which erodes the enamel and causes stress to the roots;
- decreased blood supply—the vasoconstriction action of the drug reduces the supply of blood and nutrients to the mouth area; and

- dehydration—stimulants reduce salivary secretions and cause dry mouth conditions (xerostomia). A reduction in saliva results in tartar buildup and increased bacterial action.

Users habitually speak of tactile sensations or of bugs crawling on them or under the surface of the skin. Some actually hallucinate and see the bugs. Others describe a sensation of the skin being on fire. They create sores when they scratch and pick at these irritations.

7.9 Chemicals

The chemicals used to manufacture methamphetamine can be obtained through both legal and illegal means. If a particular substance that is needed is not available, another substance probably can be substituted for it. The required chemicals are precursors, reagents, solvents and catalysts.

A. Precursors

A precursor is a chemical that is essential to the production of the controlled substance and for which there is no replacement. The precursor for production of methamphetamine today generally is ephedrine or pseudoephedrine. There are a number of products that contain various amounts of ephedrine/pseudoephedrine, but the most common source for clandestine lab operators is OTC cold medications.

B. Reagents

Reagents create chemical reactions. Introduced into the precursor or later mixtures, they generate chemical change. The common reagent chemicals used in the production of meth are anhydrous ammonia, salt, iodine, hydrochloric acid, muriatic acid, sodium hydroxide, and sulfuric acid.

C. Solvents

In the methamphetamine manufacturing process, a solvent causes a chemical synthesis, which produces a complex chemical compound by a series of chemical reactions. Common solvents used in the production of methamphetamine are acetone, Coleman Fuel, and the ether from engine starter fluids.

D. Catalyst

A catalyst is a chemical that speeds up a reaction process and causes it to go to greater completion. Chemical catalysts for methamphetamine production include; Red phosphorus, lithium metal and sodium metal.

7.10 Methamphetamine Labs

Clandestine methamphetamine labs are encountered in one of three conditions: operational, non-operational, or boxed. Operational meth labs are actively making the controlled substance. In non-operational labs the drug has or will be made but there is no current production. Boxed labs are non-operational, but the equipment and chemicals are stored in containers, often during transportation. Non-operational or boxed labs must be regarded as equally hazardous as operational labs.

The methods and the chemicals used in the production of the drug are constantly being modified. Whatever the manner of manufacturing, the potential for bodily harm or death is real. When a clandestine lab is inadvertently discovered, professionals who are trained to handle hazardous materials should be contacted. State and federal law enforcement agencies employ trained chemical handlers or can contact organizations that have the training and skill to safely dismantle labs. Personal and community safety is the overriding concern when dealing with a meth lab. Law enforcement officers or other first responders should:

- evacuate the area as soon as possible,
- avoid handling anything,
- avoid turning off or on any electrical devices including those operated by batteries, such as flashlights, and
- if anything was touched or handled, immediately remove affected clothing and flush the skin for at least twenty minutes.

Call for assistance to secure the scene. Contact the DEA, a local clandestine lab team or a hazmat crew. Only properly trained and equipped personnel should be allowed to enter. The most common clandestine lab hazards include:

- explosive environments with possible unseen flammables in the air,

- poisonous atmospheres,
- chemical containers that are leaking,
- guard dogs or other dangerous animals,
- hidden traps equipped with weapons, explosives and sharp devices,
- combustible pressurized cylinders,
- electrical sources of ignition,
- cramped, cluttered spaces,
- ongoing unpredictable chemical reactions, and
- chemicals that are reactive to water, air or other solvents.

Chemical odors that may identify methamphetamine labs:

- acetone aroma similar to fingernail polish remover,
- ammonia,
- ether, or
- a strong urine odor (similar to the smell of wet diapers or cat urine).

Labs may also be identified by their surroundings:

- Individuals smoking outside (due to explosive hazards inside the lab)
- Strange or sludgy looking materials
- Leftover, separated or filler material in filters, jars or other containers in trash or in the lab
- Windows, doors and other openings covered to restrict the view from the outside
- Containers with substances settling to the bottom
- No trespassing signs
- Batteries (lithium) that have been torn apart or disassembled
- Cookware with non-cooking residue
- Vehicle and pedestrian traffic (if drugs are being sold out of the lab). Visits to the site will be short in duration and during off-hours.
- Excessive amounts of over-the-counter cold medications both used and unused

- Large numbers of containers of acetone products, ether, drain openers and other solvents.
- Occupants who appear to be unemployed but seem to have plenty of money
- Occupants that deposit garbage for pick up in another neighbor's collection area
- Evidence of chemical or waste dumping such as burn pits or dead spots in the yard.

7.11 Methods

Although there are numerous variations in each method of manufacturing the drug, current illicit methamphetamine is created in one of three ways. Note that there are no standards when it comes to making meth. There is no agency that regulates these processes or dictates what the operators name their method.

A. P2P amalgam method

When outlaw motorcycle gangs controlled street methamphetamine, they relied on the P2P method, which uses phenyl-2-propanone (P2P) and methylamine as the principal precursors. Chemicals to synthesize the final product include sodium hydroxide, hydrochloric acid, mercuric chloride and isopropanol.

When the Controlled Substance Act of 1980 designated P2P as a Schedule II drug, there was a reduction in the number of labs using the P2P method. Although it is still possible to acquire P2P on the black market, the risks in doing so have resulted in a significant decline in the method. Only eleven of approximately 16,000 meth lab seizures reported to the Drug Enforcement Administration (DEA) in 2003 used the P2P method.

The P2P method requires a lengthy manufacturing time and it produces overpowering urine-like odors that prompt reports to law enforcement. The procedure is more complex, more expensive and less potent then currently used processes. In fact, the 1980 effort to reduce meth production may have led to the invention of modern methods.

B. Red phosphorus (P) reduction (hydriodic acid method, cold method)

Using ephedrine or pseudoephedrine as a precursor, the Red-P production process generates a superior form of d-methamphetamine. Several variations use different chemicals, but all are fairly simplistic.

1. Birch or Nazi method

There are numerous urban legends about the origin of the names of these methods. Although it is possible that there is some basis for the legends, there is no proof and they cannot be considered factual. For example, it is alleged that Nazi soldiers used this method during WWII. Although it is widely accepted that the German military and Hitler himself used amphetamines and/or methamphetamines, it does not establish the production methods. Thus, the method's origins remain obscure, but it does produce high purity d-methamphetamine in a relatively short time. It has become the technique of choice and currently accounts for an estimated 60 percent of production. Both the Birch and Red-P methods follow the steps outlined in Phases 1, 2, and 3.

- Phase 1: Ephedrine or pseudoephedrine is obtained from OTC cold medications. The pills are pulverized to separate the precursor from other fillers in the pill. The crushed tablets are placed into a container with a liquid solvent (methanol, denatured alcohol or water). The unwanted components of the tablet settle out leaving the active chemical.
- Phase 2: The unwanted portions are separated from the ephedrine or pseudoephedrine by pouring the mixture though a filter or by drawing off the liquid with a siphoning device.
- Phase 3: The mixture is heated to speed evaporation from the material containing the ephedrine/pseudoephedrine.

From this point there are notable differences in the Birch and Red-P methods.

- Phase 4 *(Nazi method)*: Lithium ribbon that has been removed from lithium batteries is added to the ephedrine/pseudoephedrine powder.

- Phase 5 *(Nazi method)*: Anhydrous ammonia is added to the mixture that then turns a deep blue. Water is added. The color fades as the reaction produces a strong basic solution of methamphetamine.
- Phase 6 *(Nazi method)*: A solvent such as ether is poured into a container of methamphetamine base. The oily meth base that floats to the top is separated from the fluid that settles on the bottom.
- Phase 7 and 8 are identical to the Red-P Method.

2. Red-P method (steps 4-8)

- Phase 4 *(Red-P Method)*: The extracted ephedrine/pseudoephedrine is added to hydriodic acid or iodine/iodine crystals and red phosphorus or hypophosphorus acid. The blend is held at a slow boil lasting for up to eight hours. The methamphetamine base is allowed to cool and the mixture is filtered to remove the remaining red phosphorus and iodine material.
- Phase 5 *(Red-P method)*: Lye (Sodium Hydroxide) dissolved in water or ice is added to the mixture, and a strong alkaline solution results. A can of Red Devil lye is the most common source of sodium hydroxide.
- Phase 6 *(Red-P method)*: A solvent (Coleman Fuel, ether, toluene, mineral spirits) is added and poured through a filter to extract the freebase methamphetamine. An oily layer will form, and the base will settle to the bottom.
- Phase 7 *(Red-P method)*: The solution is then processed with a hydrogen chloride gas generator. Pure crystals of methamphetamine form.
- Phase 8 *(Red-P method)*: The crystal methamphetamine is filtered out of the liquid solution, dried, and prepared for sale or use.

7.12 Conclusion

The confident, euphoric feelings that a user experiences when methamphetamine crosses the blood brain barrier, together with the availability of the drug, have boosted the numbers of abusers. Government measures to control methamphetamine production and use are important, but they are unlikely to suffice as control measures. Building bridges between public services agencies including but not limited to law enforcement, drug courts, treatment providers and prevention specialists will be needed to cope with methamphetamine proliferation. Community awareness, with the ultimate goal of making methamphetamine use unacceptable, is imperative.

References

Anglin, M.D., Burke, C., Perrochet, B., Stamper, E., and Dawud-Noursi, S. (2000). History of the methamphetamine problem. *J Psychoactive Drugs*, 32, 2,137-141.

Burns, M.(Ed.) (2003.) *Medical-legal aspects of drugs*. Tuscon, AZ: Lawyers & Judges Publishing Company, Inc.

DAWN (2002). *Amphetamine and methamphetamine emergency department visits*, 2002. Substance Abuse and Mental Health Services Administration's (SAMHSA) Drug Abuse Warning Network.

Drug Identification Bible (2004/2005 Edition). Grand Junction, CO: Amera-Chem, Inc. Retrieved from: http://www.drugbible.com.

Fester, U. (1999). *Secrets of methamphetamine manufacture*. Port Townsend, WA: Loompanics Unlimited.

Goldstein, A. (2001). *Addiction from biology to drug policy*. New York: Oxford University Press.

Guevara, R. (2003). "Facing the methamphetamine problem in the United States." Testimony before the subcommittee on Criminal Justice, Drug Policy and Human Resources. Retrieved from: http://www.usdoj.gov/dea/pubs/cngrtest/ct071803.htm.

Johnston, L.D., O'Malley, P.M., Bachman, J.G., and Schulenberg, J.E. (2004). *Monitoring the future national survey results on drug use, 1975-2003. Volume I: Secondary school students*, p. 545. (NIH Publication No. 04-5507). Bethesda, MD: National Institute on Drug Abuse.

Johnston, L.D., O'Malley, P.M., Bachman, J.G., and Schulenberg, J.E. (2004). *Monitoring the future national results on adolescent drug use: Overview of key findings, 2003*, p. 59 (NIH Publication No. 04-5506). Bethesda, MD: National Institute on Drug Abuse.

Johnston, L. D., O'Malley, P. M., and Bachman, J. G. (2003). *Monitoring the Future national survey results on adolescent drug use: Overview of key findings, 2002*, p. 56 (NIH Publication No. 03-5374). Bethesda, MD: National Institute on Drug Abuse.

Jones, D. (2004) Meth presence surges 68% in workplace drug tests *USA TODAY*, July 21. Retrieved from: http://www.usatoday.com/money/workplace/2004-07-21-meth_x.htm.

Kuhn, C., Swartzwelder, S., and Wilson, W. (1998). *Buzzed: The straight facts about the most used and abused drugs from alcohol to ecstasy*. New York: W. W. Norton.

National Drug Control Strategy *February 2003 Table 71. Methamphetamine Lab Seizures 1995-2002*. Retrieved from: http://www.whitehousedrugpolicy. gov/publications/policy/ndcs03/table71.html.

Nimble, J. (1994). *The construction and operation of clandestine drug laboratories*. Port Townsend, WA: Loompanics Unlimited.

Office of National Drug Control Policy, Drug Policy Information Clearinghouse Fact Sheet, Methamphetamine, November 2003. Retrieved from: http://www.whitehousedrugpolicy.gov/publications/factsht/metamph/.

Chapter 8

Jimson Weed, Inhalants, and Hallucinogens

Morris Odell

Synopsis

8.1 Introduction

This chapter reviews a group of chemically disparate substances that cause, as a common feature, confused mental states accompanied by hallucinations. Hallucinations may be described as perceptions that appear to be real despite obvious evidence to the contrary. Most hallucinogenic drugs produce visual hallucinations, but they may also disturb the other senses. The user often lacks insight about the unreality of hallucinations and thus may believe they are real with terrifying, distressing and sometimes dangerous results.

Hallucinations occur for many reasons, not always related to acute intoxication with drugs. Certain diseases can produce them, as in schizophrenia where auditory hallucinations are a common symptom. They may also occur in acute brain syndromes caused by injury or disease and in association with alcohol abuse. The alcohol withdrawal syndrome, delirium tremens, is a classic example. Also, hallucinations are associated with certain drugs used legitimately in medical practice, especially with anaesthetics.

Because their effects are similar to the effects of certain diseases and because of their association with the search for religious or spiritual experiences, hallucinogenic substances have been given different names reflecting their effects. Common names include hallucinogen, psychedelic (literally "mind manifesting"), psychotomimetic (mimicking psychosis) and entheogenic (literally "the god within").

Some of these drugs such as nitrous oxide and the anti-cholinergics are used medically, but most of the substances discussed here are not used therapeutically. This means there is no legal source of properly synthesized pure drug and most, if not all, supplies are illicit. As a consequence, it is rarely possible to know what doses users have taken and whether they actually have taken what they thought they were getting. This is especially the case with some of the hallucinogens, which makes it difficult to rely on subjective descriptions of their effects. Illicit drugs are of unknown purity and dose, and the amounts and activities of any impurities are completely arbitrary. Even when it is possible to obtain a sample of either the drug or body fluid of a user, the analysis of the sample is neither easy nor inexpensive, especially when unusual substances are involved. For example, the short lifetime within the body of volatile or gaseous inhalants, together with specialized requirements for collection and storage of specimens, make laboratory investigation very difficult.

A general question about all drugs is whether they have deleterious effects on normal activities of life, including driving. The answer must take into account that the primary reason for taking psychoactive drugs is to induce an alteration in normal perception, consciousness and function. Almost invariably such changes degrade the person's normal level of functioning, typically inducing a degree of stupor or an agitated or temporary psychotic state.

Most of the inhaled drugs discussed here are not known to be frequent causes of drug-related driving impairment. This, however, cannot be taken as evidence that they have no effect. Rather, because of the circumstances where they are used and because of their short duration of action, the likelihood of a person driving while impaired by these substances is very small. On the other hand, the hallucinogens, including *Datura*, are much longer acting and very disabling when exerting their maximum effects. They are not a significant cause of driver impairment compared to more common drugs including alcohol, but their effects are so intense that people who do attempt to drive after taking them are usually incapable of proper control of a motor vehicle. Whether the impairment is detectable by the usual means of documenting drugged driving, such as the Standardized Field Sobriety Tests or a Drug Recognition Expert (DRE) evaluation, depends on the specific substance, the dose taken, and the elapsed time since the drug was ingested. During the phase of acute effects, there usually is no doubt that the driver is severely affected either by drugs or psychiatric illness, and medical assessment is advised. Laboratory detection of these substances in body fluids may not always be possible.

8.2 Jimson Weed

Jimson weed is a common name for the plant *Datura stramonium*, which is a member of the same botanical family as potatoes, eggplant and the deadly nightshade (Arnett, 1995). It is native to Asia but has come to have a wide distribution in other parts of the world including Australia and North America. As a common weed, it is known by local names including Angel's trumpet, Devil's trumpet, Thorn apple, stink weed and many others. Although the term Jimson weed refers specifically to one species, there are others, particularly but not exclusively in the genus *Datura*, with different appearances and very similar properties.

Jimson weed is an annual plant with characteristic trumpet shaped flowers and a spiky green seedpod. The leaves are said to have a foul odour. The seeds are small, kidney-shaped, and contain the highest amount of the toxic alkaloids.

The toxic effects of this plant are caused by a number of alkaloids with anti-cholinergic properties. These are distributed throughout the plant in different forms and include mainly hyoscyamine (in the leaves, roots and seeds) (Miraldi, Masti, Ferri, and Barni Comparini, 2001), and hyoscine (in the roots). The racemic form of hyoscyamine known as atropine is used for legitimate purposes in medicine, including the production of pupillary dilation (mydriasis) in ophthalmology and to increase heart rate in cardiology. The l-isomer of hyoscine is scopolamine, which is used in ophthalmology, anaesthesia and for the prevention of motion sickness. It also has been used as a "truth drug" because of its stupor inducing properties. Atropine and scopolamine are metabolized by the liver, and about half the dose is excreted unchanged in the urine. The half-life in blood is on the order of three to four hours although the effects on target organs such as the eye can be much longer. The alkaloids can be detected with toxicological screens of blood and urine.

These substances act by competitively blocking the action of the neurotransmitter acetylcholine at sites known as muscarinic receptors, both in the central nervous system (CNS) and in peripheral tissues. In the CNS, muscarinic blockade produces a toxic delirium with hallucinations. The peripheral receptors are part of the parasympathetic autonomic nervous system and are responsible for the control of functions such as pupillary constriction, focusing of the eye, sweating and temperature control, salivation, intestinal motility, bladder contraction, and the control of cardiac muscle. Blockade of these sites produces the opposite effect to that of acetylcholine or substances such as organophosphate insecticides and "nerve gases," which act by inhibiting the natural destruction of acetylcholine. For this reason, *Datura* extract has been proposed as prophylaxis or emergency treatment for poisoning with organophosphates (Bania, Chu, Bailes, and O'Neill, 2004).

The clinical state produced by anti-cholinergic poisoning has been traditionally described as: "Blind as a bat, mad as a hatter, red as a beet, hot as a hare, dry as a bone, the bowel and bladder lose their tone and the heart runs alone." Each of these describes the effect of blockade of the autonomic functions described above. The peripheral effects include mydriasis with cycloplegia (a dilated pupil unresponsive to light), flushed warm dry skin, a dry mouth, paralysis of the bowel and bladder, jerky movements and a rapid heartbeat with either high or low blood pressure. Centrally there is a confused state with combativeness and hallucinations, which may progress to coma and respiratory arrest. *Datura* poisoning is an unpleasant experience, and fatalities may occur because of incoordination and risk taking activities as well as direct toxic effects (Boumba, Mitselou, and Vougiouklakis, 2004).

Treatment of *Datura* poisoning requires correction of thermal and body fluid imbalances. Patients need to be monitored closely as there may have been co-administration of other drugs requiring specific treatment. They may be treated with anticholinesterase drugs such as physostigmine, which act to increase the amount of acetylcholine available by inhibiting the enzyme that removes it. This is a potentially toxic treatment and should not be used outside a hospital. The gastrointestinal paralysis theoretically increases the potential toxicity because of retention of ingested material; however, dealing with it has not been shown to reduce the duration of treatment required (Salen, Shih, Sierzenski, and Reed, 2003).

Jimson weed is not a commonly used hallucinogenic drug. Gardeners may be accidentally exposed to parts of the plant or the sap (Havelius and Asman, 2002) or users may be unaware of its poisonous nature (Chang, Wu, Deng, Lee, Chin, and Liao, 1999). Atropine abuse for its mydriatic effects has also been described (Odell, 1998). Purposeful abuse of the plant usually occurs in teenagers who ingest parts of the plant for its euphoric and hallucinogenic effects. Because of the unknown and highly variable concentration of alkaloids, this can result in serious intoxication and death. *Datura* poisoning sometimes occurs in clusters or mini-epidemics, resulting from publicity that does not adequately stress the serious consequences. It may also occur as the result of ingestion of plant products through ignorance rather than intentionally (Balikova, 2002).

Datura is used by several different methods including smoking the leaves, ingestion of parts of the plant including the seeds, or by the preparation of an infusion or herbal tea. The alkaloids are well absorbed by all these routes, and the effects are usually apparent within an hour. The duration of the effects may be more than a day because of the long action of some of the alkaloids together with delayed absorption.

The possession and use of *Datura stramonium* is not illegal in most jurisdictions. There are many places where the plant is classified under local noxious weed laws that authorize its destruction by the agricultural authorities. Extracts of the plant contain substances that are classified as therapeutic drugs in their pure form and are subject to local drugs and poisons laws.

8.3 Inhalants

The term "inhalants" is used to describe a varied group of substances that are abused by the inhalation of their vapours or gases (Anderson and Loomis, 2003; Brouette and Anton, 2001; Flanagan, Ruprah, Meredith, and Ramsey, 1990). Their mechanisms of action vary widely so the basis for their effects on the user is diverse (Balster, 1998). Some substances have effects similar to small doses of general anaesthetics, some affect the endogenous opiate system or other neurotransmitters, and others act peripherally by affecting smooth muscle and the dynamics of circulation. There is an almost limitless number of substances that can be abused in this way, but they can be classified into three broad groups; solvents, volatile nitrites and nitrous oxide.

A. Solvent inhalation

Organic solvents are the largest and most diverse group of abused volatile substances. They are used in industry and agriculture for an enormous number of purposes, and there is literally no limit to the potential for them to be abused. Because of their widespread industrial use, it is impossible for most of these substances to be regulated or for their possession to be a criminal offence, although some jurisdictions have attempted to control the sale of aerosol paints and glues to minors.

The organic solvents include aliphatic hydrocarbons (for example butane, propane, hexane), aromatic hydrocarbons (toluene [Filley, Halliday, and Kleinschmidt-DeMasters, 2004], xylene), mixtures of these (petrol or gasoline [Cairney, Maruff, Burns, Currie, and Currie, 2004], LPG), halogenated organic compounds (chloroform, trichloroethylene, methyl chloride and a huge number of similar compounds), and oxygenated organic compounds (acetone, ethers and ketones). Many of these inhalants are abused in the form of manufactured products (LoVecchio and Fulton, 2001) and may contain other toxic substances that are ingested together with the solvent. These include heavy metals in paint pigments, lead compounds in gasoline, perfumes, insecticides, and a wide range of other industrial chemicals not usually abused on their own but capable of causing toxic effects. Abuse of medical or veterinary (Capraro, Wiley, and Tucker, 2001) inhaled drugs is also known but is uncommon. The removal of fluorocarbon propellants from asthma sprays may reduce their abuse potential (Prasher and Corbett, 1990). Inhalants may be used alone, or there may be co-administration of other drugs such as alcohol and tobacco.

Abuse of volatile substances is primarily a problem among young people from childhood through adolescence to early adulthood. This means that most users are in good health at the time of abuse and that co-morbidities are not usually a problem when interpreting the effects. Volatile abuse may be a transient or experimental phenomenon in many users who then either abandon the practice or graduate to other drugs as their peer group ages and other drugs become more fashionable and available. The practice appears to go through periods when it is common, and then there are times when its popularity wanes. Reliable information regarding the prevalence of abuse is difficult to obtain. There are enormous differences between findings in different communities depending on location, social class, and times of investigation. One Australian study found that the average age of users was 17.6 years and that 2.6 percent of all respondents had used inhalants at some time in their lives (AIHW, 2002). The proportion among teens in some communities may be as high as 25 percent; however, it is hard to be confident that studies do not suffer from sampling error. A study in the American state of Virginia found a constant death rate between 1987 and 1996 with the majority of deaths from inhalant abuse being in males aged twenty-two years (Bowen, Daniel, and Balster, 1999). Other studies have reported that inhalant abuse is an increasing problem especially in socially disadvantaged groups. Petrol (gasoline) sniffing is a serious and chronic problem in some Australian Aboriginal communities.

A small group of older users continue to abuse solvents. Studies of these people as well as studies of people exposed to solvents in the workplace have led to an understanding of the chronic effects of solvent abuse.

Volatiles may be abused in a number of ways, all aimed at maximizing the concentration of the substance in inspired air. When the substances are solvents in products such as glue or paint, the source is often placed on a rag or in a plastic bag and inhaled by holding the bag around the mouth and nose. This practice goes by various local names including "bagging," "chroming" and "huffing." Users often have a characteristic staining or rash in the exposed facial areas. Other methods include breathing vapours from an open container and spraying the contents of aerosol containers or gas refills onto material or directly into the mouth.

Inhalation is a very efficient method of ingesting a drug. The substance quickly passes into the bloodstream, bypassing the usual mechanisms of digestion and first pass metabolism in the liver. The rapid onset of effects is one of the reasons inhalation is a desirable practice for its adherents. Users experience an almost instantaneous "rush" as the substance is carried to the brain, followed by a period of euphoria, disinhibition and hallucinations. They may also become agitated and perform aggressive, dangerous or risky acts. Inhalants may also be used to enhance sexual feeling and performance (Gowitt and Hanzlick, 1992). The effects are usually short lived as the volatile substance is rapidly cleared from the circulation, but they can be prolonged by further inhalation. Less desirable effects include ataxia, confusion, nausea and vomiting as well as loss of consciousness. These effects are caused not only by the substance directly but also by hypoxia and hypercapnia as a result of re-breathing expired air. In most cases, recovery is rapid once the subject breathes clean air.

There are a huge number of toxic effects of solvent abuse, involving every part of the body. The effects of specific substances vary and will not be detailed here because of space limitations. Useful tables are included in the reviews by Flanagan (1990) and Brouette (2001). Because of the varied use of volatiles, it is preferable to have a broad understanding of the principles of solvent toxicity. Users exhibit a large number of physical signs and effects related to the local effects of the inhaled substance. These include:

- skin staining, rashes and ulceration, especially around the nose and mouth (Hwang, Himel, and Edlick, 1996)
- stains and residue on clothing
- contact dermatitis
- nausea and vomiting
- nose bleeds
- halitosis as well as the characteristic odour of the inhalant
- increased salivary and bronchial secretions causing sneezing and coughing
- conjunctivitis
- traumatic injuries as a result of activities while intoxicated

Internal and chronic effects include:

- disturbance of electrolytes and other body fluid components
- a general reduction in concentration and cognitive functioning (this is difficult to differentiate from other causes of intellectual dysfunction in many solvent abusers) (Dornig, Baumeister, Peters, and von der Beek, 2002)
- depression
- irritability and other mental disturbances (Miller, Mycyk, Leikin, and Ruland, 2002) including paranoia
- neuropsychological deficits including gait disturbance

- parkinsonism
- peripheral neuropathy
- chronic liver, kidney or heart damage
- bone marrow depression and fatal aplastic anaemia
- A dysmorphic syndrome similar to fetal alcohol syndrome has been described in the offspring of female solvent abusers, however, it is often difficult to reliably exclude the use of alcohol during pregnancy in this group.

Death during volatile abuse occurs by a number of mechanisms, which may be difficult to distinguish even at autopsy. The rebreathing procedure induces hypoxia that may persist and become fatal if the person loses consciousness with the plastic bag or other container (Byard, Chivell, and Gilbert, 2003) *in situ*. Many inhaled substances cause respiratory depression as part of their action, further contributing to this mechanism. If vomiting occurs, aspiration of vomitus is a serious risk. Hydrocarbons such as those in gasoline can cause pneumonitis. Some substances such as chloroform or methylene chloride are metabolized to toxic substances including phosgene and carbon monoxide. Many volatile substances act to directly induce cardiac arrhythmias (Williams and Cole, 1998) or coronary artery spasm. Halogenated hydrocarbons with anaesthetic properties are well known to sensitize the heart to the effect of catecholamines such as adrenaline. Thus it is dangerous to startle or chase a person acutely intoxicated with these substances for fear of triggering a fatal arrhythmia. Other causes of death include anaphylaxis and rapid liver or kidney failure (McIntyre and Long, 1992) from direct toxicity or idiosyncratic sensitivities. Many abused volatile substances are extremely flammable and the vapours can form explosive mixtures with air. This is an obvious danger if people are smoking.

As would be expected, the widely varying physical and pharmacological properties of abused substances cause enormous variation in the way these substances behave in the body and the interpretation of toxicology tests. Also, only limited data are available regarding the behaviour of certain substances especially in human subjects. Many volatile substances are only present in body fluids for a short time and are either excreted unchanged in expired air, metabolized to some other substance, or they may be stored in the tissues for a longer period if they are lipid soluble.

This makes toxicological investigation difficult, especially in the living where some time may elapse between ingestion of the substance and the opportunity for sample collection. Usually it is possible to determine that living subjects have been using volatile intoxicants by the circumstances, clinical observations and the existence of paraphernalia such as used containers, plastic bags, and paint residue.

Toxicology is most useful in fatal cases where metabolism and elimination cease with the victim's death. In these cases residues may be detected in body fluids such as blood and urine, and in tissues especially liver and brain. Since many substances of interest are volatile, collection of specimens needs to use techniques that minimize loss. These include tight sealing of containers, avoidance of empty headspace as much as possible, avoidance of plastic containers, and refrigeration of the specimen. Expert opinion should be sought following analysis especially in cases where volatile substances may occur naturally. Examples of this are acetone in diabetics and volatile products (including alcohol) in decomposed bodies.

In contrast to alcohol and a small number of other drugs, very little is known about blood concentrations of most volatile abused substances. It generally is not possible to correlate toxicology results with effects, times or amounts ingested.

Control of the problem of volatile abuse has been attempted in different ways. The large number of abused substances and their presence in so many commonly available products make it impossible to legally restrict access to every possible inhalant. It is also not practical to outlaw their use as enforcement would be virtually impossible. In some jurisdictions, restrictions have been placed on the sale of certain glues and paint sprays to minors, but since this does not prevent them from obtaining other substances such as gasoline, it "shifts the problem sideways."

Educational programs attempt to show the dangers of inhalation with the intention of discouraging young people from adopting the practice. They also have tried to educate intractable users about "safer" techniques such as never inhaling alone, seeking medical attention, and finding a safe place to use inhalants. Harm minimization campaigns for this extremely dangerous practice are sometimes seen as legitimizing it and remain controversial (Age Education Unit, 2002).

B. Volatile nitrites (Romanelli, Smith, Thornton, and Pomeroy, 2004)

These include amyl, isopropyl, butyl and isobutyl nitrites which are available as industrial chemicals as well as in solutions sold in sex shops under suggestive trade names. The sale of nitrites is restricted in some jurisdictions, but they are available by mail order and on the Internet. In attempts to circumvent restrictions of the sale of nitrites, they sometimes are sold in mixtures with other substances such as perfumes and are labeled as room fresheners or video head cleaner. Generically, the nitrites are a group of drugs that act by relaxing smooth muscle. They are used in medical practice to dilate blood vessels and cause a rapid reduction of blood pressure and relief of angina.

Nitrites are used to produce a sensation of euphoria and to enhance sexual experience. Because of their effects on blood pressure, they cause a feeling of light-headedness which may be associated with disinhibition and heightened sexual arousal. They are also said to relax the anal sphincter and enhance the sensations and duration of orgasm. The effects are felt very quickly after inhalation but only last a few minutes, resulting in frequent repetition of drug use. Nitrite use has been most common in homosexual communities and at dance parties and raves, but their popularity has decreased with the availability of other drugs and concerns about their relationship to HIV disease.

Amyl nitrite, the only volatile nitrite now available for medical purposes, has very limited applications. It was originally sold in small, sheathed glass vials or pearls intended to be broken under the nose of the recipient when required. These vials are popularly known as "poppers." When vaporized, the liquid has a characteristic odor, pleasant to some and distasteful to others.

The acute side effects of nitrite inhalation are related to their effects on blood pressure and smooth muscle as well as any hypersensitivities or skin reactions. Users may experience fainting, nausea, headaches, flushing, loss of bowel control and dizziness. Long-term users may suffer from anemia and problems due to chemical effects on hemoglobin in red blood cells. Nitrites react with hemoglobin to produce methaemogobin, which does not transfer oxygen. This causes "chemical asphyxia" with symptoms of lethargy and cyanosis that can be life threatening. Paradoxically, this property of nitrites is used to treat cyanide poisoning which affects hemoglobin in a different way. A yellow, crusty facial eruption in chronic users is probably caused by the effects of nitric acid on skin proteins.

Nitrites have a significant interaction with sildenafil (Viagra) and allied drugs that results in severe hypotension (low blood pressure). This is a potential problem in persons taking these drugs and nitrites together for their effects on sexual function.

Nitrites have been suspected of having an adverse effect on the immune system and were investigated as a cause of AIDS before the HIV was identified. They are also metabolized to nitrosamines, which are carcinogenic. It is possible that the use of nitrites may worsen the progression of HIV related disorders, especially Kaposi's sarcoma, but no published studies have proven such a link. It is more likely that the common factor of receptive anal intercourse and other unsafe sexual practices in gay men accounts for the association between nitrite use and Kaposi's sarcoma.

C. Nitrous oxide

Nitrous oxide, a colorless odorless gas, is used in medicine, obstetrics and dentistry as an anesthetic. In less pure form it is used for boosting the power of automobile racing engines. It is also used as a propellant in pressurized dispensers of foods such as whipped cream.

Nitrous oxide was first used for recreational purposes in the late 18th century when it was known as "laughing gas," and special parties were held to allow people to use it. Many writers about the abuse potential of this gas have been unable to resist bad puns in their titles because of this (Sandoval, 1993). It was later found to be an effective anesthetic when inhaled at higher concentrations. It is not, however, powerful enough to induce full surgical anesthesia on its own and is used in anesthetics mixed with oxygen and other agents. Pure nitrous oxide is sold for medical purposes as a pressurized liquid, and it is also available as a 50 percent mixture with oxygen known as Entonox.

Although the gas is likely to be abused by medical and dental professionals and students because of their easy access, this is not common, possibly because of its short action and the need for expensive non-portable equipment to store and dispense it (Gillman, 1992). It is abused by non-medical users in the form of whipped cream dispenser bulbs (Ng and Frith, 2002) or bulk supplies to the food processing industry.

The effects of nitrous oxide are the result of its action on neurotransmitter systems especially the endorphin system. When inhaled, nitrous oxide produces a feeling of tingling and euphoria that some people find unpleasant but others enjoy. The experience includes feelings of dissociation, dizziness, warmth, analgesia and auditory hallucinations. Users may giggle and laugh uncontrollably. There is no evidence of any addiction potential or withdrawal syndrome. Because of the gas's limited solubility in body fluids, the effects cease within a few minutes after exposure making it ideal for use in dentistry and minor surgical procedures.

Nitrous oxide is a relatively safe drug, but danger arises from the possibility of accidental hypoxia with prolonged inhalation. When it has been used for some time at high concentrations, large amounts appear in the alveoli of the lung afterwards as it "washes out" of the body. This may displace oxygen causing transient asphyxia even after use of the gas has ceased. Deaths from nitrous oxide abuse are uncommon, but when they do occur, the cause is usually hypoxia (Wagner, Clark, Wesche, Doedens, and Lloyd, 1992). This was the reported cause of at least eleven workplace deaths in the U.S. between 1984 and 1987, which makes it a very minor cause of occupational death (Suruda and McGlothin, 1990). A rare case of suicide by this means has also been reported (Chadly, Marc, Barres, and Durigon, 1989).

Although there are few toxic effects from short term or episodic use, long-term users can develop a neurological syndrome because of an interaction of nitrous oxide with vitamin B12 (Butzkueven and King, 2000). This causes inactivation of the vitamin and certain enzymes associated with it and results in a degenerative syndrome of the posterior columns of the spinal cord. Affected individuals experience gait disturbance with tingling and numbness in the hands and feet. The condition may be mistaken for a psychiatric disorder because of the unusual constellation of symptoms and signs (Brett, 1997). There may also be a degree of bone marrow suppression as vitamin B12 is required for red blood cell production. The symptoms usually respond well to treatment with injections of vitamin B12 and the co-factor methionine.

D. Hallucinogenic drugs (Nichols, 2004; Laing, 2003)

Many drugs are capable of inducing hallucinations, but this section will discuss only the "classical" hallucinogens. These are exemplified by certain naturally occurring alkaloids traditionally used for this purpose and synthetic drugs with actions similar to lysergic acid diethylamide (LSD).

Natural substances have been used for thousands of years to induce altered states of awareness for ritualistic or religious reasons. There are many substances capable of inducing what can loosely be termed "altered states of awareness." This is a broad term and could even include intoxication with ethanol or cannabis as well as the effects of *Datura* described in Section 8.2. Plants used purely for hallucinogenic purposes include the Peyote cactus (mescaline), certain mushrooms (psilocybin), and other unidentified plant extracts. Bufotenine is an unusual hallucinogen because of its origin in the poisonous skin secretions of the cane toad *Bufo marinus*.

Interest in hallucinogens was re-kindled in the mid 20th century with the publication of accounts of their effects. The most influential of these was probably Aldous Huxley's literary description of his experiences with mescaline.[1] The history of synthetic hallucinogens begins with Alfred Hofmann's synthesis of LSD in 1938 and his experiences with it from 1943 (Hofmann, no date). Although it was available for psychiatric treatment and other purposes, it remained little more than a curiosity until it underwent a renaissance in the 1960s when the hippie movement took it up. It was used extensively during that time despite being made illegal. Since then, many other substances have been synthesized and investigated for hallucinogenic activity.

No discussion of hallucinogens is complete without mentioning Dr. Alexander Shulgin who has devoted his career as a pharmacologist and chemist to the investigation of mind-altering chemicals. He is the principal author of two comprehensive books detailing the synthesis and effects of these substances (Shulgin, 1997; Shulgin, 1991).

Many hallucinogens belong to two broad chemical classes, the phenethylamine (or phenylethylamine) derivatives that include mescaline as well as amphetamine derivatives such as MDMA (Ecstasy); and the tryptamine derivatives that include substances such as DMT, psilocybin, bufotenine and the neurotransmitter serotonin. A third group includes LSD and some naturally occurring alkaloids. There are many possible "designer" modifications to these basic structures and new substances are continually appearing. For example, "Foxy methoxy" (Meatherall and Sharma, 2003) is yet another substituted tryptamine. All of these drugs share essentially similar effects and are of interest mainly because of their social and legal ramifications. Few of them have been subjected to rigorous scientific investigation.

The mechanism of action of hallucinogens interests investigators because of the spectacular effects of very small doses, and the similarity between effects of hallucinogens and psychotic illnesses. Many of the drug effects can be antagonized by anti-psychotic drugs used in the same way as for the treatment of established mental illness. The current theory is that hallucinogens enhance or mimic the action of serotonin (5-hydroxy-tryptamine or 5-HT), which is an important neurotransmitter in the CNS. Some drugs act on 5-HT receptors directly, and others may act via a catecholamine pathway to control serotonin containing cells in other parts of the nervous system. There are several subtypes of 5-HT receptors, and differential action at these receptors may explain the differences in effects between particular drugs. This mechanism has also been proposed as a possible explanation for apparent antagonism of the subjective response to alcohol intoxication that is reported by users of LSD and other hallucinogens (Barrett, Archambault, Engelberg, and Pihl, 2000).

The effects of hallucinogens can be divided into physical effects and psychopharmacological effects. The physical effects are rarely a problem with small doses taken for their hallucinogenic effects. The effects are similar to those of many other psychoactive drugs, including drowsiness, tremor, blurred vision and confusion. LSD has sympathomimetic effects and causes dilated pupils, piloerection and other effects mediated by catecholamines. Some of the hallucinogens, such as LSD, are not physically toxic even in large doses, and they do not induce addiction or a physical withdrawal syndrome. Others, especially those based on phenethylamine can have pronounced amphetamine-like activity and cause typical sympathetic nervous system effects that can be fatal in overdose. The toxic effects are described in the review by Buchanan (1988) and include hyperthermia, hypertension and seizures. Many of the designer hallucinogens have an unknown and usually unresearched potential for toxicity. Users of these drugs, which include substances sold as scientific laboratory reagents, run the risk of toxic effects that may be permanent. Although not associated with hallucinogens, the classic example of this was the permanent Parkinsonism caused by MPTP, an impurity in illicit MPPP which is an opiate analogue (Buchanan and Brown, 1988).

Hallucinogenic drugs are sold in a multitude of forms depending on their source and the culture within which they are used. Naturally occurring hallucinogens are produced in the form of dried plant or mushroom parts that are ingested, smoked or made into an infusion. Many synthetic hallucinogens are produced in illicit laboratories in the form of tablets or capsules, often with identifying logos embossed into the tablet. LSD is active in very small doses on the order of tens of micrograms and has traditionally been sold in the form of small pieces of gelatin or blotting paper impregnated with the drug. These carry printed logos related to the drug culture. The dosage forms of illicit drugs are subject to rapid change by the clandestine laboratories that produce them. From time to time, law enforcement authorities publish posters showing images of these items to assist in their identification.

Hallucinogen abuse stems from the psychopharmacological effects of the drugs. They alter perception, most commonly vision and hearing although other modalities may also be affected. Users report amplification of sensory input resulting in intensification of colors and vivid hallucinations that are extremely variable in extent. They also experience mood alterations with distortions in time sense and feelings of depersonalization. They may experience intense ecstatic, mystical, transcendental, and spiritual feelings (de Rios, Grob, and Baker, 2002). A common neural mechanism between hallucinogenic drug effects and mystical experiences, involving 5-HT pathways, has been proposed to explain why this occurs (Goodman, 2002). Such a pathway could also explain the frequent occurrence of religious delusions in people suffering from psychiatric conditions associated with disturbances of serotonin levels.

Users of hallucinogens may also experience "bad trips" with unpleasant panic states, paranoia, frightening hallucinations, and feelings of insanity. The drugs' effects are highly dependent on the personality and expectations of the user as well as on the environment in which they are used. This means that the results may not be reproducible, even in the same subject, at different times. The multiplicity of subjective accounts about the action of these drugs makes scientific investigation difficult. The psychoactive effects are essentially subjective, irreproducible, unmeasurable and unverifiable. The many urban legends surrounding hallucinogen use include bizarre effects such as attempting to fly from tall buildings or staring at the sun. Most of these case reports are of doubtful veracity especially when one takes into account the interesting social history of the hallucinogens. Efforts to systematically describe these effects are probably not of great value, as aptly summarized by Shulgin (1997):

> In the case of LSD, it seems presumptuous to attempt to select typical comments for quotation. Literally thousands of reports are in the literature, from early exploratory research, to clinical applications for treatment of autism, of alcoholism, or mental illness, to assisting in psychotherapy and in the dying process, to the adventures of the military in both intelligence and chemical warfare, to innumerable anecdotal tales of pleasure and pain. Dozens of books have been devoted to these topics.

Behavior and emotion associated with hallucinogens may be indistinguishable from psychoses such as schizophrenia, and the behavior is more likely to result in serious injury or death than any direct toxicity of most hallucinogens. Users may believe they are invulnerable or have superhuman powers and carry out dangerous activities and even suicide as a result. The incidence of permanent drug induced psychotic illness, however, is believed to be very low.

One controversial effect of hallucinogens, especially LSD, is the occurrence of flashbacks or recurrent psychedelic effect sometimes years after using the drug. This condition has been named "Hallucinogen Persisting Perception Disorder" or HPPD (Hapern and Harrison, 2003). The criteria for its diagnosis were set out initially in DSM-III in 1986 and refined further in DSM-IV in 1994 (APA, 1994). The diagnosis requires the occurrence of disabling hallucinogenic effects after using these drugs together with the exclusion of other drug effects or psychiatric illness. Many studies have been done to try to understand this condition, but they have been hampered by the subjective nature of the phenomena and difficulties excluding other causes for perceptual distortions. HPPD is said to be more common in people who have used LSD illegally compared to these who have taken controlled doses in a research setting. It has not been widely reported after use of more modern hallucinogens, and there are great differences in the reporting rates for different hallucinogens, some of which are chemically related. In cases where people satisfy the diagnostic criteria and are disabled by the condition, treatment is similar to that for other psychiatric conditions including psychosis.

Hallucinogenic drugs are not a major concern in the overall spectrum of illicit drug abuse in most western societies in the early 21st century. The reasons include the intensity of the experiences, the non-addictive nature of most hallucinogens, which limits their illicit commercial utility, and their long duration of action. They are relatively scarce in most communities compared to alcohol, cannabis, opiates and amphetamines, including MDMA. From time to time, however, certain hallucinogens become popular and are used at dances and rave parties, but most do not have a long "commercial life."

Most well known synthetic hallucinogens such as LSD have been illegal for many years, and all supplies are manufactured in illicit laboratories. In attempts to circumvent prohibitions, modified compounds based on the basic phenethylamine or tryptamine structure have been synthesized and sold as designer drugs. These are touted as being legal on the basis that they are not listed on schedules of prohibited substances. They often are available from legitimate chemical suppliers and are sold legally, even to the extent of being available by order via the Internet. Some jurisdictions have countered this by scheduling generic descriptions of "analogues" of hallucinogenic substances in their Drugs and Poisons legislation and by restricting the sale of certain chemical precursors used in the synthesis of illicit drugs. The long and sometimes colorful history of efforts to legally prohibit the manufacture and use of drugs is described in detail in the excellent reference by Laing (2003).

Endnotes

1. Huxley, A. *"The Doors of Perception"* first published by Chatto & Windus London (1954) and subsequently by many others. The companion volume *"Heaven and Hell"* appeared two years later.

References

Age Education Unit. (2002). *Chroming: Children at risk.* Retrieved August 16, 2004 from: http://www.education.theage.com.au/pagedetail. asp?intpageid= 124&strsection=students&intsectionid=0.

American Psychiatric Association (APA). (1994) *Diagnostic and statistical manual of mental disorders: DSM IV*. Washington D.C.: American Psychiatric Press, Inc.

Anderson, C.E., and Loomis, G.A. (2003). Recognition and prevention of inhalant abuse. *Am. Fam. Physician*, 68, 5, 869-874.

Arnett, A.M. (1995). Jimson weed poisoning. *Clinical Toxicology Review*, 8, 3, December 1995. Retrieved on February 19, 2005 from: http://www.maripoisoncenter.com/ctr/9512jimsonweed.html.

Australian Institute of Health and Welfare (AIHW). (2002). *2001 national drug household survey first results*. Canberra: AIHW.

Balikova, M. (2002). Collective poisoning with hallucinogenous herbal tea. *Forensic Sci Int.*, 128, 1-2, 50-52.

Balster, R.L. (1998). Neural basis of inhalant abuse. *Drug and Alcohol Dependence*, 51, 207-214.

Bania, T.C., Chu, J., Bailes, D., and O'Neill, M. (2004). Jimson weed extract as a protective agent in severe organophosphate toxicity. *Acad. Emerg. Med.*, 11, 4, 335-338.

Barrett, S.P., Archambault, J., Engelberg, M., and Pihl, R.O. (2000). Hallucinogenic drugs attenuate the subjective response to alcohol in humans. *Hum. Psychopharmacol. Clin. Exp.*, 15, 559-565.

Boumba, V.A., Mitselou, A., Vougiouklakis, T. (2004). Fatal poisoning from Datura stramonium seeds. *Vet. Hum. Toxicol.*, 46, 2, 81-82.

Bowen, S.E., Daniel, J., and Balster, R.L. (1999). Deaths associated with inhalant abuse in Virginia from 1987 to 1996. *Drug Alcohol Depend.*, 53, 3, 239-245.

Brett, A. (1997). Myeloneuropathy from whipped cream bulbs presenting as a conversion disorder. *Aust. NZ. J. Psychiatry*, 31, 1, 131-132.

Brouette, T., and Anton, R. (2001). Clinical review of inhalants. *Am. J. Addiction*, 10, 79-94.

Buchanan, J.F., and Brown, C.R. (1988). Designer drugs: A problem in clinical toxicology. *Med. Toxicol.*, 3, 1, 1-17.

Butzkueven, H., and King, J.O. (2000). Nitrous oxide myelopathy in an abuser of whipped cream bulbs. *J. Clin. Neuroscience*, 7, 1, 73-75.

Byard, R.W., Chivell, W.C., and Gilbert, J.D. (2003). Unusual facial markings and lethal mechanisms in a series of gasoline inhalation deaths. *Am. J. Forensic Med. Pathol.*, 24, 3, 298-302.

Cairney, S., Maruff, P., Burns, C.B., Currie, J., and Currie, B.J. (2004). Neurological and cognitive impairment associated with leaded gasoline encephalopathy. *Drug Alcohol Depend.*, 73, 2, 83-188.

Capraro, A.J., Wiley, J.F., and Tucker, J.R. (2001). Severe intoxication from xylazine inhalation. *Pediatr. Emerg. Care*, 17, 6, 447-448.

Chadly, A., Marc, B., Barres, D., and Durigon, M. (1989). Suicide by nitrous oxide poisoning. *Am. J. Forensic. Med. Pathol.*, 10, 4, 330-331.

Chang, S.S., Wu, M.L., Deng, J.F., Lee, C.C., Chin, T.F., and Liao, S.J. (1999). Poisoning by Datura leaves used as edible wild vegetables. *Vet. Hum. Toxicol.*, 41, 4, 242-245.

de Rios, M.D., Grob, C.S., and Baker, J.R. (2002). Hallucinogens and redemption. *J Psychoactive Drugs*, 34, 3, 239-248.

Doring, G., Baumeister, F.A., Peters, J., and von der Beek, J. (2002). Butane abuse associated encephalopathy. *Klin. Padiatr.*, 21, 4-5, 295-298.

Filley, C.M., Halliday, W., and Kleinschmidt-DeMasters, B.K. (2004). The effects of toluene on the central nervous system. *J. Neuropathol. Exp. Neurol.*, 63, 1, 1-12.

Flanagan, R.J., Ruprah, M., Meredith, T.J., and Ramsey, J.D. (1990). An introduction to the clinical toxicology of volatile substances. *Drug Safety*, 5, 5, 359-383.

Gillman, M.A. (1992). Nitrous oxide abuse in perspective. *Clin. Neuropharmacol.*, 1, 5(4), 297-306.

Goodman, N. (2002). The serotonergic system and mysticism: Could LSD and the non-drug-induced mystical experience share common neural mechanisms? *J Psychoactive Drugs*, 34,3, 263-72.

Gowitt, G.T., and Hanzlick, R.L. (1992). Atypical auto-erotic deaths. *Am. J. Forensic Med. Pathol.*, 13, 2, 115-119.

Hapern, J.H., and Harrison, G.P. (2003). Hallucinogen persisting perception disorder: What do we know after 50 years? *Drug Alcohol Depend.*, 69, 109-119.

Havelius, U., and Asman, P. (2002). Accidental mydriasis from exposure to Angel's Trumpet *(Datura suavolens)*. *Acta. Ophthalmol. Scand.*, 80, 3, 332-335.

Hofmann, A. (no date). *LSD - my problem child.* Retrieved August 16, 2004 from: http://www.flashback.se/archive/my_problem_child/index.html.

Hwang, J.C., Himel, H.N., and Edlich, R.F. (1996). Frostbite of the face after recreational misuse of nitrous oxide. *Burns*, 22, 2, 152-153.

Laing, R.R. (Ed.) (2003). *Hallucinogens: A forensic drug handbook.* Amsterdam: Boston: Academic Press.

LoVecchio, F., and Fulton, S.E. (2001). Ventricular fibrillation following inhalation of Glade air freshener. *Eur. J. Emerg. Med.*, 8, 2, 153-154.

McIntyre, A.S., and Long, R.G. (1992). Fatal fulminant liver failure in a 'solvent abuser'. *Postgrad. Med. J.*, 68, 795, 29-30.

Meatheral, R., and Sharma, P. (2003). Foxy, a designer tryptamine hallucinogen. *J. Anal. Toxicol.*, 27, 313-317.

Miller, P.W., Mycyk, M.B., Leikin, J.B., and Ruland, S.D. (2002). An unusual presentation of inhalant abuse with dissociative amnesia. *Vet. Hum. Toxicol.*, 44, 1, 17-19.

Miraldi, E., Masti, A., Ferri, S., and Barni-Comparini, I. (2001). Distribution of hyoscyamine and scopolamine in Datura stramonium. *Fitoterapia*, 72, 6, 664-668.

Ng, J., and Frith, R. (2002). Nanging. *Lancet*, 360, 384.

Nichols, D.E. (2004). Hallucinogens. *Pharmacology and Therapeutics*, 101, 131-181.

Odell, M.S. (1998). Drug-induced anisocoria in two detainees. *J. Clin. For. Med*, 5, 1, 10-12.

Prasher, V.P., and Corbett, J.A. (1990). Aerosol addiction. *Br. J. Psychiatry*, 157, 922-924.

Romanelli, F., Smith, K.M., Thornton, M.D., and Pomeroy, C. (2004). Poppers: Epidemiology and clinical management of inhaled nitrite abuse. *Pharmacotherapy 24*, 1, 69-78.

Salen, P., Shih, R., Sierzenski, P., and Reed, J. (2003). Effect of physostigmine and gastric lavage in a Datura stramonium-induced anticholinergic poisoning epidemic. *Am. J. Emerg. Med.*, 21, 4, 316-317.

Sandoval, V.A. (1993). Nitrous oxide: A serious look at laughing gas. *Tex. Dent. J.*, 110(5), 13-16.

Shulgin, A., and Shulgin, A. (1991). *PIHKAL: A chemical love story*. Berkeley, CA: Transform Press.

_____, (1997). *TIHKAL : The continuation*. Berkeley, CA: Transform Press.

Suruda, A.J., and McGlothin, J.D. (1990). Fatal abuse of nitrous oxide in the workplace. *J. Occup. Med.*, 32, 8, 682-684.

Wagner, S.A., Clark, M.A., Wesche, D.L., Doedens, D.J., and Lloyd, A.W. (1992). Asphyxial deaths from the recreational use of nitrous oxide. *J. Forensic Sci.*, 3,74, 1008-1015.

Williams, D.R., and Cole, S.J. (1998). Ventricular fibrillation following butane gas inhalation. *Resuscitation*, 37,1, 43-45.

Chapter 9

PCP (Phencyclidine)

Clark John

9.1 Overview and Classification

Phencyclidine (PCP), a controlled substance under the federal Schedule I, is an interesting, dangerous, and bizarre drug of abuse. It is classified as a general anesthetic, or dissociative anesthetic. For the purposes of drug influence, it is classified as a separate category together with its many analogs (close chemical cousins), and ketamine.

PCP and its analogs are sometimes referred to as psychedelic anesthetics. More commonly, they are classified as hallucinogens, because individuals under their influence often experience hallucinations. For purposes of recognizing drug influence, however, the classification as a hallucinogen can prove confusing. For example, the eye signs of PCP are markedly different than those of more traditional hallucinogens such as LSD.

9.2 Origin and History

PCP was developed by the pharmaceutical company, Parke-Davis, in the late 1950s as a surgical anesthetic for humans and was patented under the trade name Sernyl in 1963. Like many other drugs of abuse, it was created for a legitimate purpose, and it held great promise as a surgical anesthetic because of its unique ability to block pain without depressing vital signs. Initially, it was considered to be a wonderful discovery.

Due to the undesirable post-operative effects experienced by some patients, it was discontinued as an anesthetic for humans in 1967. It was re-patented as a veterinary surgical anesthetic under the trade name Sernylan in 1968, but all legitimate manufacture of PCP was discontinued in 1978. Illicit manufacture continues at the present time in clandestine drug laboratories. Table 9.1 lists common street names for the drug.

PCP	PCP-Other Drug Combinations		
	PCP-Marijuana	PCP-Cocaine	PCP-Heroin
Dust	Love boat	Space base	Fireball
Angel dust	Boat		
Sherm	Lovely		
Juice, water	KJ (crystal joint)		
Dip	CJ (crystal joint)		
Wet, wet daddy			
Supergrass			
Killer weed			
Enbalming fluid			
Rocket fuel			
Wack			
Ozone			

Table 9.1 Street Names for PCP

9.3 Name Identification of PCP

PCP is an initialism; i.e., an acronym that cannot be pronounced as a word. The initials as well as the word, phencyclidine, are derived from the drug's chemical name, 1-(1-phenylcyclohexyl) piperidine. The drug is a member of the arylcyclohexylamine family of drugs.

9.4 Identification of PCP by Appearance and Packaging

PCP commonly is an amber liquid with a noxious chemical odor or a crystalline powder. The odor is difficult to contain completely and often leads to discovery of the concealed drug. Users frequently ingest PCP by smoking tobacco cigarettes or marijuana joints that have been dipped into the liquid. Once the cigarette or joint dries, a stain or a crystalline sheen on the cigarette reveals that it has been dipped with PCP.

Liquid PCP is typically packaged in small glass vials with plastic screw-on tops. When a large amount is transported, it may be disguised as apple juice in commercially labeled apple juice jars or in baby bottles. The juice jars likely will be in shopping bags with other groceries, and the baby bottles in diaper bags with other baby items. These are simple ways to try to conceal a dangerous drug.

9.5 PCP- Related Behavior

When an individual under the influence of PCP acts out in public places, the media report the bizarre behavior, the unusual strength, and the violence. The activity, confusion, and disoriented state appear similar to a psychotic episode, and the term, psychotomimetic, which means that a drug state mimics a psychosis, is appropriately applied to the effects of this drug. As it leaves the body by metabolism and excretion, the psychosis-like drug state gradually resolves, usually within four to six hours. Some users of PCP, of course, do not display psychotic behavior. If they use a smaller amount or have developed tolerance, or both, they will appear to be intoxicated but will not be completely out of control.

PCP is lipid soluble, and it creates cyclic behavior in the individual who uses it. Because the drug moves back and forth between lipid stores and the bloodstream, behavior and degree of impairment vary widely and unpredictably. A dangerous event that occurs without warning is a sudden violent outburst by an individual who has been in a catatonic state. The individual who has been totally non-communicative, rigid, and blankly staring can suddenly "go off" into a violent outburst. In an attempt to prevent these outbursts, police officers routinely reduce sensory stimulation of PCP-influenced individuals who are in custody. The stimulation of bright lights, loud noises, or physical touching seems to precipitate violent episodes.

Media reports draw the public's attention to incidents that involve some degree of public nudity. Such behavior is the result of the combination of high body temperature and a confused and disoriented mental state. The individuals experience uncomfortable body heat but fail to recognize that undressing and being nude in public is unacceptable to citizens and the authorities. In addition to removing their clothing, they may try to cool their bodies by swimming naked in public lakes or in the backyard pools of strangers. Because of the amnesic effects of the drug, they probably will not remember that they behaved in strange ways.

9.6 Signs and Symptoms of Influence

Because the signs of PCP influence are bizarre and obvious, citizens sometimes can identify users and report them to the police in a timely manner. On the other hand, law enforcement personnel must recognize specific signs and symptoms, which may or may not be readily observable. For example, PCP causes significant elevation of pulse rate, blood pressure, and body temperature. Effects on the eyes are remarkably distinct. The eyes jerk involuntarily when the person is told to visually follow a stimulus across a horizontal plane (horizontal gaze nystagmus or HGN). It is unique to PCP that the jerking begins with only slight deviation from a straight-ahead angle of gaze. Jerking may also occur when a stimulus is moved vertically (vertical gaze nystagmus or VGN). The eyes will not converge normally as they attempt to follow a stimulus brought in toward the bridge of the nose. Pupil size and reaction to light stimuli are not affected.

Profound muscle rigidity, which causes an individual to display robotic-like movements, is a hallmark of PCP, as is a blank stare. The latter causes an individual to appear to be in a hypnotic trance. Not all signs appear in all individuals on all occasions of use, but when they do occur, they specifically and strongly indicate PCP influence. Non-communication is another hallmark. Responses, if any, are slow, inappropriate, and repetitive. The signs associated with analogs are indistinguishable from those of PCP although they may differ in duration and intensity.

Increased body temperature causes profuse sweating that is inconsistent with the ambient temperature and level of activity. Clothing may be saturated with sweat, and the individual may be partially undressed even in cold weather. Users feel detached from reality, from the environment, and from themselves. They report "out of body" experiences and hallucinations in the form of illusions and delusions. The individual who experiences an illusion sees something that does not really exist or sees a distortion of something that does exist. The deluded individual holds a false belief. Seeing God probably is an illusion. Believing oneself to be God is a delusion.

PCP-influenced individuals sometimes exhibit unusual strength. They lift great weights and break open locked handcuffs. These remarkable feats appear to be the result of extreme disorientation and confusion, the lack of pain sensations, and increased adrenaline production.

9.7 Danger is Real

Safety is a concern for anyone who must deal with an individual under the influence of PCP. There is danger for the user, for the person who must confront and control that individual, and for the general public. The fact that a person under the influence of an anesthetic such as PCP does not feel pain gives rise to justifiable concern. A person who feels no pain is a formidable combatant, and the most prudent course of action is avoidance of an altercation. It generally is unwise to provoke, either intentionally or unwittingly, an individual who is under the influence of PCP.

9.8 A Contamination Hazard

Contact with liquid PCP poses a high risk of dangerous contamination. Transdermal absorption; i.e., absorption though the skin, can occur with even brief contact. Fortunately, the liquid emits a strong chemical odor, and if the odor is recognized and heeded, appropriate action can be taken to deal safely with both the substance and the individual. The chemical odor readily escapes many containers. This first warning of PCP's presence has foiled a number of attempts to smuggle liquid PCP aboard commercial airliners. The attempts failed when the odor escaped screw top containers and was detected by airline personnel.

9.9 Methods of Administration

Smoking is a common method for ingesting PCP although methods differ by locales. A Sherman cigarette, parsley, or marijuana is dipped or sprayed with liquid PCP and smoked. Crystalline PCP can be sprinkled on marijuana for smoking. It also can be injected, dropped into the eye with an eyedropper, taken orally, or insufflated (snorted).

9.10 PCP Production

Legitimate manufacture of PCP was discontinued in 1978, and the drug that is on the street today is illicitly manufactured in clandestine drug laboratories. Production requires only a simple three-step recipe, a modest investment in chemicals, and some rudimentary containers and implements. The process becomes more difficult and more expensive, however, with restriction on piperidine, which is one of the two main precursor chemicals, cyclohexanone and piperidine. These are needed to make the PCC crystals, which are an essential component of the process.

The simple manufacturing process is not without risks, however, and accidents due to poisonous gases, violent explosions and fire are not uncommon. Los Angeles based gang members control the manufacture and the distribution of PCP.

9.11 Driving Under the Influence

PCP significantly impairs the ability to operate a motor vehicle. A person under the influence of an anesthetic cannot process information from multiple sources in a timely and accurate manner, as required for safe driving. Crashes involving PCP suspects often are bizarre and catastrophic. PCP-influenced drivers have been known, for example, to stop in the roadway in the midst of heavy traffic, to enter and drive the wrong way on freeways, and to drive on pedestrian walkways.

9.12 Lethal Consequences

Although fatal overdoses with PCP are rare, they are occasionally reported by medical examiners. The popular combination of PCP and crack cocaine is particularly likely to be fatal. Nonetheless, individuals under the influence of PCP actually are more likely to die as a result of what has been termed behavioral toxicity. That is, death results not from the effects of an overdose on the body but from behaviors that are directly attributable to the drug. For example, an extremely disoriented individual may participate in and be oblivious to the extreme danger of an activity. Severe

anxiety, aggression, panic, paranoia and rage can also have lethal outcomes.

9.13 Ketamine: An Overview

Like PCP, ketamine is a general anesthetic, and a dissociative anesthetic,
but it is the less potent of the two. Like PCP, it belongs to the
arylcyclohexylamine family of drugs. It is used as an anesthetic for pedi-
atric and burn patients and as a battlefield anesthetic. In the latter arena, its
characteristics of rapid onset, effective blocking of pain, and increased
vital signs are believed to save many lives in combat situations.

Ketamine was discovered in 1962 by an investigator at Wayne State
University as he searched for anesthetics that would be alternatives to
PCP. It is a controlled substance under the federal Schedule III, and it has
been marketed legally by Parke-Davis since 1970. Although there is no
known illicit manufacture, the illicit market is served by diversion of the
pharmaceutical product. The quantity smuggled into the United States
from Mexico has increased dramatically during recent years, because the
illicit demand for the drug has risen. Since the mid-1990s, abuse by adolescents and young adults has moved it from a fairly obscure market to a
position as formidable drug of abuse. Youthful users are known as a K-
Heads. K-hole and K-land are terms for where users are when they are
under the influence. A dose or hit is referred to as a "bump." Table 9.2 lists
common street names for ketamine.

Pharmaceutical liquid ketamine can be dehydrated to produce a powder simply by heating the liquid. As a fine, white, crystalline powder, it
appears duller and more powdery than cocaine. A standard 10 ml vial of
liquid ketamine produces approximately one gram of powder. (For comparison, a packet of artificial sweetener contains one gram.) This powder
can then be adulterated with other white powder substances to enhance
profits. Lidocaine, a topical anesthetic, is sometimes used for that purpose. Individual doses of approximately 1/5 gram are packaged in small
zip-lock bag and sold for ingestion by insufflation. Liquid ketamine can
be injected intravenously or intramuscularly. The signs and symptoms associated with ketamine use may be indistinguishable from those of PCP
use and depend upon the dose, tolerance, and method of ingestion.

Trade Names	Street Names	Combinations with Other Drugs	
		Ketamine - MDMA	Ketamine - Cocaine
Ketaset	K	Kitty Flipping	Calvin Klein
Ketalar	Special K	Product 19	
Ketaject	Super K		
Ketavet	Cat valium		
Vetamine	Vitamin K		
Vetaket			
Vetalar			

Table 9.2 Ketamine hydrochloride, Ketamine 2-(2-chlorophenyl)-2-(methylamino)-cyclohexanone

9.14 Conclusions

PCP is a dangerous and potentially addicting drug. Individuals who are under its influence are unsafe drivers, and their drug use creates great risk of harm to themselves and to others in virtually any circumstance of use. Although ketamine, a related drug, is less potent, it has become an abused substance nonetheless with dose-related effects similar to those of PCP.

Chapter 10

Gamma Hydroxy Butyrate (GHB)

Trinka Porrata

10.1 Introduction

Gamma hydroxy butyrate (GHB) is most often characterized as a central nervous system (CNS) depressant and is so listed in legislation and law enforcement training bulletins, but it isn't a classic, consistent CNS depressant. Physicians and drug recognition experts (DREs) examining someone who has taken GHB may be puzzled to find that the person's heart rate and blood pressure are elevated, not depressed as expected with most depressants. They might suspect that some other drug is also affecting the individual's vital signs, but GHB may be the only drug found in the blood system. Heart rate can go up or down with GHB. It is perhaps best called a behavioral depressant for those on the outside looking in. On the other hand, Dr. Wallace Winters, an early investigator of GHB, categorized it as a CNS excitant with PCP and ketamine (Porrata, 2003).

During the 1960s, Dr. Winters, a neuropharmacology research scientist at the UCLA Brain Research Institute, was studying the neurophysiological correlates of wakefulness and sleep in the context of the action of

GHB & Misc Names	GBL	BD	GHV (not all confirmed)
Alcover	2(3H) furanone	1,4 Butanediol	4-Methyl valerate
Alpha G-3	dihydro	1,4 butylene glycol	4-Pentanolide
Aminos	Blast	1,4 dihydroxybutan	4SLeep
Anectamine	BLO	glycol	Gamma
Cherry meth	Blow	1,4 tetramenthylene	hydroxyvalerate
Easy lay	Blue Moon	glycol	Great4Sleep
Fantasy (NZ)	Blue Nitro	AminoFlex	Liquid Relaxation
G	Blue Nitro Vitality	Biocopia PM	Midnight Blue
G caps	Chimney Magic	Biosul	Neutralize (or BD?)
Gamma OH	Eclipse	BlueRaine	Serenity II (or BD)
Gamma 10	Fingernail polish	Borametz	Sodium 4-
Gamma hydrate	remover	Butylene glycol	hydroxyvalerate
Gamma	Firewater	BVM	SomaSleep
hydroxybutyrate	Furanone	Dormir	Sublimiss
Georgia home boy	Furanone dihydro	Enliven	Tranquili G
GHB	Furanone Extreme	Enliven celluplex	Valeric acid
GHBers	FuroMax	Fantasy (NZ)	"Valerian" (not same
GHBeers	Gamma Butyl	Fingernail polish	as valerian root
GHBuddy	Lactone	remover	extract though
Gina	Gamma	FX Cherry Bomb	related)
Great Hormones @	Butyrolactone	FX Lemon Drop	
Bedtime	Gamma G	FX Orange	
Grievous bodily	Gamma Ram	FX Rush	
harm	GBL	Fubar	
G-riffick	Gen X	GHRE (GH	
Heaven (UK)	GH Gold (GHG)	releasing extract)	
Jib	GH Relief	G3	
Liquid E	GH Release	hurricane	
Liquid X	GH Revitalizer	Inner G	
Liquid ecstasy	Helping Hand	Jet	
Natural sleep 500	Contact Cement	Liquid Gold	
Organic Quaalude	Remover	Midnight	
Oxy sleep	Insom-X	Miracle Cleaning	
RenewG	Invigorate	Cloth	
Salty water	Jolt	Mystic	
Scoop	Knock out	NeuroMod	
Soap	Lactone	N-Force	
Sodium oxybate	Liquid Libido	NRG3 Weight belt	
Somatomax PM	Nu-Life	cleaner	
Somsanit	Once Removed Nail	Omega-G	
Swirl	Polish Remover	One4B (NZ)	
Vita G	(reformulated in 04)	Pine needle extract	
Vitality	Original Removed	Pro G	
Water	Patron's Nails Polish	Promusol	
Women's Viagra	Remover Pads	Puritech	
Xyrem	Reactive	Rejuv@night	
	Regeneraize	Rejoov	

Table 10.1 *GHB Name Chart*

GHB & Misc Names	GBL	BD	GHV (not all confirmed)

Somatize
hGH releasers
Insom-X
Longevity
GH Revitalizer
 	
TERMS:
Carpeting out
Throwing down
Scooping out
Swirling down
	Remforce
	R.E.M. Nite (says BD
	  but tested positive
	  for GBL)
	Renewsolvent
	RenewTrient
	RenewTrient caps
	Rest-eze
	Revivarant
	Revivarant-G
	Take Over (cleaner)
	Verve
	Verve 5.0
	V-3
	V35
	Woodman's Pride
	Floor Stripper
	  (mixture)
	Zip Stripper II
	  (mixture)
		Remedy G or GH
		R.E.M. Nite
		Rest-Q
		Revitalize Plus
		Serenity
		Serenity II
		  (or valeric)
		SolVent
		Soma Solutions
		SomatoPro
		Somax
		Sucol B
		Tetramethylene
		  glycol
		Thunder
		Thunder II
		Thunder Nectar
		Ultimate Euphoria
		(Kaizen)
		Ultradiol
		V35
		Weight Belt Cleaner
		White Magic
		X-12
		Zen	

Table 10.1 (cont.) GHB Name Chart

anesthetic agents on the brain. He included GHB as a study drug, believing it to be a depressant and anesthetic.

During the first stage of research, an error was made in converting a dose for rats into a dose for a cat. The cat experienced a seizure, an atypical outcome for a CNS depressant overdose. Depressants typically cause respiratory depression and possibly death but not seizures. The investigators reassessed GHB and concluded that it is a cataleptic anesthetic, not a depressant.

Dr. Winters had been examining the normal progression of events in the brain and in behavior as a patient goes deeper into anesthesia. He commented that, "... an anesthetic to the surgeon is an agent that puts you into a state where he can do whatever he wants" (Portia, 2003), and it was a common assumption that all anesthetics were depressants with basically the same mechanism of action. With increasing dose, respiratory depression progresses through several stages into the extreme stage, death. His research demonstrated, however, that not all anesthetics behave in this way.

A profound non-responsive state can be produced by depression of the nervous system. The state can also be produced by such an extreme hyper-excited state of the nervous system that the individual does not respond to external stimuli. PCP, ketamine and GHB produce a continuum of increasing CNS excitation leading to hyper-excitation and loss of response. These are cataleptic anesthetics, which produce an increased rate of firing of neurons in the brain that exceeds a recognizable pattern of activity. Messages cease to have significance to the nervous system, the brain cannot integrate the activity of the neurons, and there is a failure to respond. "Catalepsy" refers to the condition of peculiar muscular rigidity in which the body and limbs keep any position in which they are placed. This differs from the condition of "cataplexy," for which GHB is sometimes used as a treatment. It can reduce cataplexy attacks reportedly by about 70 percent. Cataplexy is a debilitating medical condition in which a person suddenly feels weak and collapses at moments of strong emotion such as laughter, anger, fear or surprise. In so collapsing, people with cataplexy may injure themselves. Unfortunately, GHB abusers and addicts experience comparable episodes of sudden, dramatic loss of muscle control, often resulting in injuries.

GHB can produce a profound unresponsive state or the grand mal seizures that the research group observed in cats. By increasing successive doses of GHB, they were able to characterize the steps leading up to grand mal seizure state. In low doses there was some enhancement of the electroencephalogram (EEG) indicators of a wakeful state, somewhat like the effect of an amphetamine, and the cats were more alert. As the doses were increased, drug induced euphoria was followed by agitation, hallucinations, and distorted perceptions.

Typically, the cats vomited before going into the catatonic state in which they were immobile. Their pupils dilated, and their bodies became rigid. In a state presumed to be hallucinogenic, they exhibited abnormal, anti-gravity postures (body positions not consistent with simply being unconscious or asleep) and seemed to be visually tracking events not obvious to others in the environment. As dose and effects increased, "intimate bursts" of activity in the brain, such as those seen in petit mal seizure, occurred. The bursts became continuous with a cataleptic state and finally became a classic grand mal seizure. Flattened and rigid, the cats were non-responsive except for myoclonic jerking. This continuum of effects that was observed in cats is consistent with reported clinical symptoms of adverse reactions to GHB.

Dr. Winters described their observations: "We saw bizarre behavior. Cats are elegant animals, so you can easily tell when their posture is abnormal" (Portia, 2003). It is relevant to note that these were valuable research animals. They were not being given maximum doses for the purpose of finding fatal drug levels, and they were not being dosed frequently enough to study tolerance or dependence.

During the cataleptic state associated with GHB, it would be possible to perform surgery, but the drug is not believed to be a good analgesic. It probably does not significantly relieve pain. Although some degree of pain relief results from the loss of response, the non-responsive patients cannot acknowledge whatever pain they continue to experience.

PCP also had been developed as an anesthetic. Dr. Winters noted its characteristics to be similar to GHB, but it is a more potent drug, and the progression through the continuum of effects was much more rapid than with GHB.

Because it does not depress a patient's vital functions, PCP was an initially promising anesthetic, but its use was short-lived. Patients in clinical trials, who were given PCP, exhibited bizarre post-operative psychotic reactions. Some thought they had died and subsequently experienced profound problems with reality. The pharmaceutical company withdrew PCP. An analog that has similar properties but appeared to be safer was then developed. That drug, ketamine, was approved for geriatrics, pediatrics, and veterinary medicine, and it is currently used as an anesthetic. It also is widely abused, and its most common nickname is "Special K."

The UCLA research group gave sub-hallucinogenic doses of ketamine to rats for several days and then examined their EEGs one month later. Dr. Winters described the findings, "Our study didn't get much attention, but it blew me away. Low doses for several days produced epileptic foci in the brain. It frightened me" (Portia, 2003). Epilepsy is a brain disorder in which clusters of nerve cells, or neurons, in the brain sometimes signal abnormally, causing strange sensations, emotions, behavior or sometimes convulsions, muscle spasms, and loss of consciousness. Epileptic foci refer to those points in the brain where these abnormal signals originate.

Dr. Winters considered ketamine to be a safe drug in medical settings where the dose is titrated and the patients' responses are monitored by an anesthesiologist. Those circumstances of medical use, of course, cannot be compared to the circumstances of recreational use of ketamine.

Meanwhile, recognizing the abuse potential of GHB through his research, Dr. Winters worried that it would indeed hit the abuse circuit. His only surprise is that it took so long.

GHB entered the drug marketplace during the 1980s. It was first touted as an anabolic steroid replacement, but soon it was also claimed to be a food supplement, a legal high, a sleep aid, an anti-depressant, and a weight control aid. Though there is little scientific evidence to support any of these claims, it was sold over the counter (OTC) as a dietary supplement.

GHB was banned from OTC sales in 1990 by the Food and Drug Administration, but it was not scheduled as an illegal drug, This left it in a state of limbo; it was not to be sold over the counter, and the FDA could take legal action against anyone manufacturing GHB, but there were no penalties for possession or use of GHB. Distribution and sales continued, and its adverse effects were largely overlooked in those early years due to a lack of information, as well as to the fact that laboratories could not test for its presence in body fluids. At first, it was a drug used by bodybuilders, but its use expanded into nightclubs and other social venues during the early nineties, and law enforcement began to take notice of overdoses.

In 1996 a sentinel GHB event for the Los Angeles Police Department (LAPD) occurred on a summer night in Hollywood. Four young men, ages sixteen to twenty years, were found unconscious in the 400 block of Fairfax Avenue. They had consumed GHB and were in various stages of respiratory arrest. Two required resuscitation. In the long term, GHB impacted more than the four users that night.

One of the first responders later described the eerie scene. The officers encountered not only the four unconscious youth but also many others in various stages of overdose or influence. They were moving about in slow motion, staggering, or lying on the ground. The officers asked for paramedics. They asked for more paramedics. Finally, the radio message was, "Clear the station, we need people out here."

The youngest of the four unconscious individuals later stated that he consumed twelve beers, several diet pills, and two swigs of the GHB that was offered to the group in a gallon jug. He recalls nothing from the moment of ingestion until he awoke in a hospital bed, but friends told him that after drinking from the jug he was grinning ear-to-ear with his eyes rolling and flirting with females in the crowd. Then he collapsed. He appeared to be dead, but paramedics were able to revive him. This son of a retired LAPD officer entered and successfully completed drug rehabilitation. Prior to the incident, his father hadn't known that his sixteen-year old son had tried even alcohol.

The only one of the foursome who did not lapse into a coma, a nineteen year old, stated he had used GHB on other occasions. He said that, depending on how much is consumed and what other drugs are consumed, "You feel good for up to about two hours and then you sleep." He added, "It's easy to get. There's no punishment if you get caught, so it's cool" (Porrata, 2002).

Whether GHB can be described as cool is arguable, but it now is unquestionably illegal. Rhode Island and Georgia were the first states to make GHB an illegal substance. The Hollywood incident prompted legislative action, and a 1997 California law made both the drug and its analogs illegal. It became illegal federally in March 2000.

GHB overdoses continued to occur in California through 1996, including multiple incidents in the Hollywood area of Los Angeles and in Orange County, and it was becoming a drug of choice elsewhere. In an Australian teen club, ten users collapsed and five of those were placed on life support. In all of these incidents, one-third to one-half of those who collapsed required drastic measures by paramedics and remained on life support for some time thereafter. It should be noted that these reported overdoses were witnessed, and medical assistance was summoned. If GHB use occurs in other circumstances, perhaps in a vehicle or at home alone, where there are no witnesses to call paramedics, the outcome may be less favorable.

GHB is an addictive drug with a severe withdrawal potential. The frequency of its involvement in abuse and addiction likely is underestimated, because drug-use surveys don't routinely obtain information about its use. GHB users may not participate as survey respondents, because many don't fit the stereotypical drug abuser profile. An interview with a crack-cocaine addict may yield critical information about cocaine abuse, but the GHB user is unlikely to be interviewed or, if he is, to be asked about the use of GHB. Also, GHB is not readily measured in body fluids due to rapid elimination and limited testing capabilities.

10.2 Drug-Facilitated Sexual Assault (DFSA)

GHB is the fastest growing of more than an estimated forty drugs that are used to facilitate sexual assault, and it puts victims at the highest risk of death. Both men and women are victims, and their companions may also be drugged, simply to get them out of the way. The victims may be male or female, young or old, the settings may be Raves, sleazy bars, or expensive restaurants. DFSA respects no social boundaries.

The media frequently use the phrase "date rape drug" when reporting sexual assaults in which GHB, flunitrazepam (Rohypnol or "roofies") or other drugs played a role. Drug-facilitated sexual assaults occur. Acquaintance rapes occur. Sometimes drug-facilitated acquaintance rapes occur, but "date rate drug" is a misnomer. DFSA is a sexual assault during which a drug incapacitates the victim thereby denying her or him the ability to give or withhold consent. Because the assault may or may not be associated with a date, the term "rape drug" is more accurate.

Myths abound. DFSA is not a simple act of rendering the intended victim unconscious. The original Mickey Finn drug, chloral hydrate, accomplished that, but the drugs being used today do more. Depending on the particular drug and the specific amount, the victim may seem to participate or to be the aggressor early in the attack. GHB is known for its sexual enhancement capabilities, and a woman, who has unwittingly ingested GHB, may behave in ways that are quite atypical for her. For example, she may interact suggestively with a stranger, enter a wet T-shirt contest, or expose her breasts to bystanders. Later she will neither remember what she did nor believe accounts of her conduct.

A victim awakens with little or no memory of what has happened, dazed and puzzled by the evidence of sexual activity. This confusion can result in delay as the victim tries to recall events, perhaps seeking information from a companion or someone who was present. When she finally comprehends and reports to the police that she has been sexually assaulted, valuable time for collecting evidence has been lost.

A newspaper account of a victim's claim that she was drugged and raped may report that the results of a test for date rape drugs were negative. Though the account is not inaccurate, it is incomplete and misleading. A negative toxicology report means that a drug wasn't found, but it does not differentiate between the drug having never been present and the drug having left the body before evidence was obtained. Each drug has its own profile of symptoms and duration in body fluids. GHB, currently the drug most often used in DFSA other than alcohol, dissipates from the system quickly.

Hospitals perform preliminary screening tests, but they do not determine definitively whether a drug was present. Even analyses by forensic crime labs do not exhaust all possibilities in a sexual assault case, because of limited funding for equipment and training. The television portrayal of toxicologists' access to technology is seldom, if ever, the reality of the criminal justice system.

The February 3, 2003, issue of *Newsweek* (Smalley, 2003) and the December 2002 issue of *Glamour* (Whitley, 2002) published articles about GHB rape. Possibly they provided a sense of vindication for victims whose stories had not been told or had been told but disbelieved and ignored. The articles also focused attention on mishandled cases. After each article appeared, Project GHB (www.projectghb.org), a nonprofit organization dedicated to education about the drug GHB, received many e-mails and telephone calls from victims, as well as from detectives and prosecutors determined to handle cases more appropriately. A lack of information and training hampers police officers, prosecutors and judges and sometimes forestalls justice for victims.

Consider a DUI arrest that proceeded properly but that was followed by an inadequate investigation. There was significant evidence that the arrestee was the victim of a drug-facilitated rape. A bartender provided crucial information about events prior to the victim's departure from the bar. The police department, however, did not acknowledge that a crime had occurred. They interviewed the suspect, apparently considered him credible, and subsequently indicated during a phone call to the victim and her husband that they believed she had lied about engaging in consensual sex with the suspect. Had the marriage been unstable, that phone call might have been followed by domestic violence. In another state, the husband of a DFSA victim committed suicide shortly after a police officer told him that he believed the sex had been consensual.

At best, DFSA offenders are not easily apprehended, and the difficulties of bringing charges against them are compounded by the loss of both memory and evidence. Case complexities are a byproduct of the effects of the drugs employed and unfortunately, the medical and law enforcement communities and the judicial system are not universally knowledgeable about the drug.

10.3 GHB and Driving

Because GHB is difficult to identify, abusers and addicts often evade arrest for DUI. If arrested, they may not be prosecuted. If prosecuted, they may receive minimal penalty. Given the drug's ambiguous history and status, the defense may be able to rely on its legal sale as a dietary supplement. Strangely, the court may overlook the fact that the offender drank a product labeled inkjet cartridge cleaner, paint stripper, or fingernail polish remover.

A traffic school instructor who mentioned GHB in a session reported that she was stunned by a student's observation that unlike alcohol, one can party on GHB and the system won't detect it. Though the system may not catch it, the risks are real. The drug was involved in head-on collisions in Ohio, Virginia, Florida, New Jersey, and Georgia. Innocent parties, including a two year old, died in those crashes.

The behaviors of GHB-influenced drivers have been captured by police car videos. In a video from Florida, an officer tries to talk to a driver he had stopped for erratic driving. The young man can be seen leaning over at the waist lower and lower until he collapses onto the ground. Had he not been stopped, he likely would have collapsed while he was driving. The officer recognized that a bottle on the car seat contained a GHB analog.

In another case, documented on a Florida National Guard training tape, a car was observed zigzagging across four lanes of traffic. After the car was stopped, a video by the second officer on the scene recorded the driver's condition. He stepped out, immediately plummeted to the ground, and broke his ankle at that moment. Throughout the remainder of the taped episode, he appears aware that something was wrong with his ankle. He reached for it as he exhibited random, brief and sudden cataplexy attacks. He repeatedly stood, fell to the ground, and immediately bounced up saying, "I'm all right." The baffled officers thought some medical condition was causing his unusual behavior, and they instructed him again and again to sit down. He denied having taken anything or having a medical problem, but he finally did sit on the car seat, reached down to his ankle, and fell out of the car onto his head on the pavement. At the hospital, drug screens revealed no alcohol or other drugs, and he was released. He later sought out and thanked the officers for getting him off the road and confided that he had been on GHB. The officers recommended that the urine sample be submitted for further testing, but the department declined the extra expense.

A Florida case drew media attention. A twenty-one-year-old female, in her first contact with an officer while under the influence of GHB, passed out behind the wheel of her car. She was ticketed for careless driving. The officer, who had no knowledge of GHB, reported it as a traffic accident due to loss of control for unknown reasons. Two weeks later, the same young woman was found passed out at a red light, and she didn't respond when the officer opened the door. By the time paramedics arrived, however, the GHB effects had resolved abruptly, as they typically do approximately four hours after ingestion, and she talked in a normal manner. Alcohol was not involved, and she would have been released without charge had she not blurted out that she was on GHB. Although she was charged with driving under the influence, she was released from jail, still in possession of her driver's license. She had been out of jail less than twelve hours when she put two shots of GHB into a bottle of ice tea, drank it, and began to drive to a friend's house. She was observed swerving back and forth across the centerline and passing on the grass to the right of other vehicles. Her trip ended when she hit a vehicle head-on. A fifty-four-year-old woman in the other vehicle died (Davis, 2002).

Fluid specimens generally are tested for GHB only by specific request, but relatively few officers recognize the signs and symptoms that warrant the request. The largest numbers of GHB-related deaths and addiction cases in the U.S. have been reported from Florida. Between December 1, 2000 and July 31, 2001, the Florida Department of Law Enforcement tested for drugs in 1,941 DUI cases and tested for GHB in thirty cases. The Pinellas-Pasco Medical Examiner's Office tests for GHB if requested or if the driver is under age forty. They found GHB in 8 percent of the specimens obtained from suspected drug DUI drivers (Davis, 2002).

Note, however, that the age of GHB addicts extends to age sixty-five.

William C. Head, a defense attorney, who has published a book of strategies for avoiding drunk driving convictions, in speaking about his clients charged with GHB offenses said "I just won one in a city court in Atlanta where there was enough GHB (in the driver) to stop an elephant" (Davis, 2002). Regrettably, his claim probably is true.

A victim, who has unwittingly ingested GHB and attempts to drive, may be arrested for DUI. The arresting officer may suspect that her allegation of being drugged or raped is a ploy to avoid a DUI charge. In such an incident in a southwestern state, the officer ordered the hospital not to examine a victim for rape after she was released from jail on a DUI charge. Although her disarrayed clothing and other factors were inconsistent with just a traffic accident, the officer was adamant in his belief she was trying to avoid the DUI. She went elsewhere for examination and testing, and sexual activity was documented. The case became a major issue in local newspapers when the DUI charge was pursued but the rape issue was ignored. The publicity ceased when the DUI charge was dropped and confidentiality was mandated. Losing the opportunity to obtain evidence of an alleged crime is never appropriate. The evidence that would have been obtained with the rape examination would have supported either her allegation of a crime or the officer's belief that she was lying.

A New England rape victim, a married woman, was booked for DUI after a traffic accident. The officers noted in their report of the incident that she had not been wearing underpants, that her slacks were on backwards, and that she was wearing a tiny T-shirt. The shirt, which belonged to her young son, had been in her car. In their search of the vehicle, the officers overlooked the adult-size T-shirt she had worn, as well as her bloody underpants. The bartender confirmed that she consumed only two drinks and became visibly intoxicated within minutes after the second drink. He testified that another patron, who he knew was not a friend of the victim, took her car keys and said he would take care of her. The officers initially ignored this woman's claim that she had been raped. When they finally interviewed the suspect, he admitted that he had engaged in sex with her but assured them that it was consensual. During her DUI trial, the victim testified that she had been raped. In response, the judge gave her the maximum fine, suspended her driver's license and warned her to "stay out of places like that" (Personal Communication, August, 2002).

10.4 GHB and Robbery

GHB can effectively incapacitate victims for purposes of robbery. Once the individual is under the influence of the drug, credit cards, cash, and other valuables can easily be taken. GHB in the drinks of a person who is winning in a casino virtually insures that the winnings can be stolen in a parking lot or hotel room.

10.5 Addiction

GHB abuse and addiction is believed to be widespread in the athletic world and especially in bodybuilding where use began in the mid 1980s. The editor of one bodybuilding magazine declined to either talk to me about it or to publish an article about assistance for GHB addiction. His reason? He stated that he doesn't want anyone to think of GHB addiction as a bodybuilder's disease.

Since December 1998, more than 1,000 addicts have contacted the GHB Addiction Helpline operated by Project GHB. The emails and calls have come from nearly every state in the U.S. and from twelve other countries. Many of the callers acknowledged that they are athletes, mostly bodybuilders. Initially most take it at bedtime, believing that it will enhance growth hormone and steroid production while they sleep. Some take it with ephedrine and caffeine prior to a strenuous workout session, because the buzz enables them to dissociate from the workout. Possibly the death in 2003 of a bodybuilder, who had been both Mr. America and Mr. USA, will serve as a warning (Donald, 2004).

In a telephone contact with Project GHB's Helpline, this bodybuilder (and father of a young son) had asked for help. He didn't want to die, and he was convinced that GHB would kill him if he continued using it. He also knew that most addiction treatment centers have had no experience with this bizarre drug, and he was fearful of entering treatment. His death was attributed to GHB withdrawal syndrome.

Viewing it initially as a near perfect supplement, not a drug, its benefits are touted and users encourage others to try it. Unfortunately, regular use can lead to addiction within weeks and is common with four to eight months of use. Occasional users are at risk of rape, overdose and death, but they are not likely to become addicted. It is the daily use of GHB, whether as an anti-depressant, a sleep aid, a workout aid, weight loss product, or an anti-aging substance that sharply increases the risk of addiction. First, GHB may be taken as a sleep aid. Then a morning "wake up" dose is needed. Before long, it is needed just to cope with the day's demands. Eventually, the user's need for the *perfect supplement* extends around the clock, and he or she has become an addict almost without recognition of the addictive process.

When the second stage of GHB use develops, the user may be the last to recognize it. Friends, spouses, and co-workers observe bizarre behavior changes, which they do not understand. The "head snap" that often occurs about fifteen minutes after taking a dose sometimes is so violent as to break a bathroom mirror. A user may twitch briefly or in some cases for several minutes. Strange behaviors and blackouts become frequent, especially after heavier nighttime doses.

Treatment is both different from and more difficult than the treatment for addiction to many other drugs. The delay of a dose by more than a few hours triggers withdrawal symptoms, including profuse sweating, inability to sleep, anxiety attacks and soaring blood pressure and pulse. Patients, who seem to be doing well, are sometimes released too soon, because treatment professionals are unfamiliar with the time course of GHB withdrawal. In the second phase of withdrawal, which can begin on day four or five, the addict experiences severe symptoms, including hallucinations, an altered mental state, and extreme depression. In Seattle, a frantic wife finally found her husband on the streets after he was released from a treatment center on day three. He was confused, hallucinating, and at risk of wandering into traffic.

The most efficacious treatment of GHB withdrawal has not been fully defined, but benzodiazepines or barbiturates and antipsychotic drugs appear to be useful. Although tapering GHB doses prior to detoxification can reduce the severity of withdrawal, the reduction can be dangerous. Many individuals are unable to tolerate withdrawal symptoms, and attempting to detoxify without medical assistance is not recommended. Since GHB is routinely transported in water bottles and sports drink bottles, patients should not be allowed to bring liquids into a treatment facility. The drug may also be in containers of cleaning products, dietary supplements, nasal spray or eye drops.

10.6 Senior Citizens at Risk

GHB is prescribed as an antidepressant in some European countries. Reports to Project GHB indicate that those with prior mental health issues often find that it seems to work at first but then becomes a source of deepened anxiety and depression. It is advertised and sold via the Internet as an anti-aging medication. Not surprisingly, the latter usage attracts the interest of senior citizens, and some obtain it from sons and grandsons or from alternative medicine sources. A website known only to select customers was dismantled by Northern California narcotics agents. It served a community of alternative medicine practitioners and could not be found by searching the web for GHB. The owners are being prosecuted for illegal distribution of GHB.

10.7 GHB Analogs

GHB analogs are illegal federally and in states with analog laws that make them illegal for human consumption. The California law defines an illegal analog as being of "substantially similar chemical structure or same or similar effects."

The primary GHB analogs include gamma butyrolactone [GBL or 2 (3H) furanone dihydro] and 1,4 butanediol [BD, aka tetramethylene glycol]. These two chemicals, along with several others, have been recognized as analogs of GHB since the early 1960s. GBL is a federally listed precursor. California law lists it as a precursor and additionally as an analog. Numerous statements issued by the FDA, DEA, and California's food and drug agency declare both substances to be analogs of GHB and unapproved drugs.

Because there are legitimate industrial uses for these substances, the offense of possession of GHB analogs requires a nexus to human consumption. The demonstration of a nexus typically is not difficult. The products are marketed as weight belt or inkjet cartridge cleaner or as a plant food, none of which are safe for ingestion. The directions for use, however, reveal that they are intended for human consumption. Phrases such as "no aftertaste," "in case of accidental ingestion," or "mint flavoring added" reflect an expectation of ingestion and are at odds with the industry standard of adding an unpleasant flavor or odor to dangerous substances.

There are no significant differences between the effects of GHB and the effects of the analogs GBL and BD. The user experiences identical symptoms and urine specimens will contain GHB. The third analog, gamma valerolactone or gamma hydroxy valerate (GVL/GHV) does not convert to GHB, but it binds to the same receptor sites and produces similar physiological effects. Few laboratories can test for the latter substance, and the analog laws have not yet been tested with this one.

Dr. Winters developed a list of active and inactive GHB analogs, dividing them into straight chain and lactone (closed ring) analogs. GBL is an oxygen substituted ring analog under the lactone category. GBL is the precursor. The addition of sodium hydroxide, lye, or baking soda produces GHB. It is also an active analog that the body converts to GHB. BD falls into the straight chain category under the subdivision, simple and substituted alcohols. It is not a precursor in the manufacturing process, but it is enzymatically converted by the body into GHB.

The chemicals 2,3 butanediol and 1,3 butanediol are inactive GHB analogs, straight chain, substituted alcohols. These products are not expected to produce the same intoxicating effects on the brain, but they are potentially fatal and can produce incapacitating illness that can facilitate sexual assault.

10.8 Testing Issues

Law enforcement needs to be able to test for GHB in the field, but this is a difficult issue. Several field test kits have been marketed, but they cannot identify the analogs, resulting in a high rate of false negative results. One separate test kit now exists for GBL, but there are no test kits for BD.

Test devices represented as a method of protection against assault require careful evaluation. Typically, they are coasters or strips of paper that purportedly test for one or two of the forty drugs that are used to facilitate sexual assault. A test strip may give some indication that a drink doesn't contain GHB or ketamine, but they will fail in milk products, dark wine or diluted drinks. They provide no information about a drink containing a GHB analog or some other incapacitating drug. There is a risk that these devices will give women a false sense of security and undermine their vigilance.

GHB is eliminated from the body rapidly and cannot be found in blood after about four hours or in urine after about twelve hours. For this reason, it is imperative in rape and driving cases to obtain specimens as soon as possible. Since delays can result in a loss of evidence, obtaining the evidence specimen should be a first priority during investigations. If a specimen is negative, an analysis of the timeline of events will be necessary to establish whether the specimen was obtained when GHB could have been found. Although time can be a critical variable with all drugs, it is most crucial with GHB. Urine is the best specimen in all rape cases.

In death cases, blood is not the specimen of choice, because GHB can be created in the blood after death. The amount can be significant if the body was not discovered promptly after death. Also, if the person was in a comatose state for a prolonged period before dying, GHB will have been processed out of the blood. Since the drug is not altered post-mortem in urine and vitreous fluid, those are the better specimens in fatalities.

Screening tests for GHB are not available, and hospitals must await laboratory results to determine whether an overdose or rape was GHB-related. Rapid screening methods are in development, however, and may be available in 2005.

Hair testing for GHB is a promising method for cases that lack toxicological evidence. The tests are in use in some European countries and are expected to soon become available in the United States. The tests are expensive, but the hair sample can be obtained thirty to ninety days after a crime, and thus the method will provide an additional way to determine whether GHB played a role in a crime (Kintz, Cirimele, Jamey, and Ludes, 2003).

10.9 Xyrem Approval and Diversion

In 2002 the Food and Drug Administration approved GHB under the name Xyrem (sodium oxybate) for treatment of the combined condition of narcolepsy and cataplexy. Although it has also been recommended for treatment of narcolepsy alone, the FDA deemed it not efficacious for reducing daytime sleepiness and the committee recommended that it be banned from off label use. This recommendation to prohibit use for anything other than narcolepsy and cataplexy was not adopted. Although the regulation of Xyrem distribution appears to be stringent, it is not a foolproof system. GHB addicts have reported to Project GHB that they were able to obtain Xyrem, and a Xyrem bottle was found at a rape scene. Legitimate use by narcolepsy/cataplexy patients who will take it only at bedtime should not contribute to DUI, but off label use for other conditions might do so. Claims of therapeutic use should be supported with a prescription, but a prescription does not permit impaired driving.

10.10 Conclusion

Known primarily as a party drug or the rape drug, GHB's impact cannot be denied. The individuals whose deaths have been attributed to GHB ranged in age from thirteen to seventy-seven years. Rape victims have been ages thirteen to seventy years. Addicts are ages eighteen to sixty-five years, and about 85 percent are male. The total number of GHB related deaths is unknown, because there is no systematic reporting mechanism. Project GHB's unofficial tally is over 300, a number believed to be an undercount. GHB has been used in domestic violence, arson, insurance fraud, murder and attempted murder. It is a challenging drug for users, law enforcement, and society. Training of criminal justice professionals, standards for investigation of sexual assaults, and improved testing and analysis methods are critical needs for treatment and enforcement.

References

Davis, R. and Dennis, B. (2002). Liquid death. *St. Petersburg Times*, January 20.

Donald, M. (2004) "R.I.P.ped: Even former Mr. America Mike Scacella wasn't strong enough to beat the horrors of GHB addiction." *Dallas Observer* (Electronic version), March 25.

Kintz, P., Cirimele, V., Jamey, C., and Ludes, B. (2003) Testing for GHB in hair by GC/MS/MS after a single exposure: Application to document sexual assault." *Journal of Forensic Science*, 2003, 48, 1.

Miotto, K. and Roth, B. (2001) "Gamma Hydroxybutyrate detoxification." Texas Commission on Alcohol and Drug Abuse. http://www.tcada.state.tx.us.

Nordenberg. T. (2000) The Death of the party: All the rave, GHB's Hazards Go Unheeded. *FDA Consumer Magazine*, 2000, 34, 2, 14-20.

Porrata, T. (2002). Gamma Hydroxybutyrate, old drug - new tricks. *Austin College Health Education*, http://www.austincollege.edu.

Porrata, T. (2003). Personal interview with Dr. Wallace Winters for Project GHB and Voice of the Victims documentaries. San Diego, CA.

Smalley, S. (2003) The perfect crime. *Newsweek*, February 3, p 2.

Whitley, G. (2002). He drugged and raped me — and I couldn't prove it. *Glamour Magazine*, December, p. 214.

Chapter 11

Anabolic-Androgenic Steroids

Joel M. Mayer

Synopsis
11.1 Introduction
11.2 Pharmacology and Physiology
11.3 Undesirable Side Effects
11.4 Steroids and Aggression
11.5 Analysis in Biological Matrices
11.6 Summary
References

11.1 Introduction

Anabolic-androgenic steroids (AASs) are synthetic derivatives of the naturally occurring hormone testosterone (T). AASs were originally developed for therapeutic uses to provide anabolic activity with negligible androgenic effects. 'Anabolic' is derived from the term anabolism, which denotes any constructive metabolic process by which organisms convert substances into other components of the organism's chemical architecture. 'Androgenic' is derived from the term androgen(s) that are the class of sex hormones associated with the development and maintenance of the secondary male sex characteristics, sperm induction, and sexual differentiation. AASs are four-ringed structures with nineteen carbon atoms that make up the androstane backbone. They are related chemically to a range of other hormones that find therapeutic applications ranging from birth control to fertility regulation and anticancer agents. Through its androgenic activity, testosterone restores sex drive in men and possibly in women. Through its anabolic effects it boosts muscle mass in men and women. Testosterone has a pronounced anabolic effect on the musculoskeletal system resulting in several phenomena including an increase in lean body mass, a dose-dependent hypertrophy of muscle fibers and an increase in muscle strength.

Scientists have questioned the anabolic effects of AASs for decades, but recent investigations of the effects of supraphysiologic doses support the efficacy of these regimens to produce effects on the musculoskeletal system similar to those seen qualitatively with T. This has been confirmed in the sports world by the detection of banned steroids in the urine of athletes who developed unusual physiques in very short periods and subsequently won major sporting events. For athletes in world-class competitions and especially in the professional arenas, illegal steroids are a powerful lure, despite the risk of adverse effects.

Recent clinical studies have discovered novel therapeutic uses for physiologic doses of AAS without any significant adverse effects in the short term. The medical benefits of low therapeutic doses of AAS stand in sharp contrast, however, to the potential health risks associated with the administration of supraphysiologic doses. The latter are self-administered not only by elite athletes, strength trainers, and body builders, but also by a growing number of recreational users, including adolescent boys and girls. Surveys indicate that 15 to 30 percent of weight trainers attending gyms and health clubs use AASs. Other AAS users are non-competitive recreational body builders, or non-athletes, who use these drugs for cosmetic purposes rather than to enhance sports performance. Many American users are male teens and college athletes, and use among females has grown recently.

The 1935 discovery of a process for synthesizing the hormone T from cholesterol greatly accelerated scientific investigations into its effects. T rapidly became noted for its anabolic properties in increasing muscle size and strength, and in its androgenic properties of increasing virilization and aggression. In the early 1950s, suspicion developed in international sporting circles that some countries had private and state-sponsored programs of steroid administration consisting initially of T. Other synthetic analogues were included later as they were developed by pharmaceutical companies to treat patients in a 'catabolic state' (wasting conditions) with drugs that offered an enhanced anabolic action dissociated from the androgenic effects. Nandrolone (19-nortestosterone) was the first such synthetic analogue of T to show enough anabolic-androgenic dissociation in animal experiments to justify its introduction as a therapeutic agent. By convention, the prefix 'nor' in the chemical name indicates that a methyl group consisting of one carbon and two hydrogen atoms was removed from the original T at a substituent chain on the carbon-19 position. To-day, there are approximately sixty different AASs that vary in their chemical structure, physiologic effects, and metabolic fate in the human body.

During the 1960s, a number of deaths related to the use of stimulants occurred in sports competitions. As a result, in 1967 the International Olympic Committee (IOC) re-established a medical commission, which banned the practice of doping using stimulant and narcotic drugs. AASs were not included in the list of banned substances despite the growing suspicion of their spreading use by athletes, probably because it was not clear that the use of these steroids conferred a special advantage on users, and because there were no adequate analytical procedures for detecting them in biological tissues and fluids. Today, highly specific techniques are available to IOC-accredited laboratories for the detection of AASs and their metabolites. As analytical techniques improved, so did the ingenuity of users who sought to escape detection. In the early days, adulteration of the urine samples used for testing was somewhat successful, but the development of sensitive and specific tests for AASs provided, in part, the impetus to switch to other anabolic agents. In addition, regulatory activities in many countries put AASs on controlled and banned schedules driving their use underground and increasing the popularity of non-AAS agents.

One group of substances that gained popularity, as a substitute for AASs, is known as 'dietary supplements' or 'prohormones', these being androstenedione, androstenediol, and their corresponding 19-nor analogues. These are marketed as substances that can enhance muscle building. The oral administration of large doses of prohormones, such as dehydroepiandrosterone (DHEA), which can act as chemical precursors to the production of T outside the testes, has been promoted as an effective mechanism to increase the circulating concentrations of T in the blood. Although many Internet sites tout the anabolic efficacy of these substances, it has not been demonstrated that they enhance sporting performance, increase strength and power, or muscle size. Prohormones are beginning to come under regulation in the United States.

Medical strategies designed to reverse catabolism in critical illness may include the use of insulin to increase skeletal muscle protein synthesis, and the anabolic effect is thought to be mediated, in part, through an increase in the body of free insulin-like growth factor-1 (IGF-1), which increases glucose and amino acid uptake and reduces protein breakdown. Some outlets that sell prohormones also sell IGF-1 and human growth hormone (HGH), either alone or in various formulations. These suppliers point to the known anabolic properties of these hormones and encourage their use to restore youthfulness, strength, and sexual potency.

During the 1990s, concerns developed over the possible undesirable effects of AASs on behaviours such as aggression, impulsivity, and personality changes. In 1992, a murder charge was reduced to manslaughter after it was confirmed that the offender had been using AASs. The so-called 'M4 rapist' in the United Kingdom committed rape and murder and claimed that his behavior was due to the use of AASs. This and similar cases led the press to coin the term 'roid rage.' Extensive research into this aspect of steroid use in human and animals points to linkages between AASs, testosterone, and other neurosteroids and neurotransmitters in the expression of aggressive behavior. It is clear, however, that such linkages are complex and cannot be separated from social, environmental, and lifestyle factors that contribute to individuals temperament, attitudes, and behaviors.

11.2 Pharmacology and Physiology

Testosterone is the primary male hormone synthesized in the testes. It is responsible for the secondary sexual characteristics that transform boys into men, and for the sexual dimorphism of men and women. In addition, T leads to sexual differentiation in the central nervous system (CNS). In laboratory animals it is clear that the CNS is inherently female unless exposed to testicular hormones. Manipulation of the hormonal environment during perinatal development permanently alters both the structure and function of the CNS. Exposing females to testicular hormones masculinizes components of the CNS, whereas prenatal chemical or surgical castration of the male allows the development of a more female-like CNS. In mammals, the sexual differentiation of the CNS has a significant role in shaping sexual preference and other reproductive behaviors, food intake, body weight, learning strategies, and aggressive behavior.

In the adult human male T regulates a range of biochemical and physiologic processes including muscle protein metabolism, formation of red blood cells, and bone metabolism. During adult life, the average male produces up to 7 milligrams of T daily and about 130 grams by the age of seventy-five. The normal concentration of plasma T in males is 300-1000 nanograms per 100 millilitres, but the average concentration falls by age seventy-five to about 50 percent of that at age twenty. In women T concentrations are about one tenth of those found in men.

T is the active ingredient in AASs and is released from various chemical forms as a result of biotransformation in the body. Chemically there are two main groups of AASs, 17α alkylated derivatives of T, and those that are derived through esterification of the 17β-hydroxyl groups. Most orally active AASs formulations are the 17α derivatives. The 17β molecules are more lipid soluble. Because it is lipid soluble, the latter is suitable for intramuscular injection as a clear suspension, for transdermal administration using a patch, or for topical application as a gel or a cream. The 17β esters are hydrolyzed to free T in the body, which binds to the androgen receptor (AR) in various target tissues to exert both androgenic and anabolic effects, and is then reduced to 5α-dihydrotestosterone, an androgen with higher biological activity in the brain compared to T, or aromatizes to estrogens such as 17β-estradiol, which can bind to brain estrogen receptors. It is not thought that the 17α alkylated steroids are converted to dihydrotestosterone or estradiol, although other androgenic and estrogenic metabolic products may be formed. Their efficacies as oral preparations are related to their resistance to hepatic biotransformation and to the first pass effect as they are being absorbed from the gastrointestinal tract. This effectively acts to increase their oral bioavailability. The various chemical analogues of testosterone have been useful pharmacologically to alter the relative anabolic-androgenic potency, slow the rate and change the pattern of biotransformation, or decrease the degree of aromatization to estradiol. All AASs possess anabolic and androgenic activity at various ratios, and none are absolutely selective for one activity or the other. For example, testosterone has an anabolic to androgenic ratio of one, whereas the ratio for nandrolone is ten, and that for stanozolol is thirty. Table 11.1 lists some of the common AASs in use today.

The action of AASs in stimulating growth of skeletal muscle in subjects, such as women and children with low circulating T, is undisputed. It is now generally accepted that supraphysiologic doses of T and AAS combined with exercise can result in significant increases in lean muscle mass and strength in men to a greater extent than either intervention alone. The larger observational studies of AAS users suggest that drug regimens fol-

Oral Agents	Injectable/Topical Agents
17α-alkyl derivatives	17β-ester derivatives
Methandrostenolone	Testosterone esters, e.g., cypionate, propionate
Methyltestosterone	Nandrolone esters, e.g., decanoate
Stanozolol	Drostanolone
Bolasterone	Methandriol
Ethylestrenol	Methonolone
Danazol	Trenbolone
Fluoxymesterone	Dromostanolone
Mesterolone	Oxymetholone

Figure Table 11.1 *Anabolic-androgenic steroids in common use.*

low a typical pattern. The athletic use involves combinations of different oral and injectable AASs. These are 'stacked' to create a mega-dose regimen that is self-administered during drug cycles that can last four to fifteen weeks. The time interval between cycles varies depending on personal preference, attempts to escape detection, and attempts to introduce washout periods. These strategies are designed to provide optimal anabolic impact and to prevent desensitization and androgenic receptor (AR) up-regulation from attenuating steroid effects. Some users will switch from one cocktail to another, and some super users will continue steroid administration without any breaks. The latter approach is likely to produce a greater incidence of undesirable side effects.

Conventional wisdom and practices suggest that efficacious supraphysiologic doses of T and AAS should be one milligram per kilogram body weight per day. This results in the administration of upwards of 400 milligrams per week. Physiologic replacement doses of T may be equivalent to this regimen, but are often lower than that. The therapeutic applications of T therapy are to restore hormone concentrations in hypogonadal men to increase lean muscle mass and bone density, to initiate delayed puberty, to augment muscle mass in older men, and to improve mood and alleviate depression. T therapy is also used in the treatment of severe wasting or catabolism associated with critical illnesses such as severe burns, HIV/AIDS, kidney and hepatic failure, and cancer. The overall anabolic effect is complex as it may involve mechanisms related to the activation of the AR, and also mechanisms that involve the neuroendocrine axes to include the stimulation of HGH and IGF-1. Some athletes claim that the administration of AASs enables faster recovery from post-game and training-related fatigue. This may be mediated through antagonism of the catabolic effect of high concentrations of endogenous cortisol that are a natural consequence of the stress produced by the severe physical activity.

The oral ingestion of steroid prohormones (DHEA, androstenediones and androstenediols) may not have anabolic impact equivalent to that seen with T or AAS possibly because their effect is mitigated by their conversion to T in the periphery. For instance, the ingestion of DHEA will result in an increase in circulating DHEA itself, but it is not resolved whether this is associated with a corresponding increase in plasma T. This is not surprising, because in the adult male the overall peripheral contribution of prohormones to circulating T is extremely small. Indeed, normal pathways of biotransformation of steroid prohormones will likely increase circulating estrogen concentrations, and hence mega doses of these substances for men may have adverse effects associated with raised estrogen, e.g., increased risk of the development of gynecomastia (femininization). In young adult women, an increase in performance may be possible following the ingestion of these supplements, because circulating T would be expected to increase since there is no testicular contribution.

11.3 Undesirable Side Effects

The severity of undesirable effects associated with AAS administration depends on the gender, the type of steroid or pattern of stacking, and the dose and duration of exposure. No adverse effects following an acute overdose with AAS have been reported. With pharmacological or supraphysiologic doses, however, the risks increase and adverse reactions have been noted. Liver dysfunction is cited as a result of chronic administration of large doses of AASs, especially with the orally administered 17α alkylated derivatives. This is typically manifested in elevated liver enzyme levels that are accepted as diagnostic indicators of impaired hepatic function. This is confounded, however, by observations that exercise alone can increase the activity of these enzymes.

Several case reports and studies point to cardiovascular negative effects including changes in the lipoprotein profile where low-density lipoprotein LDL-cholesterol is raised and high-density lipoprotein HDL-cholesterol is lowered. There are also reports of elevated blood pressure in AAS users, arrhythmias, and most notably left ventricular hypertrophy known as 'athlete's heart'.

Dermatologic changes such as acne, striae, alopecia, and hirsutism are induced by the action of dihydrotestosterone on androgen receptors in skin and sebaceous glands. High doses of AAS cause acne by increasing skin surface lipids and the cutaneous population of propionibacteria acnes. Cutaneous striae are the result of rapid weight gain and impaired collagen elasticity caused by AAS.

Chronic administration of AASs leads to disturbances of the hypothalamic-pituitary-gonadal axis resulting in gender-specific effects. In males, this endocrine suppression can lead to testicular atrophy, low sperm count, and changes in libido. Impotence often occurs after cessation of a steroid cycle. One also encounters depression of release of luteinizing hormone (LH) and follicle-stimulating hormone (FSH). Lower than normal concentrations of LH in the urine have been used as indirect markers of AAS ingestion. Although there is no evidence that the administration of androgens in hypogonadal or normal men leads to the development of benign prostatic hyperplasia or the progression of pre-clinical to clinical prostatic carcinoma, such may be the case for men receiving T for replacement therapy. This suggests that users of supraphysiologic doses of AAS face higher than normal risks of prostate hyperplasia or cancer. In women, the reproductive-endocrine-related side effects may include hirsutism and masculinization, voice deepening, menstrual irregularities, altered libido, and reduced breast size. Ironically, depending on the type of AAS that males use and on the extent to which 17β-estradiol or other estrogens are formed in the body, they face the opposite risk of breast enlargement.

The impaired collagen metabolism may result in loss of elasticity that has been linked to skin striae and to tendon rupture. AASs appear to induce reversible changes in the biomechanical properties of tendon, producing stiffer, less elastic tendon, but the ultimate strength of the tendon is not affected. The act of repeatedly administering any substance by intramuscular injection has the potential to create tissue inflammation, sepsis, and scarring, especially when the illegality of steroid use drives the activity underground leading to the use and sharing of non-sterile needles, syringes, and vials. Finally, it has been suggested that affective and psychotic disorders may occur at a higher prevalence in steroid users compared to non-user control subjects.

11.4 Steroids and Aggression

Aggression is a complex behavior that has many definitions including an overt behavior with the intention of inflicting damage or other unpleasantness upon another individual. Early anecdotal accounts of personality changes, short tempers, and loss of control over behavior by AAS users triggered animal and human research into the possible link between these elements. This occurred at a time when studies had begun to show a direct relation between high plasma T concentrations and aggression. It is now recognized that aggression encompasses non-homogenous behaviors ranging from episodic events to severe psychopathology and involving *inter alia* elements of impulsivity, a desire to dominate, self-control, and violent tendencies. In addition, environmental and socioeconomic factors must be included in the analysis of the impact of AAS on aggressive behavior.

One of the most replicated findings in psychology is the observation of lower 5-hydroxyindoleacetic acid (5-HIAA) in the brain and cerebrospinal fluid of subjects with impulsive aggression and suicidal behavior. 5-HIAA is the principal metabolite of the neurotransmitter serotonin, and low 5-HIAA is typically indicative of low levels of serotonin. The brainstem serotonergic system is the most widely distributed system with pathways in the brain that project diffusely to a variety of brain regions that control a wide range of functions. In humans and other mammals, clinical studies identify serotonin as a major modulator of emotional behavior, impulsivity, and aggression. Moreover, T modulates serotonergic receptor activity in a way that directly affects aggression, fear, and anxiety. Clearly, aggressive behavior is not only linked to androgenic activity but also to serotonin, and it has been hypothesized that the interaction between high T and low serotonin plays a key role in aggressive behavior. Since AASs mediate their effects through T and the androgenic receptor, it seems logical to ask the question whether the behavioural effects of AASs are also related to serotonin.

Men in general are more aggressive than women, and women have much lower T levels than men. High T men present a picture of delinquency, substance abuse, and a tendency towards antisocial and excess aggressive behavior, though the latter does not necessarily express itself in criminality. The conclusion derived from accumulating evidence in humans and animals indicates that high T levels in both men and women are related to dominance-related aggression, not by directly eliciting violence but by altering the probability that aggression is shown in a particular situation under specific combination of external and internal cues. When T is converted in the body to 5α-dihydrotestosterone, it acts on the androgen receptor but when converted to estradiol by the aromatase enzyme it acts on the estrogen receptor. Scientific evidence suggests that the effects of T in mediating aggression occur after aromatization.

Animal experiments into the effects of AASs on aggression reveal a complex picture. The effects of AAS on aggression are sex-, species-, and compound-specific. For example, the administration of T in supraphysiologic doses enhances aggression, whereas stanozolol fails to do so. Estrogens, as well as T, stimulate aggressive behaviors in animals. It is possible that the differential effects of various AASs on aggression reflect differences in the abilities of these substances to act at androgen and estrogen receptors, and overall behavior is then the result of a balance between estrogen and androgen receptor-mediated signaling.

Anecdotal accounts and structured interviews of offenders who have implicated AAS use for their actions, and recent studies of non-offender steroid users, point to a link between AAS and enhanced aggression. This takes the form of impulsive violent behavior, moodiness, irritability, apparent loss of control, and episodic fighting that is triggered by minor events. These reports suffer from several confounding factors that limit our ability to conclusively determine what role AAS plays in aggressive behavior. Although every effort was made to remove biased self-reporting in offender interviews, it is difficult to remove the possibility that the men exaggerated their reports of the effects of steroids in the hopes of improving their legal position, as did the M4 rapist. In many studies that attempt to examine the possible effect of AAS use on aggression and criminality in humans, the data do not include a full history of steroid taking or of blood or plasma concentrations of AAS at times relevant to the study. Moreover, the groups of steroid users usually assessed for enhanced aggression include athletes, strength trainers, body builders, or other men who operate in a highly physical environment in a variety of roles. In sports, increased aggression may be regarded as a desirable attribute that can be harnessed to improve training and performance in competitions. It is not clear, however, whether a personal choice of other strength-requiring environments or careers points to a personality that is already predisposed to aggression that may express itself in undesirable or antisocial behavior. Steroid use may, therefore, simply unmask inherent tendencies rather than create them. While one cannot dismiss the data that point to a possible link between AAS use and aggression, ranging from minor temper flare-ups to homicidal behaviour, the scientific evidence available in support of this proposition is less than decisive. Withdrawal from AASs may also precipitate moodiness, irritability, and feelings of depression, which may have a negative impact on the ability to effectively interact with the social environment.

The question that remains to be answered is whether 'roid rage' is truly triggered by a recent cycle or past administration of AAS, or whether the situation is much more complex involving personalities that are shaped by socioeconomic backgrounds and brains that operate with different neuronal circuitries and neurotransmitter concentrations. An interaction among these factors may be a more likely scenario, and additional research is required to resolve the issue.

11.5 Analysis in Biological Matrices

In 1969, the first application of radioimmunoassay (RIA) for the detection and measurement of steroids in biological fluids was published. This technique involves a measurement of the degree of interaction between known amounts of an antibody that was raised in animals and designed to recognize steroid-like molecules and the steroid(s) of interest in a biological matrix. RIA offers speed and low-cost testing and for many years it has been the workhorse of rapid drug screening. Nonetheless, due to its relatively low specificity compared to other techniques, a more probative analysis has to be deployed when the results of the test are presented in the legal arena.

Over the past years many clinical, forensic, and IOC-accredited laboratories have developed analytical techniques using gas chromatography/mass spectrometry (GC/MS) that provide the necessary confirmation and identification of AASs. This approach consists of isolation of the steroid(s) of interest from a biological matrix, followed by instrument analysis that incorporates chromatographic separation and detection of each steroid molecule by a selective mass detector. This is now the required standard in this type of analysis though RIA and other immunoglobulin-based technique can still be deployed as presumptive tests to screen large numbers of samples. A positive RIA result must always be followed by GC/MS analysis.

Urine is the sample of choice for steroid detection as it is for many other drug screening tests, because it presents a body compartment that captures in large amounts the products that are cleared from the blood in the normal process of detoxification. Relative to the blood, urine will have larger amounts of drugs or their metabolites at some time after exposure, administration, or ingestion. This makes drug use easier to detect. In addition, collection of urine samples is easier and less invasive than collection of blood samples.

Given the metabolic fate of AASs in the human body, very small amounts of the parent steroid normally appear in the urine, and much larger amounts of the AAS metabolite are found in free form or as conjugate with endogenous glucuronic acid. This means that analysis for AAS in the urine usually involves a test for a metabolite. This also means that the detection time since the last exposure is greater for a urine sample, because the actual blood or plasma concentration may fall below a limit of instrument detection as the time elapsed between ingestion and sample collection increases. Despite significant advances in steroid testing, caution must always be exercised in the interpretation of test results. For instance, the purity of prohormones sold over the Internet is not guaranteed. Androstenedione supplements have been found contaminated with 19-norandrostenedione in sufficient quantities to cause a positive urine test result for 19-norandrosterone, which is the standard marker for detecting nandrolone use.

AAS users who attempt to escape detection may adulterate their urine samples in an effort to foil the test by introducing agents such as gluteraldehyde, bleach, or Drano®, by causing severe diuresis through drinking copious amounts of various 'teas' just prior to providing a sample, or by ingesting drugs that will enhance urinary steroid excretion. These strategies may interfere with the immunoglobulin-based test, but not usually with the GC/MS test. In order to ensure the integrity of the process, scientists monitor other aspects of 'healthy' urine such as, temperature on collection, the pH, creatinine concentration, and specific gravity. AAS use has also been tracked using T/LH ratios, or the T/E (T/EpiT) ratio. The latter was adopted by the IOC and is based on the GC/MS determination of the ratio of T to its 17α-epimer, epitestosterone (EpiT) following release from the glucuronic acid conjugate and isolation from the urine. An epimer is either of the two mirror images of the same molecule that differ with respect to the configuration around one asymmetric carbon atom. In healthy men and women, the median T/E ratio approximates unity, but supraphysiologic doses of T increase urinary excretion of T, and the laboratory threshold for this ratio that generates a positive doping report has been established as six. Microbial contamination and activity in improperly stored urine samples does not appear to produce significant concentrations of newly formed T, and the addition of suitable chemical preservative to each sample to prevent microbial action is a straightforward way of overcoming quasi-legal difficulties.

AAS analysis in blood is being established as an additional biological matrix with results that provide drug-taking information closer to the event in question. The detection time following the end of a cycle may be reduced when testing in blood compared to urine testing, the latter being more likely to provide information about the past and not necessarily the present. Whether blood testing will facilitate the detection of AAS administration remains to be seen, but it could be helpful in assessing whether natural androgens had been administered.

Scalp hair has been used forensically to determine whether drug administration took place at some time in the past. The protocols that have been established for the collection and analysis of such samples can be applied successfully to AAS testing. Given that the turnover rate for incorporation of xenobiotics into hair is markedly different than that seen with blood and urine, it must be understood that a negative finding in hair is not mutually exclusive to a positive finding in blood or urine of the parent substance or its metabolite, and should not be used to introduce ambiguity into the interpretive process when all these biological matrices are collected and analyzed.

11.6 Summary

The use of anabolic-androgenic steroids is likely to continue for medical and non-medical reasons. Although many questions dealing with the disposition, effects, and analysis of these substances have been answered, much remains to be researched. Of particular ongoing interest is whether the undesirable psychological and behavioral effects pose a risk to users and society at large, and whether this can be conclusively probated in a legal context. Since the behavioral effects are difficult to separate from other factors, more work needs to be done in this area. The research is complicated by new information that shows that there is likely a complex interaction between endogenous androgens and other steroids and neural and neuroendocrine pathway involving a range of neurohormones and neurotransmitters. The reality is that AAS users will also ingest a range of other substances to supplant or counter some of steroid effects. These include ephedrine or amphetamines to stimulate fat loss; insulin and insulin-like growth factors for enhanced anabolic effect; human chorionic gonadotrophin to restore endogenous testosterone; dehydroepiandrosterone, androstenedione, and androstenediol as steroid precursors; opioids to relive pain following training and sporting events; gammahydroxybutyrate as a sedative aid and possibly to release HGH; tamoxifen to prevent estradiol- and estrogen-induced gynecomastia (feminization). Many of these substances can alter behavior as part of the pharmacological spectrum of effects, and contribute to the final phenomenology of AAS use.

References

Birger, M., Swartz, M., Cohen, D., Alesh, Y., Grishpan, C., and Kotelr, M. (2003). Aggression: The testosterone-serotonin link.

Isr Med Assoc J, 5, 653-658.

Choi, P.Y.L. and Pope, H.G. (1994). Violence towards women and illicit androgenic-anabolic steroid use.

Ann Clin Psychiatry, 6, 1, 21-25.

Christiansen, K. (2001). Behavioural effects of androgen in men and women. *J Endocrinol, 170,* 39-48.

Clark, A.S., and Henderson, L.P. (2003). Behavioral and physiological responses to anabolic-androgenic steroids.

Neuroscience and Biobehavioral Rev., 27, 413-436.

Daly, R.C., Su, T-P., Schmidt, P.J., Pagliaro, M., Pickar, D., and Rubinow, D.R. (2003). Neuroendocrine and behavioral effects of high-dose anabolic steroids administration in male normal volunteers. *Psychoneuroendocrinology, 28,* 317-331.

Evans, N.A. (2004). Current concepts in anabolic-androgenic steroids. *Am J Sports Med, 32,* 2, 534-542.

Hadley, J.S., and Hinds, C.J. (2002). Anabolic strategies in critical illness. *Current Opinion Pharmacol, 2,* 700-707.

Kicman, A., and Gower, D.B. (2003). Anabolic steroids in sport: biochemical, clinical and analytical perspective. *Ann Clin Biochem, 40,* 321-356.

Midgley, S.J., and Davies, J.B. (2001). Levels of aggression among a group of anabolic-androgenic steroid users. *Med Sci Law, 41,* 4, 309-314.

Perry, P.J., Kutscher, E.C., Lund, B.C., Yates, W.R., Holman, T.L., and Demers, L. (2003). Measures of aggression and mood changes in male weightlifters with and without androgenic anabolic steroid use. *J Forens Sci, 48,* 3, 1-6.

Pope, H.G., and Katz, D.L. (1988). Affective and psychotic symptoms associated with anabolic steroid use. *Am J Psychiatry, 145,* 4, 487-490.

Shahidi, N.T. (2001). A review of the chemistry, biological action, and clinical applications of anabolic-androgenic steroids. *Clin Ther, 23,* 9, 1355-1390.

Todd, T. (1987). Anabolic steroids: The gremlins of sport. *J Sport History, 14,* 87-107.

Yesalis, C.E., Baruskiewicz, C.K., Kopstein, A.N., and Bahrke, M.S. (1997). Trends in anabolic-androgenic steroid use among adolescents. *Arch Pediatr Adolesc Med, 151,* 1197-1206.

Chapter 12

The Turkish Experience in the Development of Laws and Policies Regarding Alcohol- and Drug-Impairment

Sevil Atasoy and Tanil M. Baskan

12.1 Introduction

Turkey's rate of road traffic accidents is three to six times higher than that of European Union nations. Nearly 200 thousand people lost their lives and 2.5 million people were injured over the last thirty years, which means that one out of every 250 Turkish citizens died and one out of every twenty was injured.

The overall road share of the total transport market increased from 35 to 93 percent between 1950 and 2000, and the total number of drivers' licenses rose by 130 percent, reaching 13 million. From 1983 to 1993, the number of accidents grew at an average rate of 14 percent per year, more than twice the growth rate of vehicle kilometers driven (6 percent). Drivers were culpable in 90 percent of the 2002 traffic accidents. The death toll will probably continue to increase in future years as traffic increases. Currently, losses due to injuries and property damage are on the order of 2 percent of GDP (State Institute of Statistics, 2003; Swedish National Road Consulting BA (Sweroad), 2001; Turkish Grand National Assembly, 2000).

Although traffic accidents make news headlines nearly every day, there is a general insensitivity towards the issue. Many citizens appear to perceive the penalized driver as "a person out of luck who was caught by the police" and not as someone who broke the law. To raise citizens' awareness about road safety and accident prevention, the first Saturday in May is an annual "International Road Safety Day," and the following week is "Road Traffic Week." The year 2004 was declared "Traffic Safety Year" by the Prime Minister's Office. Despite these efforts, the yearly total of high severity casualties remained stable for the last three years.

The issue of road safety has been moving up the policy agenda in Turkey. The government, with the support of the World Bank, recently completed a medium term strategy to address this issue. The strategy has been endorsed by the Traffic Safety Highway Council, headed by the Prime Minister (The World Bank, 2003). In parallel, a strategic alliance was formed between the Dutch program, Partners for Roads, and the World Bank to develop safe road design and to facilitate the transfer of knowledge (The World Bank Group, 2004).

Driving while impaired—whether by alcohol, by other drugs, or by a combination thereof—is a major threat to road safety. This chapter reviews the Turkish experience in the development of laws and policies regarding alcohol and drug-impairment. It also presents alcohol and drug consumption data and statistical information about traffic accidents.

12.2 Brief Description of the Country

Turkey's total land area is 814,578 square kilometers with 3 percent of the area located in southeastern Europe (Thrace). The rest is in southwestern Asia (Anatolia) bordering the Black Sea between Bulgaria and Georgia, and the Aegean and the Mediterranean Seas between Greece and Syria. Turkey's land borders Armenia (268 km), Azerbaijan (9 km), Bulgaria (240 km), Georgia (252 km), Greece (206 km), Iran (499 km), Iraq (352 km), and Syria (822 km).

The mid 2004 estimate of Turkey's population is 70.8 million people. Almost half reside in the coastal regions, while the interior areas are less populated. The country has eighty-one cities. Nineteen cities have over one million inhabitants. One seventh of the population resides in Istanbul. Since the 1960s, Turkey has had a high rate of urbanization.

The age group up to eighteen years makes up 40 percent of the populaton and eighteen to sixty-four years old constitute almost 54 percent. The median age is 27.1 years. The annual population growth rate is 1.13 percent, and the birthrate is 17.22 births per 1,000. The gender ratio is approximately 103 males to 100 females (State Institute of Statistics, 2002).

12.3 Consumption of Alcohol and Drugs in Turkey
A. Alcohol consumption

An alcohol beverage is defined by law as a product, including beer, wine, liquor, and mixed drinks, containing at least one-half percent alcohol by volume. The legal age for drinking or buying any type of alcoholic beverage on or off the premises is eighteen years, but the age restriction is not effectively enforced. There are no restrictions on hours or days of sale, but there are restrictions on types and location of outlets. Special permission is required to sell alcoholic beverages in shops and supermarkets.

A state monopoly on production and distribution of alcohol beverages was lifted in 2002. The production and distribution of beer and wine require licenses, as does the sale of alcoholic beverages in parks, cafes, and restaurants. Alcohol advertising is banned in national and private broadcasting, but it is allowed in printed media and cinemas. In addition, sports and youth event sponsorship is banned for the wine and spirits industries but not for beer. Alcohol consumption is banned in health care establishments, educational buildings, government offices, sporting and leisure events, public transport and workplaces. Laws require that labels specify alcohol content, but do not require health warnings on containers and bottles (World Health Organization, 2004).

Trends per capita alcohol consumption per year by adults (age fifteen and older) show an increase from 0.8 liters of absolute alcohol in 1970 to 1.5.liters in 1980. A decline was observed during the 1980s followed by an increase that was attributable to a significant rise in beer consumption (World Health Organization, 1999).

A 1995 study examined alcohol use by 2,636 Instanbul students (1,502 boys, 1,134 girls, ages fifteen to sixteen years). During the previous twelve months, 51 percent had drunk alcohol and 24 percent had been intoxicated. Lifetime prevalence of alcohol use was 61 percent (boys 62 percent, girls 60 percent). A more comprehensive study was conducted in 2003 as part of the National Assessment studies. A total of 4,182 sixteen-year-old boys and girls were surveyed in randomly selected public, private and vocational secondary schools in six cities: Istanbul, Ankara, Izmir, Samsun, Diyarbakir and Adana.

Almost half of the respondents reported having smoked cigarettes within the past twelve months, and 35 percent reported alcohol use, more boys than girls. Sixteen percent reported that they had been drunk on one or two occasions during the previous twelve-month period. Almost 20 percent reported alcohol use in the past thirty days with 10 percent indicating use on one or two occasions. More than 15 percent reported having had more than five drinks in a row, and around 8 percent said they had been drunk one or two times during the thirty days prior to the survey (United Nations Office on Drugs and Crime, 2004a).

B. Drug abuse data

Although drug use is increasing in Turkey, studies conducted in the treatment community and in prison settings indicate that the prevalence of drug-related problems is lower in Turkey than in many European and Asian countries. Cannabis is the most frequently used drug, followed by inhalants, synthetic opiates and heroin. There is also strong evidence of an increasing use of Ecstasy among young people in the urban centers.

The most extensive drug abuse research in Turkey to date is a study conducted by UNODC in cooperation with the Government of Turkey (United Nations Office on Drugs and Crime, 2004a). With the cooperation of six universities, data were collected over an eight-month period. The Institute of Forensic Sciences of Istanbul University coordinated data collection in Istanbul, Samsun, Diyarbakir and Adana. The results can be summarized as follows: among sixteen-year-old secondary school students (n = 4,182) 6 percent of the boys and 2 percent of girls have used cannabis, 4 percent of all students aged sixteen years have used inhalants, and 3 percent have used tranquilizers without a doctor's prescription. An additional 3 percent have used anabolic steroids, and 2 percent have used ecstasy. Most of the first time use had occurred quite recently, i.e. when the students were sixteen years of age. Most students had heard of cocaine, heroin, cannabis, ecstasy, and tranquilizers. Marijuana or hashish had been used by 3 percent of the students in the last twelve months, and stimulants had been used during that period by more than 2 percent.

To determine the patterns and dynamics of problem drug use in Turkey, another study interviewed 588 drug abusers in community, treatment, and prison settings. Interviews with 261 key informants used a structured questionnaire in a face-to-face setting. The annual prevalence of drug abuse as percentage of the population aged fifteen to sixty-four by drug was found to be cannabis 1.8 percent, cocaine and ecstasy 0.3 percent, amphetamines 0.2 percent, inhalants 0.06 percent, and opiates 0.05 percent. (United Nations Office on Drugs and Crime, 2004a; United Nations Office on Drugs and Crime, 2004b).

C. Treatment demand

Between 1997 and 2002, the highest demand nationally for treatment by drug was for heroin and other opioids, followed by inhalants and cannabis. Drugs for which there was less demand for treatment included benzodiazepines, barbiturates, amphetamines, cocaine, and ecstasy. More than a third of the individuals who entered treatment had used a benzodiazepine as a secondary drug, and 27 percent had used cannabis as a secondary drug. Males accounted for almost 92 percent of the admissions to treatment programs (United Nations Office on Drugs and Crime, 2003).

12.4 Road Traffic Accident Statistics

The total length of public roads in Turkey is 62,863 km. The length of all motorways is 1,773 km. The number of motor vehicles is 9,821,000 and the number of motorized two-wheelers is 1,047,000. The number of passenger cars and station wagons is 5,679,000 (2002 International Road Traffic and Accident Database, 2004). The current drivers' license system does not comply with European Community regulations and the Vienna Agreement. The license information does not include the type of vehicles that the licensee is permitted to drive, or the expiration date of the license (Economic Commission for Europe: Inland Transport Committee, 2004).

As a natural result of using the road transport extensively (the market share of road transport was 93 percent in 2002), the heavy motor vehicle usage is high. For every heavy motor vehicle, there are 2.89 cars in Turkey, whereas this rate is 1:19.65 in Germany, 1:11.81 in Austria and 1:11:63 in Bulgaria. The high usage and the large number of heavy vehicles leads to an increase in the number of traffic accidents, deaths and injuries (General Directorate of Security Traffic Research Center, 2001).

The General Directorate of Security, Traffic Division of the Ministry of Internal Affairs (referred to hereafter as police) is responsible for road safety in urban areas. Traffic Teams of the General Command of Gendarmerie (referred hereafter to as gendarmerie) is responsible for road safety in rural areas. Police and gendarmerie investigate all injury, fatal, and hit and run traffic collisions for the purpose of documentation and prosecution.

The State Institute of Statistics collects, analyzes, and disseminates national statistics including traffic accidents. Accidents that occur in rural areas are covered, but they are not analyzed and reported in the same way as urban accidents. This lack of information is reflected in international road databases (International Road Traffic and Accident Database, 2004). Although areas covered in national traffic accident statistics have been extended in recent years, deaths that occur enroute to hospitals, in hospital emergency rooms or after discharge still are missing. Prior to 1999, no information was reported on hit and run cases. The insufficient collaboration between different agencies makes a detailed cause and outcome analysis practically impossible.

Also, accident reports by police and gendarmerie are inadequate due to incomplete investigation and data entry. Although the Official Accident

Investigation Form has a specific box for BAC entry, it does not have a section for possible drug abuse. Furthermore, not every accident is reported to police or gendarmerie. Drivers may not report an accident because they wish to avoid trial if they do not possess a driver's license, or if they are under the influence of alcohol or drugs at the time of the accident. The unreliability of official traffic accident statistics is also reflected in the World Bank supported Traffic Safety Project (Swedish National Road Consulting BA [Sweroad], 2001).

The analysis of recorded traffic accidents increased dramatically between 1990 and 2000 (Figure 12.1). The slight decrease, which can be seen in the figure for 2002, can be attributed to effective prevention activities and the improvement of black spot areas (accident prone locations).

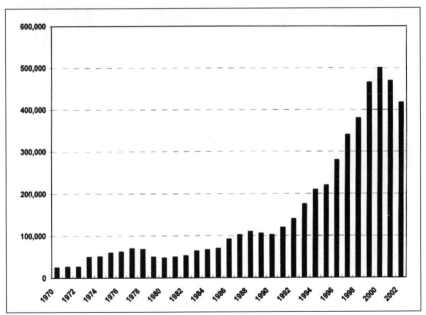

Source: State Institute of Statistics, 2003

Figure 12.1 *Traffic Accidents Recorded Between 1970 and 2002*

Approximately 88,000 injuries were recorded in 1990. The number increased by more than 50 percent during the following decade and then decreased to 116,412 persons in 2002 (Figure 12.2).

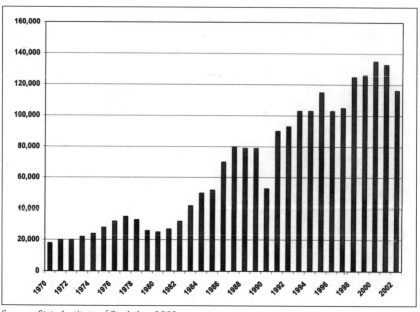

Source: State Institute of Statistics, 2003

Figure 12.2 *Injuries in Traffic Accidents Between 1970 and 2002*

The recorded number of fatalities between 1970 and 2002 shows periodic fluctuations. The death toll doubled between 1970 and 1988 reaching 7,500 persons. A significant decrease occurred after the 1990s. The decrease reflects at least in part an improvement in health services (private ambulances, hospitals, rescue teams, improved emergency room infrastructure, and better training for health services personnel). The introduction of side and front airbags, anti-lock brakes, and the increased use of seat belts also contributed to the decrease in fatalities (Figure 12.3).

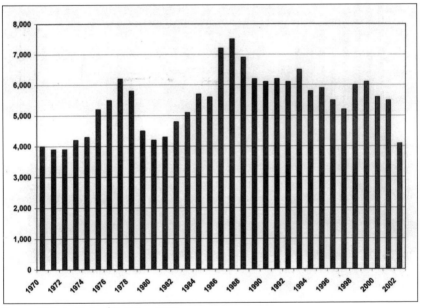

Source: State Institute of Statistics, 2003

Figure 12.3 *Fatalities in Traffic Accidents Between 1970 and 2002*

The number of fatalities in traffic accidents per 100,000 motorized vehicles has been continuously dropping since year 1970. The number of fatalities recorded at the accident sites is shown in Figure 12.4.

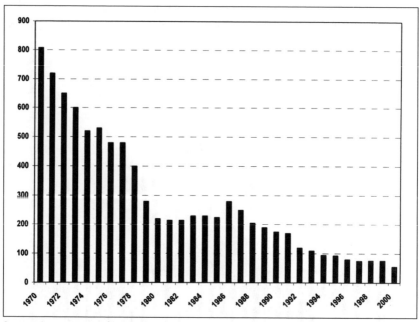

Source: State Institute of Statistics, 2003

Figure 12.4 Number Fatalities per 100,000 Motor Vehicles (Police and gendarmerie-reported fatalities at accident sites, hit and run cases and hospital statistics not included.)

Although the number of fatalities per motor vehicle decreased between 1970 and 2000, the number of traffic accidents per 100,000 persons remained unchanged between 1970 and 1985 and increased sharply thereafter (Figure 12.5).

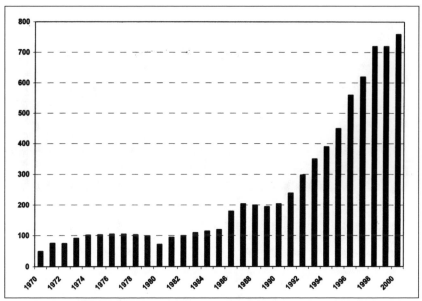

Source: State Institute of Statistics, 2003

Figure 12.5 Number of Accidents per 100,000 Inhabitants (Police and Gendarmerie-reported accidents, hit and run cases not included. Based on police and State Institute statistics.)

The number of injured per 100,000 population has increased fourfold since 1980 and exceeded 200 people per 100,000 inhabitants (Figure 12.6).

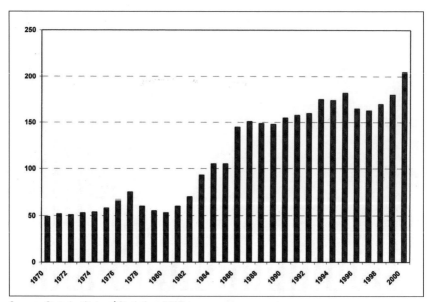

Source: State Institute of Statistics, 2003

Figure 12.6 Number of Injuries per 100,000 of the Population

The number of fatalities per 100,000 persons peaked in 1977 and 1987 and subsequently decreased (Figure 12.7).

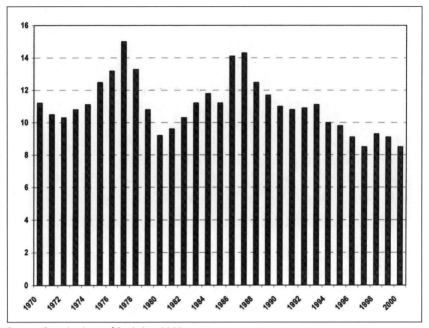

Source: State Institute of Statistics, 2003

Figure 12.7 Number of Fatalities per 100,000 Inhabitants

A. Official statistics related to driving under the influence of alcohol and drugs

Turkey has no reliable statistics on drug impaired driving, because drivers are generally tested only for blood alcohol concentration and not for drugs. This lack of reliable statistics is not due to inadequate legal provisions. Existing rules and regulations concerning road transportation cover all contemporary approaches to the prevention of drunk and drugged driving. They actually are more stringent than those of most European nations. Some provisions of the legislation raise serious questions from the human rights perspective, but that topic falls outside the scope of this chapter.

Despite the legislation that is in place, there is an overall lack of clarity about substances, methods of detection, and laboratories. As an example, drug terminology in the Highway Traffic Law and Highway Traffic Regulations is not the same as drug terminology in the Turkish Penal Code. The Highway Traffic Law (HTR) defines drugs as "narcotic drugs and mood lifting substances." The regulation to enforce the law draws a wider framework and defines drugs as "natural and synthetic psychotropic substances with numbing, sleep inducing, and mood lifting effects." The Penal Code, on the other hand, uses only the word "narcotics" and due to their penalty-increasing consequences lists heroin, cocaine, base morphine, and morphine by name.

Turkey is a party to the 1961 Single Convention of Narcotic Drugs, the 1971 Convention on Psychotropic Substances and the 1988 United Nations Convention against Illicit Traffic in Narcotic Drugs and Psychotropic Substances. Thus, although national legislation does not list substances by name, all chemicals controlled by these conventions are included.

If 'drug' is defined as chemicals that affect the activity and function of the central nervous system (CNS), it must be noted that many over-the-counter (OTC) drugs and prescription drugs act on the CNS. Several classes of drugs, including antihistamines, hypnotics, tranquilizers and tricyclic antidepressants, have been shown to impair driving skills in laboratory tests and driver-simulation studies (Movig, Mathijssen, Nagel, van Egmond, de Gier, Leufkens, and Egberts, 2004; Drummer, Gerostamoulos, Batziris, Chu, Caplehorn, Robertson, and Swann, 2004; Verster, Veldhuijzen, and Volkerts, 2004; Bramness, Skurtveit, and Morland, 2004; Druid,

Holmgren, and Ahlner, 2001; Barbone, McMahon, Davey, Morris, Reid, McDevitt, and MacDonald, 1998; Robbe, 1998; Christensen, Nielsen, and Nielsen, 1990; Smiley, 1987; Ellinwood and Heatherly, 1985; Krantz and Wannerberg, 1981; Blomberg and Preusser, 1974).

The degree of impairment resulting from a combination of any of these substances with alcohol is clear (Drummer, Gerostamoulos, Batziris, Chu, Caplehorn, Robertson, and Swann, 2003; Behrensdorff and Steentoft, 2003; Mura et al., 2003; Arora, Baraona, and Lieber, 2000; Krull, Smith, and Parsons, 1994; Macdonald and Dooley, 1993). Also, a drug-drug combination is at least as risky as moderate quantities of alcohol use (Movig et al., 2004). The H2-receptor antagonists cimetidine and ranitidine increase blood alcohol concentrations (BAC) by decreasing the first pass metabolism (Arora et al., 2000).

According to Krueger (2000), the issue of alcohol impairment has been resolved from the legal point of view. In his words, however, "in the case of drugs the situation seems to be almost hopelessly complicated... This dilemma leads to the widespread practice of the courts punishing for alcohol or other offences, even in cases where drug consumption was probably the cause of the driving violation." Psyhotropic substances under international control in accordance with the Convention on Psychotropic Substances, 1971 comprise a green list of prescription drugs. A red list includes narcotic drugs under international control in accordance with the Single Convention on Narcotic Drugs, 1961 and the Protocol of 25 March 1972 amending the Single Convention, Yellow List. The Ministry of Health declares and updates the list of drugs that are to be sold with green or red-list prescriptions. Nevertheless, drugs such as Rohypnol (Flunitrazepam), a red prescription drug, remain easily available in the black market. Flunitrazepam impairs cognitive and psychomotor functions affecting reaction time and driving skill. Its use in combination with alcohol is a particular concern due to potentiation of effects.

The misuse of drugs and their availability without prescription, from the point of view of public health, has always been an issue in Turkey. Furthermore, the problem of widespread use of prescription drugs like Akineton (biperiden) and Diazem (diazepam) by youth has arisen as an issue in the Parliament (Yazar, 1996). Many non-prescription drugs, e.g., Benadryl (diphenhydramine), which is a first generation, drowsiness-producing antihistamine, are readily available OTC, as are analgesic, antipyretic and antitussive agents that can have adverse effects on driving skills (Bramness et al., 2004; Behrensdorff et al., 2003; DuBuske, 2001; Starmer, 1985; Chesher, 1985). It is difficult to fully assess the total effects on traffic of a broad array of psychoactive substances.

Even if the scope of the problems associated with psychoactive substances were limited to illicit drugs and drugs sold with red-list and green-list prescription, a serious problem remains. The number of laboratories that perform toxicological analyses is limited, even in major cities like Istanbul and Izmir. Only alcohol analysis with breath-sampling instruments is routinely conducted.

In 2002, drivers were liable in 97 percent of 498,114 accidents that occurred in police areas. Investigation reports cite alcohol as the cause of the accident in only 1.27 percent of the cases (State Institute of Statistics, 2003). Forty-four percent of the drivers had a class B driver's license (automobile, minibus, or pick-up truck drivers), 27 percent had a class E driver's license (bus drivers), and 14 percent did not possess a driver's license. Of the drivers killed, 35 percent had class B licenses, 28 percent class E licenses, and 13 percent did not have a license. Figure 12.8 shows the number of accident-involved drivers by age and sex.

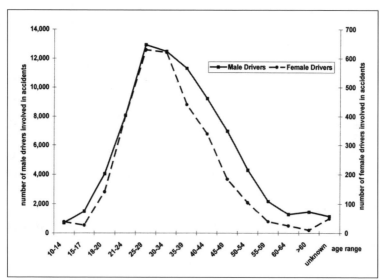

Source: State Institute of Statistics, 2003

Figure 12.8 Drivers Involved in Accidents by Age and Sex of Drivers in 2002

B. Scientific study of driving under the influence of alcohol and drugs

In a 2001 study, Aktas et al. examined the files of 1,255 traffic accident victims who were treated in the emergency room of the Ege University School of Medicine hospital. The study reported that blood alcohol was not determined for more than half of them. In 46 percent of the cases, the police, gendarmerie, or medical personnel checked for alcohol breath odor to identify the presence of alcohol, and documented any measured BACs that were between 10-15 g/dl. The authors were unable to find any information about the use of substances other than alcohol (Aktas, Kocak, Zeyfeoglu, Ilhami, and Aksu, 2002).

Police officers frequently decide to proceed with sobriety testing based on the presence or absence of an odor of alcohol. Controlled studies, however, report that decisions based on odor alone include many false negative errors. In a study by Moskowitz et al. (1999), twenty experienced officers attempted to detect an alcohol odor from fourteen subjects who were at BACs ranging from zero to 0.130 g/dl. Subjects were concealed behind a screen. Under these conditions, odor was detected two-thirds of the time for BACs below 0.08 percent and 85 percent of the time for BACs at or above 0.08 percent. After the subjects consumed food, the officers' detection of odor declined further. Ratings of the strength of the odor were unrelated to BACs, and BAC estimates did not rise above chance level. These results demonstrate that under laboratory conditions, the detection of breath alcohol odor is unreliable. This suggests a reason for the low detection rate under roadside conditions (Moskowitz, Burns, and Ferguson, 1999). These findings are consistent with a police station study (Widmark, 1932) and a roadside study (Compton, 1985).

Although Ege University School of Medicine is one of Turkey's best-equipped health institutions, only half of accident victim patients are tested for alcohol. The situation changed slightly after 2002 when the Department of Legal Medicine introduced blood alcohol testing for legal purposes. Subsequently, between June and December 2002, one-fifth of the blood samples obtained from injured drivers had BACs above 0.05 g/dl (Ozturk, Akgur, and Yemiscigil, 2003).

Aksoy et al. reviewed the autopsy reports of traffic accident cases submitted by the Istanbul branch of the Council of Legal Medicine between 1994 and 1996. Alcohol was identified in 40 percent of the blood specimens obtained from drivers and victims. The reports contained no information about substances other than alcohol (Aksoy, Birgen, Baskan, and Inanici, 1998).

Aktas et al. reviewed traffic accident cases admitted to the Department of Legal Medicine of Ege University between the years 1997 and 2001. The investigators report that none of the examination and consultation reports for 542 victims contained information about analyses for alcohol or other substances (Aktas, Kocak, and Zeyfeoglu, 2002).

Toprak et al. reported a review of 26,421 postmortem examinations at the Council of Legal Medicine of the Ministry of Justice between 1990 and 2000. Death was attributed to drug overdose in 2.3 percent of the examinations with 97 percent of those related to heroin, followed by barbiturate, benzodiazepine, cocaine and methadone. In 34 percent of the cases, two or more substances were used together. A benzodiazepine was the second drug in about 100 deaths. (Toprak, Pac, Ersoy, and Akgul, 2003).

The postmortem analysis of 3,990 intoxication-related deaths revealed differences between geographical regions. In Instanbul, alcohol was the primary cause of death in 22.7 percent of the cases, followed by 9.5 percent illicit drugs and 7.5 percent pharmaceuticals (Baser, Yayci, and Inanici, 2003).

In 2000, an evaluation of 226 intoxication cases found consumption of illicit alcohol beverages or cologne in 43.8 percent of the cases (Inanici, Birgen, and Anolay, 2000). In a similar evaluation in 1996, the ingested liquid was an illicit alcoholic beverage in 42.5 percent of the cases and cologne in 19.2 percent (Elmas, Tuzun, Imrag, and Korkut, 1996). In an evaluation of the post-mortem toxicology reports of 24,206 autopsies in Istanbul between 1992 and 2002, the cause of death was identified as methanol intoxication in 271 cases (Yayci, Agritmis, Turla, and Koc, 2003).

12.5 Legislation Regarding Driving under the Influence of Alcohol and Drugs

A. Alcohol and substance use and the Turkish criminal law

Human action that constitutes a crime consists of four elements: conduct, legality, unlawfulness, and culpability. The Turkish Criminal Law considers voluntary or involuntary intoxication within the concept of "culpability." From the perspective of intoxication, the basic requirement of criminal responsibility or culpability is that the human action must take place voluntarily. Even if an action is unlawful, if it is not carried out voluntarily, the person cannot be held liable. That link between the person and the action is the subjective element of culpability. Mental disability, being deaf, mute or of minor age, as well as the consequences of alcohol and drug use, affect culpability.

The person must be culpable at the time the crime is committed. The loss of culpability *after* committing a crime does not affect liability. If a person loses culpability *before* committing the crime, but *after* deciding to commit it, *actio libera in causa* holds him responsible. To illustrate, a person who decides to commit a crime may use alcohol or drugs to gain courage or to inhibit instincts that would prevent him from committing the crime. In such a case, the person is considered culpable for the crime.

If a person is forced to consume alcohol or drugs and then commits a crime either unintentionally or due to the effects of the alcohol or drugs, the perpetrator's criminal responsibility is determined according article 48 of the Turkish Penal Code. If the intoxication has completely eliminated the perception ability, the perpetrator does not have the capability for fault and will not receive any penalty. On the other hand, if the intoxication has diminished the culpability, the penalty will be reduced from one third to half in accordance with article 47 of Turkish Penal Code.

If alcohol or a drug is consumed voluntarily and a crime is committed either with or without prior intention to do so, it is considered to be a voluntary intoxication, and the perpetrator will be held completely responsible. If insufficient care is taken in the use of a substance that may affect the consciousness, the crime is committed by failure in duty rather than criminal intention, and a penalty is determined accordingly.

B. Highway traffic law

Traffic offenses were regulated by Municipality Law in the 1920s, Police Authorization Law between 1937 and 1953 and by the provisions of Highway Traffic Law between 1953 and 1983. The Highway Traffic Law (HTL) No. 2918 of 1983, which is still enforced, contained the first provisions for regulation of driving under influence.

The HTL objectives are traffic order on the road, the safety of life and property, and determination of the measures needed for traffic safety. Unless there is a specific provision against it, the law can be applied in public areas such as parks, gardens, parking places, bus stations or terminals, and gas or service stations. The law also applies to toll roads and commercial vehicles that provide a land connection to sea, lakes and rivers.

Article 41 of HTL, which regulates the requirements for drivers' licenses, was amended in 1996 to prohibit people sentenced for a drug-related crime from applying for a license. Harsher penalties for drink-driving offenses were enacted in 1996, allowing police to conduct preliminary breath tests and to use BACs as sufficient evidence of an offense (per se legislation). The maximum license disqualification period and the monetary fines for drunk-driving offenses were increased by almost ten times.

Article 48 of HTL regulates driving under the influence of alcohol, drugs, or mood lifting substances: "People under influence of drugs and mood lifting substances and people who have temporarily lost their safe driving skills due to alcohol consumption are prohibited from driving on the road." This article was amended in 2003 as follows:

> Technical devices shall be used by law enforcement personnel to identify the drugs and mood lifting substances, the effects of alcoholic beverages, and the blood alcohol concentrations. The determination methods and examination conditions will be arranged in the regulation that shall be prepared in accordance with the opinions of the Ministry of Health. Driving under influence of alcohol with a blood alcohol level higher than the limit level stated in the regulations will result with a suspension of the license for six months. A fee of 265 YTL (authors' note: about US $180) must be paid to reinstate a suspended license. If the same offence is committed for the second time, in a five-year period, the suspension will be two years and the driver will have to attend a driving school. Driving schools should operate according rules and regulations set forth by the Ministries of Internal Affairs and Health. A fee of 332 YTL (about US $220) must be paid to reinstate a suspended license. Driving under influence three or more times in a five-year period will result with a suspension of the license for five years. A fee of 532 YTL (about US $360) must be paid to reinstate a suspended license along with a light imprisonment penalty of not less than six months. The driver will be subjected to psycho technical and psychiatric evaluation for the establishment of fitness to drive... "Driving under influence of drugs and mood lifting substances—even if the action constitutes another

crime—is subject to six months of light imprisonment along with a financial penalty of 532 YTL (US $ 360) and a permanent cancellation of the license.

C. Enforcement of the Highway Traffic Law (HTL)

The HTL is enforced under the provisions of Highway Traffic Regulations of 1997 (HTR), which prohibit driving under influence of natural and synthetic psychotropic substances, illicit drugs, sedatives, hypnotics and mood lifting substances unrelated to amount or degree of impairment. Driving is prohibited if there is a loss of safe driving skills due to alcohol consumption.

1. Drug impaired driving

Drivers suspected of driving under the influence of substances with narcotic, hypnotic and mood-lifting effects are dispatched to a medical examiner's office where blood and urine specimens are obtained, and their condition is evaluated. If a medical examiner is not available, the specimens can be obtained at another governmental health agency with the necessary facilities. If the specimen cannot be obtained in any of these facilities, sampling can be carried out by a health professional. The specimens are submitted to the nearest governmental health agency laboratory or to a police crime laboratory.

2. Determination of blood alcohol concentration

In cases of suspected drunk driving or in property damage only (PDO) traffic accidents, the drivers' BACs are determined at the site by law enforcement personnel and are recorded in the accident report. A traffic accident with fatalities or injuries is a major offense if it involves alcohol.

In PDO cases, the driver will not be dispatched to a medical examiner or a governmental health agency for BAC measurement. If BAC can be measured on site, the results will be recorded as an addendum to the accident report. If the driver objects to the BAC measurement with the breath sampling device, a blood sample will be collected for analysis by a police crime laboratory, a medical examiner, or a governmental health agency.

The Law on the Establishment of Clinical Laboratories (1927) states that only laboratories staffed with a biochemist or microbiologist certified by the Ministry of Health are authorized to analyze biological samples. Highway Traffic Regulations, however, permit analysis by police crime laboratories, which do have have certified analysts.

D. Activities for the prevention of traffic accidents
1. Conscious negligence

Activities of the media, researchers, and private citizens have stimulated debate in the Parliament about road safety. In response to escalating numbers of traffic accidents, the media have advocated amendments of the Turkish Penal Code. The father of a girl killed in a road accident founded a non-governmental activist organization. Researchers proposed the term "conscious negligence" to define the offence of killing a person while driving (Cakmut, 1999; Yilmaz, 1994).

In January 2003, Article 45 of the Turkish Penal Code was amended to accept the term "conscious negligence," defined as voluntary and conscious conduct by a person with the knowledge that the conduct is likely to be harmful to the health or well-being of another person. An example would be speeding in a crowded urban area and causing an accident with fatalities. With a very high probability, the driver would not have wanted the accident to happen, but he could have foreseen the result. In other words, he was conscious of the fact that an accident might happen.

2. Psycho technical evaluation

Psychologists in Spain, Austria, Germany, and Hungary conduct psycho technical evaluations of drivers involved in accidents to ensure traffic safety from the human factors point of view. (Yasak, Dogruyusever, Sendag, and Oguz, 2002; Bukasa, Wenninger, and Yasak, 2000). The procedure was introduced to Turkey in 1996 (Yasak, 1997).

If a driver is convicted of driving under the influence more than three times in a five-year period, his driver's license is suspended for five years. Reinstatement requires a psycho technical evaluation and a psychiatric examination of the driver. The Highway Traffic Regulations set out the principles and rules of these required procedures, and there are authorized centers where the psycho technical evaluations are conducted. Governmental agencies and private transportation companies may take the psycho technical evaluation results into consideration in their selection of drivers, but they are not legally required to do so. Between 1996 and 2002, 12,053 drivers underwent psycho technical evaluation. Most of those (98 percent) were required due to speeding offences and only 0.62 percent were due to driving under the influence of alcohol (Trafik Arastirma Merkezi, 2004).

12.6 Activities on Accident Prevention
A. The parliamentary traffic safety commissions
The objective of several studies and surveys conducted since the late eighties has been the reduction of accident related fatalities. In 1995 and 2000 Parliamentary Traffic Safety Commissions were formed to analyze traffic accidents and recommend methods of improvement.

The 2000 commission's collaboration with universities in the preparation of a final report provided an opportunity for scholars from Istanbul University to introduce the North American Drug Evaluation and Classification Program (DECP). In this program, suspected drug-impaired drivers are evaluated by trained officers who follow a systematic and standardized twelve-step protocol, which includes the Standardized Field Sobriety Tests (EU Project Rosita, 2002; International Association of Chiefs of Police, 1999). Also, very detailed information was provided on road side drug testing (EU Project Rosita, 2002; Samyn and van Haeren, 2000; Skopp and Potsch, 1999; Kidwell, Holland, and Athanaselis, 1998; Holmgren, Loch, and Schuberth, 1985; Jonah, 1982). The 2000 commission recommended implementation of a DRE program, and a workshop on the Drug Recognition Expert approach was convened in 2003 (Page, Gould, Moeller, Jeffrey, Drummer, and Atasoy, 2004).

The commission also recommended revocation of the provision that allows sentences to be postponed and permits imprisonment sentences to be converted to a financial penalty. Finally, the commission recommended that the concept of "conscious negligence" be included in the Turkish Penal Code. After a year, the commission chairman noted a lack of interest in the report (Tan, 2001). Legislation enacted in 2003, however, did address some of the issues raised in the commission report.

B. Five-year development plans of the Prime Ministry State Planning Organization

At five-year intervals the State Planning Organization develops plans to facilitate the effective and accelerated use of resources and to insure that economic, social, and cultural services are carried out with integrity in an efficient, organized, and fast manner. Policies and objectives are analyzed and evaluated.

The first plan was developed in 1963, and presently the eighth plan is in force (Turkish Grand National Assembly, 2000). During the initial plan, a highway transportation office was established. During the second plan, a Road Transportation and Traffic General Management Agency was established to centralize all the duties related with road transportation. Nonetheless, confusion regarding the authorities and responsibilities continued, and it was decided, therefore, in the seventh term to establish a committee to coordinate the ministries. The established committee has not effectively addressed the issue of impaired driving (Pampal, Hatipoglu, and Arikan Ozturk, 2002).

C. The Traffic Research Center

A Traffic Research Center was established in 1997 under the Ministry of Interior. It conducts research in collaboration with universities and makes research-based recommendations to the authorities. The center disseminates accident prevention materials, sponsors awareness campaigns, operates a web site and makes an effort to reach the community. Although the center acknowledges driving under the influence of alcohol as one of the major causes of accidents and defends a reduction of the legal BAC, it has not acknowledged or disseminated information about the risk of driving under influence of psychoactive substances (Trafik Arastirma Merkezi, 1999).

D. Academic research
1. The Road Improvement and Traffic Safety Project

The Road Improvement and Traffic Safety Project of 1998 and 2001 with a budget of approximately $250 million U.S. was the largest traffic safety project supported by World Bank to date. Project activities were executed with the participation of Road General Management, Police

Headquarters, Ministry of Education, Ministry of Health, and Gazi University School of Medicine. SweRoad also took part with over thirty consultants from Sweden, Denmark and Finland (The World Bank, 2003; Swedish National Road Consulting BA [Sweroad], 2001).

The project's objective was the development of a national strategy for the traffic accident problem in Turkey. The goal was a 40 percent reduction in the death toll from traffic crashes by the year 2010. The project analyzed information about engineering, education, legislation, and law enforcement and offered sound recommendations for improvement. Unfortunately, the topic of impaired driving was not among the recommendations. The lack of toxicology laboratories and the problems of underfunded, understaffed crime laboratories found no place in the final document.

During the three years that have elapsed since the completion of the project, the Highway Traffic Law and the Turkish Penal Code have been amended, and infrastructure improvements have been made, such as the reduction of the black spots (accident prone locations). Hundreds of police officers have been trained and the emergency room at Gazi University in Ankara has been modernized. Although the project charted significant new directions for reducing traffic accidents, a national strategy document is still absent (Aydin, 2004).

Concerns about the project are evident in the Implementation Completion Report published by the World Bank (November 2003). The Principal Performance Ratings Section evaluated the outcome of the project as "satisfactory," the sustainability as "likely" and the institutional development impact as "modest" (The World Bank, 2003).

2. The working conditions of heavy vehicle drivers and traffic accidents project

The Traffic Research Center (Trafik Arastirma Merkezi) and Ankara Hacettepe University Department of Sociology collaborated in the conduct of a 1999 project that examined the working conditions of truck and bus drivers. Face to face interviews were conducted with 994 male drivers, ages eighteen to seventy years. The average number of relatives the drivers had to take care of was 5.6, and truck or bus driving was the only source of income for 82 percent of them. The monthly salary for the majority was less than $200 U.S.

One third of the truck drivers and 20 percent of the bus drivers consumed alcoholic beverages one to three times a week with more than two thirds preferring Raki (a dry, white aniseed type drink, distilled from grape with an ethanol content between 45-50 percent). Sixteen percent of the drivers reported chronic health problems, and one third use Gripin, a paracetamol and caffeine-containing pill, to alleviate cold symptoms and headache. The drivers also said they take Gripin to help them stay awake (Sonmez, 1999).

A similar survey of 500 heavy vehicle drivers found that 65 percent of the drivers use two to five tablets of Gripin daily for the reasons stated above. Six percent of these drivers reported diminished visual acuity after ingestion of Gripin (Yildirim, 2003). Similar results were obtained by Memisci (Memisci, 2002).

The belief that drinking coffee counteracts the negative effects of alcohol is very widespread in Turkey, and drinking coffee after a meal is a traditional behavior. Studies of the effects of caffeine on alcohol related driving impairment indicate that that caffeine may increase alertness and improve reaction time after alcohol use, but it will not completely counteract alcohol impairment (Liguori and Robinson, 2001; Drake, Roehrs, Turner, Scofield, and Roth, 2003; Marczinski and Fillmore, 2003).

Sonmez reported that the drivers of trucks drive ten hours per day, 5.5 days per week, all year around, and 35 percent stop only when they feel the need to sleep. They delay bedrest until the journey has ended. Sonmez found no statistical relation between this behavior and age, work status, or type of vehicle driven. Half of the drivers had been involved in at least one accident, and the range of number of accidents was one (73.9 percent) to five (0.4 percent) (Sonmez, 1999).

None of the aforementioned studies included questions about drug use in relation to driving, and no questions were asked about the use of sleep inducing, narcotic or stimulating substances. It is known, however, that trucks leaving the Netherlands reach a target destination in the heartland of Turkey (a distance of about 2,000 miles) without stopping and without changing the driver. It is also known that an amphetamine-like stimulant, Captagon (fenetyllin), is smuggled through Turkey by truck drivers targeting Saudi Arabian markets (Department of State, 2004). It seems likely that truck drivers use Captagon as an aid to staying awake.

References

Aksoy, E., Birgen, N., Baskan, T. M., and Inanici, M. A. (1998). Trafik kazalarina bagli olum otopsilerinin incelenmesi. In Kusadasi, Turkey: III. Adli Bilimler Kongresi.

Aktas, E. O., Kocak, A., and Zeyfeoglu, Y. (2002). Evaluation of forensic traffic cases admitted to Department of Forensic Medicine of Ege University. In Ankara, Turkey: Uluslararasi Trafik ve Yol Guvenligi Kongresi ve Fuari.

Aktas, E. O., Kocak, A., Zeyfeoglu, Y., Ilhami, S., and Aksu, H. (2002). Trafik kazasi nedeniyle Ege Universitesi Acil Servisine basvuran olgularin ozellikleri. In Ankara, Turkey: Uluslararasi Trafik ve Yol Guvenligi Kongresi ve Fuari.

Albayrak, M. (1997). Trafik kazalarinda kusur ve kusurun tesbiti. Unpublished master's thesis in Forensic Sciences, Istanbul University, Turkey.

Arora, S., Baraona, E., and Lieber, C. S. (2000). Alcohol levels are increased in social drinkers receiving ranitidine. The American Journal of Gastroenterology, 95, 208-213.

Aydin, C. (2004). Traffic Safety Project: Is the action plan to save 20,000 people going to be applied? Atilim University, Ankara, Turkey. Retrieved May 21, 2004 at: http://www.atilim.edu.tr/~caydin/trguvproj.doc.

Barbone, F., McMahon, A. D., Davey, P. G., Morris, A. D., Reid, I. C., McDevitt, D. G., and MacDonald, T. M. (1998). Association of road-traffic accidents with benzodiazepine use. The Lancet, 352, 1331-1336.

Baser, L., Yayci, N., and Inanici, M. A. (2003). The profile of deaths in Turkey due to intoxication. Forensic Science International, 136, 312.

Baskan, T. M. and Atasoy, S. (1997). Regulatory mechanisms for food safety in Turkey. In Food and Health Today, the Truth and the Myth (pp. 78-79). Singapore: The Medicolegal Society of Singapore.

Behrensdorff, I. and Steentoft, A. (2003). Medicinal and illegal drugs among Danish car drivers. Accident Analysis & Prevention, 35, 851-860.

Birgen, N., Baskan, T. M., and Inanici, M. A. (2000). Metil alkol (metanol) zehirlenmesi ve hukuksal boyutu. Adalet Dergisi, 91, 60-69.

Blomberg, R. D. and Preusser, D. F. (1974). Narcotic use and driving behavior. Accident Analysis & Prevention, 6, 23-32.

Bramness, J. G., Skurtveit, S., and Morland, J. (2004). Impairment due to intake of carisoprodol. Drug and Alcohol Dependence, 74, 311-318.

Bukasa, B., Wenninger, U., and Yasak, Y. (2000). Surucu secimi. In Izmir, Turkey: XI. Ulusal Psikoloji Kongresi.

Cakar, F. (1997). Bilirkisi kararlarini etkileyen ve ikinci kez bilirkisiye gonderilmesinde etken olan faktorlerin incelenmesi. Unpublished master's thesis in Forensic Sciences, Istanbul University, Turkey.

Cakmut, A. (1999). Trafik kazalarinda cezai sorumluluk. Unpublished master's thesis in Forensic Sciences, Istanbul University, Turkey.

Chesher, G. B. (1985). The influence of analgesic drugs in road crashes. Accident Analysis & Prevention, 17, 303-309.

Christensen, L. Q., Nielsen, L. M., and Nielsen, S. L. (1990). Traffic accidents and drivers suspected for drug influence. Forensic Science International, 45, 273-280.

Compton, R. P. (1985). Pilot test of selected DWI detection procedures for use at sobriety checkpoints (Rep. No. HS806 724).(pp. US Department of Transportation: Office of Driver and Pedestrian Research, National Highway Traffic Safety Administration.

Department of State (2004). International Narcotics Control Strategy Report. U.S.: Bureau for International Narcotics and Law Enforcement Affairs.

Drake, C. L., Roehrs, T., Turner, L., Scofield, H. M., and Roth, T. (2003). Caffeine reversal of ethanol effects on the multiple sleep latency test, memory, and psychomotor performance. Neuropsychopharmacology: Official Publication Of The American College Of Neuropsychopharmacology, 28, 371-378.

Druid, H., Holmgren, P., and Ahlner, J. (2001). Flunitrazepam: an evaluation of use, abuse and toxicity. Forensic Science International, 122, 136-141.

Drummer, O. H., Gerostamoulos, J., Batziris, H., Chu, M., Caplehorn, J., Robertson, M. D., and Swann, P. (2004). The involvement of drugs in drivers of motor vehicles killed in Australian road traffic crashes. Accident Analysis & Prevention, 36, 239-248.

Drummer, O. H., Gerostamoulos, J., Batziris, H., Chu, M., Caplehorn, J. R. M., Robertson, M. D., and Swann, P. (2003). The incidence of drugs in drivers killed in Australian road traffic crashes. Forensic Science International, 134, 154-162.

DuBuske, L. M. (2001). Pharmacokinetics/pharmacodynamics and psychomotor performance aspects of antihistamine therapies. Clinical and Applied Immunology Reviews, 1, 277-289.

Economic Commission for Europe: Inland Transport Committee (2004). Recommendation to Contracting Parties of the UN 1949 Convention on Road Traffic and the related Protocols on Road Signs and Signals and Road Markings to adhere to the 1968 "Vienna" Conventions in their latest amended versions (as approved in 2004), and to the amended 1971 European Agreements supplementing them TRANS/WP.1/2004/1. United Nations, Economic and Social Council [On-line]. Retrieved March 24, 2004 at: http://www.unece.org/trans/doc/2004/wp1/TRANS-WP1-2004-01e.pdf.

Ellinwood, J. and Heatherly, D. G. (1985). Benzodiazepines, the popular minor tranquilizers: Dynamics of effect on driving skills. Accident Analysis & Prevention, 17, 283-290.

Elmas, I., Tuzun, B., Imrag, C., and Korkut, M. (1996). Evaluation of deaths due to methyl alcohol intoxication with respect to forensic medicine. Journal of Istanbul Medical Faculty, 59, 64-69.

EU Project Rosita (2002). Roadside Testing Assessment. European Union. Retrieved February 5, 2004 at: http://www.rosita.org.

General Directorate of Security Traffic Research Center (2001). Evaluation of Traffic Accidents in Turkey and the World - II. Emniyet Genel Mudurlugu Basimevi - Ankara: Turkey.

Holmgren, P., Loch, E., and Schuberth, J. (1985). Drugs in motorists traveling Swedish roads: On-the-road-detection of intoxicated drivers and screening for drugs in these offenders. Forensic Science International, 27, 57-65.

Inanici, M. A., Birgen, N., and Anolay, N. (2000). Methyl alcohol poisoning: an autopsy study. In Spain: Proceedings of the XVIIIth Congress International Academy of Legal Medicine.

International Association of Chiefs of Police (1999). The international standards of the drug evaluation and classification program. The DEC Standards Revision Subcommittee of the Technical Advisory Panel of the IACP Highway

Safety Committee. Retrieved May 7, 2004 at: http://www.theiacp.org/ div_sec_com/sections/DRE/drestandards99.pdf.

International Road Traffic and Accident Database (2004). Selected risk values for the year 2002. OECD Road Transport Research Programme. Retrieved April 7, 2004 at: http://www.bast.de/htdocs/fachthemen/irtad/english/we2.html.

Jonah, B. A. (1982). Comparison of non-respondents and respondents in a roadside survey of driver impairment. Accident Analysis & Prevention, 14, 173-177.

Kidwell, D. A., Holland, J. C., and Athanaselis, S. (1998). Testing for drugs of abuse in saliva and sweat. Journal of Chromatography B: Biomedical Sciences and Applications, 713, 111-135.

Krantz, P. and Wannerberg, O. (1981). Occurrence of barbiturate, benzodiazepine, meprobamate, methaqualone and phenothiazine in car occupants killed in traffic accidents in the south of Sweden. Forensic Science International, 18, 141-147.

Krueger, H. P. (2000). Legal approaches to controlling drugs and improving road safety in Europe. In Sweden: International Conference on Alcohol, Drugs and Traffic Safety - ICADTS 2000.

Krull, K. R., Smith, L. T., and Parsons, O. A. (1994). Simple reaction time event-related potentials: Effects of alcohol and diazepam. Progress in Neuro-Psychopharmacology and Biological Psychiatry, 18, 1247-1260.

Liguori, A. and Robinson, J. H. (2001). Caffeine antagonism of alcohol-induced driving impairment. Drug and Alcohol Dependence, 63, 123-129.

Macdonald, S. and Dooley, S. (1993). A case-control study of driving-while-impaired offenders. Drug and Alcohol Dependence, 33, 61-71.

Marczinski, C. A. and Fillmore, T. (2003). Dissociative antagonistic effects of caffeine on alcohol-Induced impairment of behavioral control. Experimental and Clinical Psychopharmacology, 11, 228-236.

Memisci, S. (2002). Trafikte agir vasita suruculerinin kisisel hata kaynaklari. Unpublished masters' thesis. Istanbul University.

Moskowitz, H., Burns, M., and Ferguson, S. (1999). Police officers' detection of breath odors from alcohol ingestion. Accident Analysis & Prevention, 31, 175-180.

Movig, K. L. L., Mathijssen, M. P. M., Nagel, P. H. A., van Egmond, T., de Gier, J. J., Leufkens, H. G. M., and Egberts, A. C. G. (2004). Psychoactive substance use and the risk of motor vehicle accidents. Accident Analysis & Prevention, 36, 631-636.

Mura, P., Kintz, P., Ludes, B., Gaulier, J. M., Marquet, P., Martin-Dupont, S., Vincent, F., Kaddour, A., Goulle, J. P., and Nouveau, J. (2003). Comparison of the prevalence of alcohol, cannabis and other drugs between 900 injured drivers and 900 control subjects: Results of a French collaborative study. Forensic Science International, 133, 79-85.

Ozturk, P., Akgur, S. A., and Yemiscigil, A. (2003). The prevalence of ethyl alcohol in forensic cases during the six month period in Izmir. Forensic Science International, 136, 310-311.

Page, T., Gould, P., Moeller, M., Jeffrey, W., Drummer, O. H., and Atasoy, S. (2004). Drug impaired driving detection: The drug recognition expert approach. Forensic Science International, 136.

Pampal, S., Hatipoglu, S., and Arikan Ozturk, E. (2002). Bes yillik kalkinma planlarinda ulastirma sektorunun incelenmesi. In Ankara: Uluslararasi Trafik ve Yol Guvenligi Kongresi ve Fuari.

Robbe, H. (1998). Marijuana's impairing effects on driving are moderate when taken alone but severe when combined with alcohol. Human Psychopharmacology: Clinical & Experimental [Special Issue: Drugs and Driving], 13, S70-S78.

Samyn, N. and van Haeren, C. (2000). On-site testing of saliva and sweat with Drugwipe and determination of concentrations of drugs of abuse in saliva, plasma and urine of suspected users. International Journal Of Legal Medicine, 113, 150-154.

Skopp, G. and Potsch, L. (1999). Perspiration versus saliva—basic aspects concerning their use in roadside drug testing. International Journal Of Legal Medicine, 112, 213-221.

Smiley, A. (1987). Effects of minor tranquilizers and antidepressants on psychomotor performance. Journal of Clinical Psychiatry, 48, 22-28.

Sonmez, A. (1999). Agir vasita suruculerinin calisma kosullari ve trafik kazalari, uzun mesafe yuk ve yolcu tasimaciligi yapan suruculer uzerine bir calisma. Ankara: Trafik Arastirma Merkez Mudurlugu Yayinlari.

Starmer, G. (1985). Antihistamines and highway safety. Accident Analysis & Prevention, 17, 311-317.

State Institute of Statistics (2002). Census of population. Republic of Turkey, Prime Ministry. Retrieved April 8, 2004 at: http://www.die.gov.tr/konularr/ nufusSayimi.htm.

State Institute of Statistics (2003). Road Traffic Accident Statistics. Ankara: Prime Ministry, State Institute of Statistics Printing Office, Turkey.

Swedish National Road Consulting BA (Sweroad) (2001). Road Improvement and Traffic Safety Project. Ankara: Republic of Turkey Ministry of Health; Ministry of Education; Ministry of Interior Affairs.

Tan, A. (2001). Turkish Parliament Official Reports. Retrieved February 21, 2004 at: http://www.tbmm.gov.tr/tutanak/donem21/yil3/bas/b045m.htm.

The European Monitoring Centre for Drugs and Drug Addiction (2003). Drugs and driving. European Legal Database on Drugs. Retrieved June 4, 2004 at: http://eldd-cma.emcdda.eu.int/comparative_doc/Drugs_and_driving.pdf.

The World Bank (2003). Implementation complementation report(CPL-40480; SCL-4048A; SCL-40490) on a load in the amount of US$ 250 million equivalent to the Republic of Turkey for a road improvement and traffic safety project. Infrastructure and Energy Services Department Europe and Central Asia Region, Report No: 25541. Retrieved May 6, 2004 at: http:// www-wds.worldbank.org/servlet/WDSContentServer/WDSP/IB/2003/12/ 09/000090341_20031209114032/Rendered/PDF/25541.pdf.

The World Bank Group (2004). Transport sector overview. Infrastructure and energy transport. Retrieved April 3, 2004 at: http://wbln0018.worldbank.org /ECA/Transport.nsf/Countries/Turkey?Opendocument.

Toprak, S., Pac, M., Ersoy, G., and Akgul, E. (2003). Drug overdose deaths in Istanbul. Forensic Science International, 136, 310-311.

Trafik Arastirma Merkezi (1999). Trafik denetimine bilimsel yaklasim. Ankara: Emniyet Genel Mudurlugu, Trafik Hizmetleri Baskanligi.

Chapter 13

Drugs and Driving – Victoria, Australia

Martin C. Boorman and Philip Swann

13.1 Introduction

Victoria is one of six states and two territories that make up the nation of Australia. Its constitutionally based criminal justice system follows the principles of English common law. Victoria has a landmass of 227,420 square kilometres, a population of almost 5 million, almost 4 million licensed motor vehicle drivers, 3.2 million registered motor vehicles, and approximately 157,000 kilometres of roadways. Motor vehicles play a major role in the mobility of the population, and road trauma is a significant social issue. Like many other jurisdictions, Victoria is experiencing an increase of the involvement of drugs other than alcohol in road trauma. The Parliament of Victoria enacts laws that regulate motor vehicle use on the state's roads.

13.2 Legislative Framework

Throughout the western world, legislation authorizes enforcement, which is either specific deterrence based on individual driver impairment or general deterrence based on crash risk.

The impact of alcohol use and driving on road safety was first recognized, and specific deterrence legislation was introduced in Victoria in 1909. An additional forty years elapsed before the impact of other drug use on road safety was recognized. In 1949 specific deterrence legislation was enacted to include drug use, and it became an offence to drive a motor vehicle while under the influence of alcohol or drug to such an extent as to be incapable of proper control of the motor vehicle (Boorman, 2001). This driving under the influence (DUI) type offense remains a part of the legislative framework today.

Enforcement of specific deterrence legislation, which is based on individual driver impairment, has been challenged in court, and securing a conviction for a DUI drug offence is often problematic. The presentation of evidence to establish a DUI drug offence without legislative authority in the form of presumptive provisions is not a simple task. Evidence must establish that a drug was present in the driver at the time of driving, that the drug affected the driver at the time of driving, and that the effects of the drug rendered the driver incapable of controlling the vehicle properly.

The presentation of evidence to establish a DUI drug offence relies largely on expert opinion. Specifically, expert opinion is required to establish a nexus between the suspect's driving ability and the effect of the drug found in a fluid specimen obtained from the suspect. The opinion must establish that the drug rendered the suspect incapable of controlling the vehicle properly. The expert's opinion is based on observation of the suspect's behaviour and appearance and the evidence that the drug was present in the suspect. The former requires recognition of signs and symptoms of drug use, and the latter requires toxicological examination of a specimen of body fluid. Neither a defined procedure nor legislative authority existed to facilitate the gathering of such evidence prior to the 2001 specific deterrence legislation.

13.3 2001 Drug Impairment Legislation

In 1994 the Victorian Parliamentary Road Safety Committee commenced an inquiry into the effects of drugs (other than alcohol) on road safety in

Victoria. That committee made forty-one recommendations in its 1996 final report (Road Safety Committee, Parliament of Victoria, 1996). Among other matters, it recommended that a new offense of driving while impaired by a drug be introduced, a specialist working party chaired by the Victoria Police be formed to identify procedures for drug impairment testing, and drug impaired driver detection training be developed for police. In 1997, the Victorian Government supported each recommendation in principle (Government of Victoria, 1997). A working party then was formed, and its 1998 report recommended a drug impairment assessment procedure that includes the use of the Standardized Field Sobriety Tests (SFSTs) (Specialist Working Party, 1988). A specific training program for police was implemented, and legislative support for the procedure came into force in Victoria on December 1, 2000 (Parliament of Victoria, 2000).

Legislation created a new driving while impaired by a drug offense. The evidence required to establish the new offense is similar to that required for a DUI drug offense, and it is gathered under legislative authority in a structured manner with mandatory compliance by suspects and with presumptive provisions. There is a presumption of impaired driving if a drug is found in a driver, the behavior of the driver is consistent with the behavior usually associated with a person who has used the drug, and the behavior usually associated with a person who has used that drug would result in the person being unable to drive properly. This presumption is the fundamental distinction between a DUI drug offense and the new driving while impaired by a drug offense. The new offense does not require that a direct connection be established between the drug effect, behavior, and driving ability, because the connection has been established through the legislation.

The signs and symptoms of impairment and their relationship to the effects of drugs are vital information under the new legislative framework, and the legislation prescribes a structured procedure for gathering evidence to establish the cause of impairment. Evidence relevant to the suspect's behavior is a key element of the offense.

This legislation addresses not only the issue of drug impaired driving but also the issue of road safety and impaired driving generally. The consumption of alcohol, the misuse of illicit or prescribed drugs, injury, illness, infirmity, or a combination of these factors can cause driver impairment. Regardless of the cause of the impairment, the fundamental safety issue is the identification of impaired drivers and their removal from the road. The new legislation provides for identification of impaired drivers so that appropriate action can be taken. If recreational misuse of drugs is the cause of impairment, a driver is prosecuted for driving while impaired by a drug. If impairment is caused by the unintentional misuse of prescribed drugs, injury, illness, or infirmity, the driver is dealt with by an administrative driver licence procedure. In either case, the driver is removed from the road, and the question of why he or she was impaired is addressed.

A. Procedure overview

The procedure has two phases. The first phase consists of two elements that provide information about impairment, a Roadside Impairment Assessment (RIA) and a Standard Impairment Assessment (SIA). The second phase also consists of two elements, the collection of body fluid specimens for drug analysis and an information review to determine the course of action to be taken. The new procedure is closely linked with the existing alcohol impaired driver detection system.

The total system is a progressive process of gathering evidence to identify impairment and determine the cause of that impairment. Screening of a driver for the presence of alcohol is an intrinsic component of the RIA, which is the first step of the process. Thus, the RIA enables an investigator to form an opinion as to whether a driver's behavior or appearance do or do not indicate alcohol alone. If the investigator's believes that alcohol alone is impairing a driver, he need not complete the RIA but can instead follow the alcohol impaired enforcement process. If the investigator does not believe impairment is caused by alcohol alone, the RIA is completed.

The RIA, which is the basis of the investigator's opinion, relies on basic observational skills and a record of facts for presentation as evidence. A template document insures that observations are recorded in a standardized manner and provides a word picture of a driver's behavior and appearance.

In the next stage, a breath specimen is obtained for an evidential analysis to establish whether and to what extent alcohol is contributing to the driver's impairment. An SIA follows the breath testing procedure. The SIA is a structured and systematic assessment of impairment that is carried out by a specially trained police officer in a controlled environment such as a police station. The assessment is videotaped using a tripod-mounted video camera with a wide-angle lens set up by the officer conducting the assessment in the area where the assessment is carried out. The camera remains static and records the activity and sound during the assessment. The videotape is only admissible as evidence for the purpose of establishing compliance with the prescribed assessment process. It is not admissible to prove or disprove the presence of impairment. The videotapes do not come before the court unless the manner in which the assessment was carried out is in dispute. The SIA consists of four components, interview and observation, physical impairment tests, information review process, and the officer's opinion.

The interview and observation component consists of a standardized series of questions. The questions examine the circumstances that led to interception of the suspect and the suspect's recent history of illness, injury, medical treatment, and drug use.

The Physical Impairment Tests (PIT) used in the SIA are based on the SFSTs, which were identified and standardized in research conducted for the U.S. Department of Transportation, National Highway Traffic Safety Administration (Burns and Moskowitz, 1977; Tharp, Burns, and Moskowitz, 1981; Anderson, Schweitz, and Snyder, 1983). The three validated tests, Horizontal Gaze Nystagmus, Walk and Turn and One Leg Stand, when used by trained officers in a systematic and standardized manner, can identify impairment at or above a 0.05 percent above blood alcohol concentration (BAC) (Burns and Anderson, 1995). This quantification allows the comparison of impairment for reasons other than alcohol with impairment at specific BACs, the latter being widely understood and accepted. The standardized conduct and performance evaluation of the tests provides a high degree of objectivity in identifying impairment.

In the information review process, specially trained police personnel review all the available information, including the investigator's RIA report, the result of the evidential breath test, the information obtained from observations and questions, and the PIT results. The collection of observed and recorded facts is the basis for an opinion as to whether a suspect is impaired. If a drug (or drugs) is believed to be the cause of the impairment, an additional body fluid specimen is obtained. If it becomes apparent or it is suspected at any time during the SIA process that injury or illness may be the cause of the impairment, an examination by a medical practitioner is immediately arranged, or if there is serious concern about the suspect's health, he or she is transported by ambulance to an emergency medical facility.

If the police officer conducting the SIA forms the opinion that the observed impairment may be caused by a drug, a blood or urine specimen is obtained from the suspect. The investigator may require the suspect to provide either a blood or urine specimen or both. It is an offense for a suspect to refuse to provide the required specimen or specimens. The specimens are obtained by medical practitioners or health professionals and are analyzed to identify the type of any drug present in the sample. The findings of the analysis are reported to the investigator.

The complete investigation file is referred to a specialist police unit for review and determination of the action to be taken. Consultation with medical and scientific experts takes place as part of that review. In cases where impairment is established and drugs that can cause impairment are present, the driver is prosecuted. In cases where impairment is established but the impairment is attributed to something other than drug use, an administrative driver licence review is carried out.

B. Enforcement personnel training

The recognition of signs and symptoms of impairment and their relationship to the effects of drugs are vital components in the scheme of the new legislative framework. The procedures require a significant level of training for enforcement personnel. For training purposes, a computerized interactive training package in the RIA and SIA procedure has been developed for enforcement personnel. It is a modular, self-paced learning program that is confined to procedural aspects of drug impaired driver detection. It can also be used as an instructional medium. There are additional materials in electronic media for training about the specifics of the legislative requirements.

Operational police are trained at two levels. At the first level, all receive training in the RIA procedure. The six-hour RIA training program provides information about observation, recognition, and recording of evidence of drug impaired driving. At the second level, a select group of operational police is trained to use the SIA procedure. This program provides instruction about the conduct and evaluation of the PIT together with electronic training about legislative requirements and video camera operation. SIA training is a thirty-two-hour competency based program with competency reassessment at twelve-month intervals. The total number trained is limited to a number that is sufficient to provide coverage across the state.

C. Procedure evaluation

The value of the SFST battery as part of the procedure to identify impairment caused by drugs other than alcohol has been clearly demonstrated. Of those cases in which there was a determination of drug impairment and a blood specimen was obtained, 97 percent of the assessments were confirmed by analysis of the blood specimen. This level of performance is comparable to the reported 94 percent performance level of the Drug Evaluation and Classification (DEC) program used in the United States (Compton, 1986).

The value of the SFST battery in the identification of specific types of drugs has also been demonstrated. Central nervous system (CNS) depressants (benzodiazepines) were found in 68 percent of the cases, narcotic analgesics (heroin, methadone) in 49 percent of the cases, cannabis (THC) in 37 percent of the cases and CNS stimulants (amphetamines) in 26 percent of the cases. Multiple drugs were found in 69 percent of the cases.

The program operation through June 30, 2004 demonstrates that the enforcement procedure is effective in identifying and removing drug impaired drivers from the road. A total of 533 suspects have been charged with offenses under the new provisions, and 321 have been convicted with 163 cases pending in the court system. Although the procedure has been vigorously challenged in the courts, only three cases have been dismissed. No legal deficiencies have been identified in the procedure.

The procedure identified thirty-five cases of impairment that were not caused by drug use, and those cases were referred for administrative driver licence review on medical grounds. An additional eleven drivers died prior to appearance at court. All of the deaths were related to drug use.

The procedure is also revealing interesting characteristics of drug-impaired drivers. Forty four percent of the drivers were involved in non-injury collisions. Offenders are predominantly male (81 percent), and their average age is thirty years. Fifty-nine percent of the suspects reported at the time of the offense that they were unemployed. Sixty-nine percent had a history of drug use (other than alcohol), and the misuse of prescription drugs is prominent (46 percent of the cases). Suspects provide a breath test during the first RIA, and if alcohol appears to be the main reason for impairment, the investigator need not complete the RIA. Accordingly, alcohol was reported in only 8 percent of the prosecuted cases.

Thirty-one percent of the suspects did not hold a valid driver licence when detected and of those, 45 percent were driving in breach of a court disqualification order. A significant number of suspects have a conviction history, 79 percent with criminal offences and 69 percent with traffic offences, but only 30 percent have a prior drunk driving offense. Thirty-two percent of those charged with driving while impaired by a drug offence were also charged with criminal offenses. Thus, the drug-impaired drivers detected under this procedure appear to be a subset of the wider drug use population.

13.4 General Deterrence Legislation

The operation of the Victorian 2001 Drug Impairment Legislation has demonstrated that drug impaired driving is a significant road safety issue. It has also demonstrated a practical, effective and valid means for police to detect and remove drug impaired drivers from the road. The program, however, does not address cases of drug impairment where outward signs of impairment are not visible. Moreover, specific deterrence legislation does not deal with the risks to road safety from impaired drivers generally. This situation is analogous in many ways to a comparison between a driving under the influence of alcohol case and an exceeding the prescribed concentration of alcohol case.

A. Alcohol

Research conducted by Borkenstein, et al. (1964) established that a driver with a BAC of 0.05 percent has a two fold higher risk of collision compared to a driver with a zero BAC. A driver with a 0.05 percent BAC will not necessarily exhibit observable signs of impairment.

The relationship between a 0.05 percent BAC and a higher risk of collision led to general deterrence legislation, which makes it an offense to drive with a BAC at or above 0.05 percent whether or not there is evidence of impairment. On the basis of the risk associated with 0.05 percent BAC and the involvement of drivers at that alcohol level in road trauma, random alcohol screening of drivers was introduced in 1976. Random alcohol screening of drivers has two objectives, to detect errant drivers and to deter errant driver behavior. At the time of introduction, there was much scepticism about the value of such a move, and great concern was expressed over whether the benefits reaped in reduction in road trauma would outweigh the interference with civil liberties. Over time and particularly beginning in 1990 when a highly visible, highly publicized, sustained and credible enforcement program was adopted (Homel 1988; Homel, Carseldine, and Kearns, 1988), the level of alcohol involvement in road trauma has declined significantly. The initial scepticism and civil liberty concerns have diminished, and the process has been accepted. To a large degree, the success of the process is attributable to the adherence to the above-mentioned principles and the allocation of sufficient resources to support those principles.

B. Illicit drugs

The contribution of drug use by drivers to road trauma has been examined throughout the world. Research findings show that inappropriate use of drugs, particularly illicit drugs, increases the risk of collision and therefore road trauma.

In Victoria in 2001, drugs were a factor in more driver fatalities than alcohol. In 2001, 29.2 percent of blood tests of fatalities tested positive for drugs other than alcohol. In comparison, 22.3 percent of fatally injured drivers had a BAC of 0.05 percent or higher. In 2002 the proportions were 27 percent for drugs and 29 percent for alcohol. The majority of the fatally injured drug positive drivers were using illicit drugs or abusing prescription drugs rather than using drugs for legitimate medical purposes. Two illicit drugs, cannabis and methamphetamine, presented special challenges for impairment legislation. In 2001, 16.5 percent of driver fatalities had used tetrahydrocannabinol (THC) or stimulant/amphetamine type drugs, while in 2002 this figure had risen to 20.4 percent of driver fatalities.

A ten-year study of drug involvement in fatal collisions by the Victorian Institute of Forensic Medicine (VIFM) (Drummer, et al., 2004) found that drivers who use illicit drugs have an increased risk of being involved in a fatal collision compared to drug free drivers. Drivers with THC in their blood had a significantly higher likelihood of being culpable than drug-free drivers (OR 2.7, 95 percent CI 1.02-7.0). For drivers with blood THC concentrations of 5 ng/ml or higher, the odds ratio was greater and more statistically significant (OR 6.6, 95 percent CI 1.5-28.0).

There are discrete cohorts within the driving population that have a higher incidence of drug-related collisions in conjunction with a specific activity. The VIFM Australian Fatality study reported that over a ten-year period 23.3 percent of fatally injured truck drivers tested positive for stimulants whereas stimulant-positive findings were 4.1 percent of fatalities among all drivers. Amphetamine use by truck drivers increased the odds ratio to 8.8 (95 percent CI 1.0-77.8) (Drummer, et al., 2004). Their risk of crash was similar to car drivers with 0.10 percent to 0.15 percent BACs. Since deaths associated with heavy vehicles make up 20 percent of the road toll, this finding reveals a major public safety issue.

Research data also reveal that the recreational use of stimulant type drugs in association with social activities is increasing. Dance and Rave environments have emerged as social activities of the young where stimulant drugs are often substituted for alcohol. This represents another discrete cohort within the driving population. Drivers who engage in this type of social activity have a collision involvement risk almost two- and one-half times that of drivers who do not.

The impairment-based drug driving enforcement program is specific to overtly drug-impaired drivers and does not provide a high degree of general deterrence for the broader driver population. Research in several Australian states reveals that the population of drivers who use drugs believes there is less likelihood of detection when using drugs than when using alcohol (Davey, Davey and Obst, 2002). The research demonstrates a need for a general deterrence strategy directed at the drug using driver population. The general deterrence strategy of random alcohol screening yielded a significant reduction in alcohol involvement in road trauma. It appears appropriate to consider random drug screening of drivers as a measure to reduce the involvement of drug use in road trauma.

Random alcohol screening underwent a considerable period of evolution. In 1976 the process commenced with defined legislative authority to intercept drivers for alcohol screening tests at roadside. The legislation authorized the use of screening tests, but the technology was rudimentary at that time, and the tests were costly and cumbersome. A driver was detained four to five minutes at roadside, and only limited personnel were available to the program. Consequently the effectiveness of roadside alcohol screening in detecting and deterring errant drivers was limited.

Almost thirty years later, advances in alcohol screening test technology have made high volume alcohol screening possible. The tests cost less and are easier to use. Personnel are available in special purpose vehicles. The entire procedure now detains a driver for no more than one minute. Victoria police personnel perform approximately 3.5 million tests for alcohol each year. The process has become a highly effective method for detecting and deterring errant drivers.

No process has yet been defined for random drug screening of drivers, and it is new ground. The situation is comparable to 1976 immediately prior to the introduction of alcohol screening. As was the case with the introduction of random alcohol tests, implementation must begin with an acceptable process. Then as operational experience is gained and technological advancements occur, the process can be reviewed and modified accordingly.

C. Drug screening technology

Screening for drugs may be achieved with body fluids such a blood, urine, oral fluid (saliva), or sweat. Because blood sampling is a very invasive process, it is not practical for roadside testing. Also, urine is not easily obtained at roadside, and the specimens provide limited information about recent drug use. On the other hand, oral fluid provides a degree of practicality for roadside screening. Its collection is relatively non-invasive, and the specimens provide evidence of recent drug use. Research overseas and in Australia has demonstrated that oral fluid is a suitable matrix for the detection of drugs. If there has been recent use of cannabis, for example, analysis of a saliva specimen can detect the presence of THC.

The technology for screening for drugs with oral fluid is in its infancy compared to breath alcohol screening technology. The latter has been under development for the past thirty years. Obtaining specimens of oral fluid is not as simple as obtaining breath specimens, and currently available technology is not as efficient in terms of cost, time and operation.

With considerable effort underway to develop the technology, however, significant and rapid advances can be expected. Already it is possible with available technology to screen drivers at roadside for two of the most widely used drugs, methamphetamine and cannabis (THC).

Oral fluid screens for drugs only indicate whether further investigation is warranted. Confirmatory laboratory analysis to an acceptable evidential standard is required for prosecution purposes. If the presence of a drug is confirmed by laboratory analysis of an oral fluid specimen, that analytic result is acceptable for evidential purposes.

D. 2003 random saliva testing for drugs legislation

The illicit drugs used by drivers, particularly cannabis (THC) and methamphetamine, increase the risk of collision and are associated with a significant incidence of road deaths in Victoria. An impairment based legislative framework only provides for the detection of drivers with an observable level of impairment and does not address the increase in collision risk associated with drug use even though outward signs of impairment are not overtly visible. The issues are more complex than for alcohol.

The physiological, pharmacological and toxicological aspects of drug use vary from drug to drug and from one set of circumstances to another. Although research findings show a relationship between drug use and collision risk, the relationship between a specific level of a drug and its effects cannot be as readily established as with alcohol. The increased collision risk is not dependent on overtly visible signs of impairment, and specific drug levels have not been defined. Therefore, a strong argument can be made for structuring a legislative framework on the prohibition of driving when any level of an illicit drug such as cannabis (THC) or methamphetamine is present in the body. This approach is analogous with zero tolerance or prohibition of any level of alcohol for certain classes of driver.

On December 9, 2003 the Road Safety (Drug Driving) Act 2003 was enacted by the Victorian Parliament to provide a legislative framework for the random drug testing of drivers by saliva sample screening. The provisions of the Act become effective December 1, 2004. An evaluation of the program will be conducted to provide Parliament with information about the effectiveness of the program and to identify any legislative or operational changes required.

The legislative framework for drug screening is modelled on the alcohol screening process. The tactical application of the process will be a matter of operational prerogative. Flexibility to apply the process on a general basis or to specific higher risk driver cohorts will be determined at an operational level based on contemporary intelligence. Three principles of application apply. Random drug screening can be performed:

- in conjunction with general random alcohol screening operations where the operations are in areas where intelligence indicates a significant level of drug use;
- in special operations directed at high-risk drug user groups associated with the road transport industry; and
- in special operations directed at high-risk drug user groups associated with the 'dance' and 'rave' environment.

The utility of the legislative framework for alcohol screening has been demonstrated and has the added benefit that it is familiar to law enforcement, jurists and the driving population. Community acceptance of random drug screening likely will be facilitated by its similarity to a process that already enjoys community acceptance and wide support.

E. Operation of the 2003 random saliva testing for drugs legislation

The new framework is a three-stage process. The first stage involves a police officer intercepting a driver and conducting an alcohol-screening test, which will take twenty to thirty seconds using the existing procedure. The driver may be intercepted by police in a random testing operation (checkpoint) or at any time when driving. Suspicion of alcohol or drug use is not required by police to justify interception of a driver. Then a preliminary drug-screening test (first test) will be conducted at roadside. Based on the use of the currently available oral-fluid sampling technology, the preliminary drug screening will routinely take approximately five minutes for a methamphetamine and THC test. Any police officer may conduct the preliminary alcohol and drug screening tests. If the tests results are negative, the driver will not be detained further. Total detention time for a negative screen will be approximately five minutes in most cases.

In the second stage, if the preliminary drug screening indicates the presence of either or both methamphetamine and THC, the driver will be required to accompany police to a testing vehicle to provide a second oral fluid specimen. The second, evidential oral fluid will be collected and tested by a specially trained and authorized police member. In the unlikely event that this second test indicates a negative result, the driver will not be detained further. Total time of detention up to this point of the process will be approximately fifteen minutes. If the second test indicates the presence of methamphetamine or THC, the driver will be informed of the result. Additional relevant information will be obtained for the purpose instituting a charge if the presence of the drug is confirmed by laboratory analysis. The second oral fluid, evidential specimen will be divided with one part given to the driver and the other part sent to a laboratory for confirmatory analysis by gas chromatography-mass spectrometry (GC-MS). The driver will be informed of his or her driving prohibition of a specified duration. Total time of detention to complete the process will be approximately thirty minutes.

In the third and final stage of the process, if laboratory analysis confirms the presence of methamphetamine or THC in the oral fluid specimen, the driver will be charged with an offence. The result of the laboratory analysis will be presented in court as evidence to prove the charge.

13.5 Conclusion

The legislative framework and enforcement procedure adopted by Victoria in 2000 is a practical, effective and valid means for police to detect and remove drug-impaired drivers from the road. Implementation of the random drug screening enforcement and deterrent program, which is modelled on the successful alcohol-screening program, has the potential to make further significant gains in road trauma reduction in Victoria.

References

Anderson. T., Schweitz, R., and Snyder, M. (1983). Field evaluation of a behavior test battery for DWI. DOT HS-806 475. Washington, D.C.: National Highway Traffic Safety Administration.

Boorman, M. (2001). The evolution of impaired driver law: Victoria. In J. Enders and B. Dupont (Eds.) *Policing the Lucky Country*. Sydney, Australia: Hawkins Press, 158-173.

Borkenstein, R.F., Crowther, F.R., Shumate, R.P., Ziel, W.B. and Zylman, R. (1964). The role of the drinking driver in traffic accidents. Department of Police Administration, Indiana University.

Burns, M., and Anderson, T. (1995). Colorado SFST field validation study. Denver, Colorado: Colorado Department of Transportation.

Burns M., and Moskowitz, H. (1977). Psychophysical tests for DWI. DOT HS-802 424.

Washington, D.C.: National Highway Traffic Safety Administration.

Compton, R. (1986). Field evaluation of the Los Angeles Police Department drug detection procedure. DOT HS-807 012. Washington, D.C.: National Highway Traffic Safety Administration.

Davey, J., Davey, T. and Obst, P. (2002). Alcohol consumption and drug use in a sample of Australian university students. Youth Studies Australia, 21, 3, 25-32.

Drummer, O., Gerastamoulos, J., Batziris, H., Chu, M., Caplehorn, J., Robertson, M., et al. (2004). The involvement of drugs in drivers of motor vehicles killed in Australian road traffic crashes. *Accident Analysis and Prevention*, 36, 239-248.

Government of Victoria. (1997). Government response to the report of the Road Safety Committee of Parliament on the effects of drugs (other than alcohol) on road safety in Victoria. Melbourne, Australia.

Homel, R. (1988). *Policing and Punishing the Drinking Driver: A study of general and specific deterrence*. New York: Springer-Verlag.

Homel, R., Carseldine, D. and Kearns, I. (1988). Drink-driving countermeasures in Australia. *Alcohol, Drugs and Driving*, 4, 2, 113-144.

Parliament of Victoria (2000). Road Safety (Amendment) Act 2000, No. 14/2000. Melbourne, Australia.

Road Safety Committee, Parliament of Victoria. (1996). Inquiry into the effects of drugs (other than alcohol) on road safety in Victoria. Final Report. Melbourne, Australia.

Drugs (Other than Alcohol) Impaired Driving Specialist Working Party Report. (1998).Victoria Police Department: Melbourne, Australia.

Tharp, V., Burns, M., and Moskowitz, H. (1981). Development and field test of psychophysical tests for DWI arrest. DOT HS-805 864. Washington, D.C.: National Highway Traffic Safety Administration.

About the Editors

Marcelline Burns, Ph.D. earned degrees in Psychology from San Diego State University, California State University Los Angeles, and the University of California Irvine. In 2003 she retired from the Southern California Research Institute where she studied the effects of alcohol and other drugs on human performance for three decades. She and colleagues developed the Standardized Field Sobriety Tests (SFSTs), and she subsequently conducted laboratory and field studies of both the SFSTs and Drug Recognition Expert methods. She lectures, trains, and provides expert testimony on the effects of alcohol and drugs.

Thomas E. Page, M.A. earned a Bachelor of Arts degree in Industrial Psychology and a Master of Arts degree in Urban Studies from the University of Detroit. He participated in the initial development of the Drug Recognition Expert (DRE) training curriculum and was Officer-in-Charge of the Los Angeles Police Department's DRE unit from 1990 to 1999. He served as the General Chairperson of the International Association of Chiefs of Police DRE Section and as a member of that organization's DRE Technical Advisory Panel. Courts in fifteen states have found him qualified to give testimony as a drug expert.

About the Contributors

Sevil Atasoy, Ph.D. holds B.S (Chemistry, 1972), M.S. (Biochemistry, 1976) and Ph.D. (Biochemistry, 1979) degrees from Istanbul University in Turkey. She is the Director of the Istanbul University Institute of Forensic Sciences. She has conducted research at Munich, Muenster, Bremen, Berkeley, Emory and Stanford Universities, and has lectured in the United States, Europe and Asia. She writes on drug policies, drug abuse prevention, drug markets, crime scene investigation and forensic identification. She is a member of international educational organizations, and serves as an expert witness in forensic sciences. The United Nations Economic and Social Council elected her to the International Narcotics Control Board for the term 2005-2010.

Tanil M. Baskan, Ph.D. holds LLB (Law, 1990), M.A. (Forensic Sciences, 1994), and Ph.D. (Forensic Sciences, 2003) degrees from Istanbul University. He is an Assistant Professor at the Institute of Forensic Sciences of Istanbul University and is a nationally known defense lawyer. His research focuses on "Law and Policies regarding Alcohol and Drug Impairment," "Investigation of Traffic Accidents," "Scientific Evidence in Civil and Criminal Cases," "Juvenile Delinquency," "Child Abuse" and "Malpractice."

Inspector **Martin C. Boorman** is the Officer-in-Charge, Traffic Alcohol Section, Technical Unit, Victoria Police, Australia. His unit is responsible for training, policy development, legal research, and maintenance of equipment for alcohol and drug impaired driving enforcement by Victoria Police. He also serves as the police representative for development and implementation of drug-impaired driving enforcement programs in Victoria. Inspector Boorman is the recipient of the Australian Police Medal for distinguished police service to road safety.

Nina J. Emerson graduated from the University of Wisconsin Law School where she currently is the director of the Resource Center on Impaired Driving. The Center is a joint effort of the Wisconsin Department of Transportation and the Law School. As director, she provides alcohol-related data and legal information about impaired driving to judges, prosecutors, defense attorneys, law enforcement officers, educators, legislators and citizens. She conducts training programs, teaches at both the state and national level, and publishes the *Resource Center Report*, a periodic report of impaired driving issues. In addition, she has authored numerous articles for the *Wisconsin Lawyer*.

Peter Gerstenzang is the senior partner in the Albany, New York law firm of Gerstenzang, O'Hern, Hickey & Gerstenzang. His criminal defense practice ranges from Long Island to Buffalo and upstate New York and focuses on the defense of DUI cases, as well as on vehicular crimes. He serves on the faculty of the Office of Court Administration Judges Training Program and lectures for the New York State Bar Association and other defense and law enforcement organizations. He is Chairman, New York State Bar Association, Committee on Traffic Safety.

Officer Clark John is an instructor and training officer for the Narcotics Division, Los Angeles Police Department. He is certified as a Drug Recognition Expert Instructor and as an Emergency Medical Technician. He has conducted and supervised hundreds of drug evaluations to determine whether individuals were under the influence of drugs, including over 200 involving the drug phencyclidine (PCP). He has made many arrests for driving under the influence of drugs and many PCP seizures. He is a visiting instructor for the Health Sciences Department, California State University, Northridge, and California State University, Dominguez Hills. He is vice-president, California Chapter of the National Association of Drug Diversion Investigators.

Sarah Kerrigan, Ph.D. is a forensic toxicologist in private practice in Houston, Texas. She trained at the Scotland Yard Forensic Science Laboratory in London, England. Between 2001 and 2004 she was Chief of the Toxicology Bureau, Scientific Laboratory Division, New Mexico Department of Health and also was an Adjunct Professor, Pathology Department, School of Medicine, University of New Mexico. Previously, Dr. Kerrigan was a forensic toxicologist with the California Department of Justice, Sacramento, CA, and she is President of the California Association of Toxicologists. She has contributed to toxicology textbooks, published original research in medical and scientific journals, and has received more than ten awards and fellowships.

Officer Chuck Matson, Omaha Police Department, is the Coordinator of the Omaha Drug Evaluation and Classification Program. In 1996 he received the Law Enforcement Award from the National Commission Against Drunk Driving in recognition of his enforcement and education efforts. He has been accepted as an expert witness on drug effects in numerous courts. He is also the founder of "Recognizing Impairing Drugs (RID) Training," a non-profit educational and consultation service.

Joel M. Mayer, Ph.D., is the Deputy Director, Scientific Affairs, Centre of Forensic Sciences, in Toronto, Ontario, Canada. He received his doctorate in pharmacology and toxicology from the University of Toronto, where he is an appointed Assistant Professor in the Department of Pharmacology, Faculty of Medicine. His responsibilities at the Centre of Forensic Sciences include scientific management and research and development. He has been involved in thousands of criminal cases and death investigations, and has appeared as an expert witness at all levels of court in Ontario.

Morris Odell, M.D. is a forensic physician at the Victorian Institute of Forensic Medicine, Australia. His duties encompass all aspects of clinical forensic medicine including the effects of alcohol and drugs on driving. He has conducted extensive research on breath testing for alcohol and on the interpretation of blood alcohol levels. His numerous publications include papers on the role of drugs in roadway fatalities. He is president of the Australian and New Zealand Forensic Medicine Society and is a board member of the International Traffic Medicine Association.

Trinka Porrata retired from the Los Angeles Police Department after a twenty-five year career. For much of her career, she supervised street narcotics enforcement squads. As a detective, she investigated sexual assaults and child abuse. Ms. Porrata now focuses on the abuse of *club drugs*, such as GHB (gamma hydroxy butyrate), Ecstasy and LSD at Rave gatherings. She is the founder and president of Project GHB, a non-profit organization whose mission is the prevention of drug abuse and the treatment of addiction to GHB and other drugs.

Eric Sills is a partner in the law firm of Gerstenzang, O'Hern, Hickey & Gerstenzang. He served as a law clerk to retired United States Magistrate Judge Ralph W. Smith, Jr. of the United States District Court, Northern District of New York. He lectures for the New York State Bar Association and other organizations.

Philip Swann, Ph.D. earned a Ph.D. in Chemical Engineering from Melbourne (Australia) University. He has worked in the field of road safety for thirty years and currently is Manager, Drugs Alcohol and Fatigue, VicRoads, State Road Transport Authority. He is an Adjunct Professor, Faculty of Life Sciences, Swinburne University of Technology, Melbourne. His research examines the performance characteristics of saliva testing equipment, psychomotor tests for impairment, and accident risk associated with impaired driving. He contributes to the development of policy, strategy, and countermeasure programs. In 1999 he received the Australian Public Service Medal in recognition of his service in the area of Drugs, Alcohol and Fatigue.

Index

U

UCLA Brain Research Institute, 155
Under the Influence, 2–3, 165, 167,
        191, 197, 204, 207–208, 210–
        214, 224, 230, 13–15, 17–20, 23,
        25, 32–36, 46, 57, 62, 65, 68–69,
        71, 74, 77, 86–87, 97, 147, 149,
        151–153
United Nations, 194–195, 204, 219

V

Viagra, 156, 61, 136
Vicodin, 64
Volatile nitrites, 125, 130, 135

W

World Bank, 192, 197, 214–215, 222
World Health Organization, 194

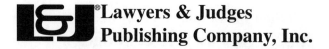

Lawyers & Judges
Publishing Company, Inc.

Medical-Legal Aspects of Alcohol,
Fourth Edition, #0888

Edited by James C. Garriott, Ph.D.

This book will help you successfully litigate cases that involve alcohol.

Medical-Legal Aspects of Alcohol, Fourth Edition is an ideal resource for anyone—an attorney, forensic scientist, medical examiner or coroner—who needs information on alcohol's disposition in the body.

Alcohol-related litigation typically pertains to arrests of drinking drivers, but also includes industrial accidents, public transport accidents and violent crimes. Even so, the medical and legal aspects of alcohol are complex topics because so many different components are present in alcohol-related cases.

It is extremely important that the alcohol analyses be preformed accurately and correctly and that the results are properly interpreted. Forensic toxicologists and pathologists are often called on to interpret the alcohol concentrations found in specimens, and at times the results are deemed meaningless because samples are mishandled, equipment is incorrectly calibrated or the results are incorrectly reported. 8 $\frac{1}{2}$" × 11", casebound, 536 pages.

Topics include

- methods for fluid analysis
- postmortem specimens
- laboratory quality assurance
- reporting of laboratory results
- workplace testing
- defending and prosecuting the drunk driver
- the legal framework of scientific evidence
- a review of breath analysis tools

- biochemistry and physiology of alcohol
- computer tools for body alcohol evaluation
- pharmacology and toxicology of ethyl alcohol
- experimental basis of psychomotor performance
- the role and responsibilities of an expert witness
- effects of alcohol combined with other drugs

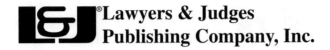

Lawyers & Judges Publishing Company, Inc.

Medical-Legal Aspects of Pain and Suffering, #6397

Edited by Patricia W. Iyer, M.S.N., RN, LNCC

There is no other book devoted to the assessment, management, and presentation of pain and suffering.

Written by experienced clinicians and attorneys, *Medical-Legal Aspects of Pain and Suffering* will help you understand how health professionals can better alleviate pain and suffering and how you can more effectively litigate claims. A unique blend of authors have contributed solid material covering a range of concerns on this hot topic. This book is loaded with practical information, medical illustrations, figures and tables, pain assessment forms, and questions for direct examination of witnesses.

Useful for healthcare professionals, claims adjusters, trial attorneys, and legal nurse consultants, this book begins by guiding you through a broad overview of key concepts and assessment tools in pain and suffering. You'll review pain management—covering psychological as well as physical pain—and issues pertaining to specific client populations and healthcare settings. Material is included for attorneys evaluating and presenting a claim involving pain and suffering that explains life care plans and the use of trial exhibits. By combining the clinical information in the first two sections with the legal strategies in the last section, this book becomes a must read. 8 $\frac{1}{2}$" × 11", casebound, 544 pages.

Topics include

- pain assessment and management
- a psychologist's view of pain and suffering
- common treatment problems
- consequences of stress
- expert fact witness testimony
- ante-mortem damages
- the intensive care unit
- life-care planning
- grief
- chronic pain
- cancer pain
- orthopaedic pain
- spinal cord injury
- wounds and burns
- organization and analysis of medical records

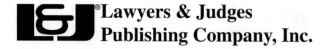
®Lawyers & Judges
Publishing Company, Inc.

Medical and Legal Aspects of Neurology, #6303

Jeffrey Wishik, M.D., J.D.

This book provides for extensive discussion of the legal and medical aspects that surround neurology.

In this book, you will find comprehensive coverage of medical tools and explanations that will allow you to understand the way neurological disorders develop. Research in the field, medical illustrations, and recent professional breakthroughs make this book necessary for anyone working in a neurology-related field.

Best of all, the book includes a range of topics so extensive that it provides not only the background for neurological diseases, but also the legal implications that result from unethical action or human error. *Medical and Legal Aspects of Neurology* covers laws, disorders, and treatments all in one compilation that closely examines the fine aspects of a complicated field. It is with the help of this resource that you can strengthen your case with the broad range of topics and the detailed explanations of each. Working without this tool limits your capabilities to be the best informed on the subject of neurology and its legal implications. 6" × 9", casebound, 348 pages.

Topics include

- the diagnostic process and testing
- the brain and higher cortical function
- chronic pain
- traumatic brain injury
- spine and nerve root disorders
- peripheral neuropathy
- seizures and epilepsy
- cerebrovascular and demyelineating diseases
- headaches
- brain and spinal cord tumors
- infectious diseases
- movement disorders
- Attention Deficit Hyperactivity Disorder

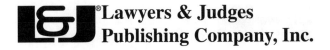

®Lawyers & Judges
Publishing Company, Inc.

Medical-Legal Aspects of the Spine, #6818

Marjorie Eskay-Auerback, M.D., J.D.

Discover this comprehensive book, complete with a discussion of the medical field, specifically the spine, and the legal implications that surround it.

This text provides beginning and intermediate-level medical information about conditions of the cervical and lumbar spine. Physical examination findings and diagnostic studies are discussed in detail. Explanations of common cervical and lumbar spine conditions, such as disc herniations, degenerative disc disease, and sprain/strain injuries are provided, along with treatment options. Non-surgical treatment, injection therapies, and surgical treatment are discussed with attention to both technique and indications. The goal of this text is to provide the reader with a practical reference to terminology frequently found in medical records and deposition testimony.

Medical-Legal Aspects of the Spine is a must-have for anyone in the field who needs to know about types of treatment, disorders, and studies that involve the spine in the legal arena, backed by accomplished medical and legal expertise. It is a comprehensive text that provides specific, important information that can alter and enhance your case. 8 $\frac{1}{2}$" × 11", casebound, approx. 130 pages.

Topics include

- back pain incidents
- providers of care
- basic anatomy and terminology of the spine
- history and physical examination of patients with neck or back pain
- imaging and other studies to evaluate the spine
- common conditions of the cervical spine
- common conditions of the lumbar spine
- surgical treatment options for cervical and lumbar spine conditions
- non-operative treatment of acute and chronic cervical and lumbar spine pain

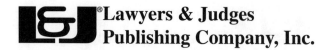

Medical-Legal Internet Directory, Third Edition, on CD-Rom #9140

Rosie Oldham, RN, LNCC

We've taken the fastest way to find medical and legal information on the Internet and made it even faster.

The Medical-Legal Internet Directory was created to save you time and energy in your search for medical and legal information on the Internet and is the one directory you will use over and over again.

The new CD-Rom version contains new websites and updated links with a description of the information it contains, and now the site is just a click away. The CD-Rom contains live links to each site so all you have to do is place the CD into your computer, look up the category you are interested in, and click. It's that simple!

Medical sites are organized alphabetically and by medical specialty, while the legal section contains more research websites, attorney directories, dictionaries, journals, schools, libraries, and much more. Broadly endorsed by national medical-legal experts, this is an invaluable reference for everyone who provides medical-legal research and litigation support.

Topics include

- bar associations
- legal directories
- dictionaries
- health law
- journals
- legal ethics

- clinical studies
- anatomy
- critical care
- dental
- geriatrics
- transplants

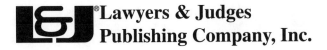

Lawyers & Judges Publishing Company, Inc.

Drug Injury: Liability, Analysis and Prevention, Second Edition, #6044

James T. O'Donnell, M.S., Pharm.D.

All of us are aware of one or more pharmaceutical and over-the-counter drugs that were pulled from the market because of the injuries they cause to the general public. Yet, every year, thousands of drug injuries occur from human error too. Physicians' ordering mistakes, pharmacists filling the wrong prescriptions, drug administration mistakes, and drug mixing make up a large portion of drug injury litigation.

This book is divided into three useful sections that cover every type of drug injury litigation. The first section deals with the manufacturing and drug-approval process. The second section examines the injuries these drugs caused and the attempted cover-ups by some of the drug companies. You will read about important litigation regarding drugs like Prozac, Accutane, Rezulin, and more. The third section looks at the mistakes that can happen in the pharmacy and malpractice claims. It also includes appendices of FDA regulations relating to drug product liability guidance for industry, use of risk minimization plans, and FDA pregnancy classifications.

You will find this text indispensable because it provides comprehensive information for attorneys, healthcare professionals, pharmacists, and those affiliated with the pharmaceutical industry. 8 $\frac{1}{2}$" × 11", casebound, approx. 1000 pages.

Topics include

- the failed system of drug warnings in America
- clinical research: testing treatments in humans
- FDA regulation of clinical investigations
- identification of regulated solid dosage forms
- nephrotoxic drugs
- evaluation of causation in drug injury cases
- the role of pharmacoepidemiology and expert testimony in drug injury
- E-Ferol disaster
- drugs for asthma, allergies, and anaphylaxis: harm from use, misuse, and nonuse

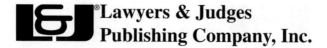

Lawyers & Judges Publishing Company, Inc.

Human Factors in Traffic Safety, #5473

Robert E. Dewar, Ph.D., CPE and Paul L. Olson, Ph.D.

There are more than 175 million licensed drivers in the United States, not including the bicyclists, motorcyclists, and pedestrians that also share the roadways. This crowding makes using the roadways safely a challenge.

Human Factors in Traffic Safety will introduce you to the various elements that affect a roadway user's response and perception. You will learn that factors such as emotion, motivation, medication, and age determine how a driver, pedestrian, bicyclist, and motorcyclist respond to emergency situations. You will also see how the roadway, vehicles, and traffic control devices are designed around drivers' limitations and how these areas can be improved.

This book will help you examine the behavior of the road user from a variety of perspectives, ranging from the design of roads and vehicles to emotional and motivational determinants of behavior. Several experts in the field of traffic safety have made contributions to this book in order to introduce you to the basics of human factors as relevant to driving and traffic safety. You will gain an understanding of this very important component of the roadway transportation: the human. This book examines the behavior of the road user from a variety of perspectives. $6^{1}/_{8}$" × $9^{1}/_{4}$", casebound, 736 pages.

Topics include:

- driver perception-response time
- fatigue and driving
- alcohol, drugs and medications
- age differences—drivers old and young
- neuropsychological, medical, and psychiatric disorders affecting motor vehicle operations
- vehicle design

- environmental factors
- railroad grade crossing accidents
- work zone accidents
- pedestrians and bicyclists
- left turn and gap acceptance crashes
- why witnesses to accidents make mistakes: the cognitive psychology of human memory

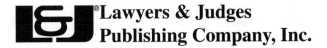

Lawyers & Judges Publishing Company, Inc.

Forensic Aspects of Chemical and Biological Terrorism, #6672

Cyril H. Wecht

History shows us how easily deadly viruses spread through populations because of travel, unrecognized symptoms, and unorganized healthcare. In today's world, people are able to travel greater distances in a short time. In only a few hours, a disease could be spread to multiple continents. In addition, technological advancements have made it easier for terrorists to produce and release chemical weapons that could be used in public areas. Therefore, in order to prevent attacks, or contain the spread of disease or chemical exposure if an attack happens, the response must be quick, organized and thorough.

Forensic Aspects of Biological and Chemical Terrorism is an eye-opening resource for healthcare professionals, 911 operators, emergency response personnel, medical examiners, coroners, hospital administrators and public health officials. It provides valuable insight into what areas need improvement, what roles each of the responders should have, and how this all can be accomplished. It also extensively covers the investigation of an attack from the signs and symptoms of various diseases and chemical exposure to how the crime scene should be handled. This timely resource is a must-have for anyone involved in public health and public safety. Foreword written by Senator Arlen Specter of Pennsylvania. 6" × 9", casebound, 450 pages.

Topics include

- identification of biological and chemical terrorism
- smallpox
- injury characteristics and treatment
- forensic toxicology
- public health aspects and protective measures
- criminal investigation
- airport security
- psychological aspects of biological and chemical terrorism
- legal considerations relating to terrorism

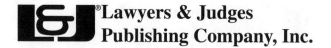

**Lawyers & Judges
Publishing Company, Inc.**

Biological and Chemical Warfare Agents
Slide Chart, #0635

Steve Weintraub

This unique slide chart provides quick information about biological and chemical agents.

On side one you will find three categories of biological agents. For each agent listed you will be able to discover whether the agent is a bacteria, toxin or virus, the historical use of the agent, treatments available and more. Side two of the chart contains information on chemical weapons.

To learn about a specific chemical or biological agent, all you have to do is slide the arrow next to the agent you are interested in. Next, read across to learn about the method of contamination and historical use, then look at the window below to find out about signs and symptoms, vaccinations and treatments. An ideal quick reference tool when learning the key points about these dangerous and deadly weapons. 8 $\frac{1}{2}$" × 11".

Topics include

- anthrax
- brucellosis
- cholera
- glanders
- plague
- Q fever
- tularemia
- typhoid fever
- typhus
- hemorrhagic feber/ebola
- smallpox

- yellow fever
- botulinus toxin
- ricin toxin
- saxitoxin
- sarin nerve gas
- VX
- tabun
- mustard gas
- hydrogen cyanide
- phosgene

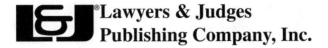

Lawyers & Judges Publishing Company, Inc.

Blood Alcohol Concentration Calculator, #0618

Steve Weintraub

This slide calculator contains up-to-date data for estimating the blood alcohol concentration of men and women from 85–300 pounds after drinking known amounts of alcoholic beverages, the number of specific mixed drinks, beers, wines or distilled spirits consumed from a known BAC level, the BAC for each hour (from 0–19) after consumption, and the number of hours required for BAC to fall to a level of choice. $6\,^1/_8$" × $9\,^1/_4$".

Drugs of Abuse Slide Chart, #0622

Steve Weintraub

This newly revised and updated calculator is loaded with information on drugs of abuse. Now one simple tool will give you trafficking penalties, street names, CSA regulatory requirements, and more. All the information contained in volumes of books and regulations is right at your fingertips. Side one lists the trade and street names of narcotics, depressants, stimulants, hallucinogens, and cannabis, along with the effects, withdrawal symptoms, and overdose effects. Also included are the medical use and physical appearance of the drug, methods of administration, detection time in urine, and physical or psychological dependence. Side two provides the CSA regulatory requirements and Federal Trafficking Penalties Guide. All information compiled from DEA, CSA, and National Institute on Drug Abuse data. $8\,^1/_2$" × 11".

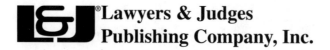

®Lawyers & Judges
Publishing Company, Inc.

PremierBAC: Blood Alcohol Concentration Software, #5606

David N. Dresser

This software program makes it a snap to calculate blood alcohol concentration.

Written by the author of *Basic Vehicle Motion Analysis*, this software has been designed with accident reconstructionists and lawyers in mind. It can calculate the person's peak blood alcohol concentration, the person's BAC after a specified time after the last drink, and it also gives you the option of using the two industry-standard equations for better accuracy.

Here is how it works. You provide the person's sex and weight, and either type in the fluid ounces and proof of the drinks, or select common drinks like brand-name beers or daiquiris from a list. The list of common beverages includes their serving size and proof so you don't have to know either of those things. You can request a BAC from a specific time since last drink, as well. Next, you choose from the two standard equations for calculating BAC: the Widmark or the NHSTA equation. You can easily perform both equations for the same person to verify accuracy. After the necessary information is entered, you will see the person's peak BAC and BAC after your specified time period. If you prefer to use the equations without the wizard to help you calculate the amount of alcohol in various drinks, you can do that too. This program is very versatile and contains very useful help screens to guide you on your way. CD-Rom.